THREE MOZART LIBRETTI
THE MARRIAGE OF FIGARO
DON GIOVANNI AND
COSÌ FAN TUTTE

Wolfgang Amadeus Mozart

Complete in Italian and English

Translated by
Robert Pack and Marjorie Lelash

DOVER PUBLICATIONS, INC.
New York

Bibliographical Note

This Dover edition, first published in 1993, is a republication of three libretti by Lorenzo da Ponte, *Le nozze di Figaro, Don Giovanni* and *Così fan tutte,* with translations of the same by Robert Pack and Marjorie Lelash, originally published as part of the volume *Mozart's Librettos* by The World Publishing Company, Cleveland, in 1961. The Italian has been tacitly corrected to conform with the Dover full scores of these operas.

Library of Congress Cataloging-in-Publication Data

Mozart, Wolfgang Amadeus, 1756–1791.
    [Operas. Librettos. English & Italian. Selections]
    Three Mozart libretti : complete in Italian and English / Wolfgang Amadeus Mozart ; translated by Robert Pack and Marjorie Lelash.
       p.   cm.
    Libretti by Lorenzo da Ponte.
    "A republication of three libretti by Lorenzo da Ponte . . . originally published as part of Mozart's librettos by the World Publishing Company, Cleveland, in 1961"—T.p. verso.
    Contents: The marriage of Figaro — Don Giovanni — Così fan tutte.
    ISBN 0-486-27726-7 (pbk.)
    1. Operas—Librettos. I. Pack, Robert, 1929– . II. Lelash, Marjorie. III. Da Ponte, Lorenzo, 1749–1838. IV. Title. V. Title: 3 Mozart libretti.
ML49.M83P213   1993
782.1'026'8—dc20   93-1233
                                                   CIP
                                                   MN

Manufactured in the United States of America
Dover Publications, Inc., 31 East 2nd Street, Mineola, N.Y. 11501

FOREWORD

In preparing these translations, we have tried to accomplish two things: first, to present the librettos of the three Mozart/Da Ponte operas as readably and as dramatically as possible, finding the natural or colloquial English phrase without falling into mannerism or dullness; second, steering a middle course between literal pedestrianism and figurative flight of fancy, to make the translations correspond to the exact meanings of the Italian texts. These two objectives naturally conflicted to some extent, but we hope that without too much loss in textual accuracy, we have succeeded in conveying the essential spirit of these three operas.

The translations will be found opposite their equivalent texts. Thus the reader can use them to follow a recorded performance, or to refresh his memory before or after a "live" rendition of any of the operas. Cuts have been made in conformance with current practice, although this, of course, varies greatly with each conductor, and with every opera house.

Certain technical points remain to be clarified. We have kept the traditional numberings of arias and ensembles because the numbers serve as convenient listening guides. However, the system of beginning another "scene" every time a new character is introduced seems antiquated and confusing, and it has not been retained. Stage directions have been held to that minimum necessary to explain the action, and some of these directions have been revised, again, in conformance with current practice. Our texts approximate as closely as possible what our readers will actually see and hear, since this book is intended not as a scholarly work but as an attempt to make the riches of Mozart's operas more accessible to a less specialized audience.

We wish to acknowledge the invaluable assistance of Miss Joan Bonime, as well as the help of Constantin Vichey and Willie Schumann.

R. P.
M. L.

CONTENTS

THE
MARRIAGE
OF
FIGARO

LE
NOZZE
DI
FIGARO

*An opera
in four acts*

*Music by
Wolfgang Amadeus Mozart
(K. 492)*

*Words by
Lorenzo da Ponte*

INTRODUCTION

Although it was begun in the autumn of 1784, only three years after *The Abduction from the Seraglio, The Marriage of Figaro* reveals Mozart in possession of his full powers as an operatic composer. Like *The Abduction, Figaro,* in addition to its timeless values, has a certain topical interest. Based on *Le Mariage de Figaro,* a play by Beaumarchais which was first performed in France in 1784 and was subsequently banned in Vienna as subversive and conducive to revolution, it also marks the first collaboration of Mozart with the great librettist Lorenzo da Ponte, who was to perform for him a service similar to that which Arrigo Boito performed for Verdi a century later. By pointing out that his libretto emphasized the human conflicts of Beaumarchais's play, rather than its political overtones —that it treated the struggle between the Count and Figaro, master and servant, as a personal conflict, rather than as an incitement to revolt—Da Ponte induced Emperor Joseph II to relax his ban and permit the opera to be performed in Vienna.

For full understanding of the plot of *Figaro,* some knowledge of Beaumarchais's earlier play, *Le Barbier de Seville,* is needed. In this play, the basis of the popular opera by Rossini, Count Almaviva, with the aid of Figaro, the resourceful barber of Seville, steals the beautiful Rosina away from her elderly guardian, Bartolo. As *The Marriage of Figaro* opens, we find that Figaro has become the Count's steward, and that the Count is beginning to neglect Rosina, now the Countess, in favor of other women—among them, Figaro's intended bride, Susanna.

The situation that evolves contains all the elements essential to true comedy. The action takes place in a small, isolated world, the Count's household, but the characters belong to a highly civilized society, and they are all playing a game of skill with all their wits. Women dominate and control the action, and point the final moral: Men must learn to see their own absurdities, and to recover their lost dignity in this recognition.

Mozart has set the story in the form of the Italian *opera buffa* of his period, with recitative instead of dialogue to advance the action, which proceeds with headlong speed. Nevertheless, every character retains his musical identity throughout the long, elaborate ensembles that are necessary to further the plot.

The characters in *Figaro* are complete human beings, more human, perhaps, than any in Mozart's subsequent operas, and very different from the somewhat flat "types" of *The Abduction from the Seraglio*. Susanna, for example, is more complex than Blonde; Blonde is always the same, but Susanna's reactions vary with her companions. Her two arias indicate the range of her nature. The first is an outpouring of her youthful merriment; the second, after its opening recitative, is an expression of her deep love for Figaro. Like Blonde, Susanna has wit and vivacity, but Mozart never lets us forget that she is a young girl in love —how much so we do not know, perhaps, until her final aria. At first she is afraid of the Count, and then she is a bit contemptuous of him; she is spiteful with Marcellina, solicitous with the Countess, mocking at Cherubino's raptures, and indignant at Basilio's insinuations.

Contrasted with Susanna, and far more complex than the nobly suffering Constanze of *The Abduction,* the Countess is a woman who, though still young and still able to enjoy life and its intrigues, laments the exigencies forced on her by her husband's philandering; her first aria shows the reflective side of her nature; in her second, she reaffirms her belief in life and in love. Figaro, although his barbs against the nobility have been softened a bit by Da Ponte, remains a colorful figure; he is inventive and energetic, and like any man in love, quick to take occasion for jealousy. The Count may be selfish, but still we find him somewhat sympathetic; we cannot hate him any more than we would hate any immature and confused young man of today. The other characters—Barbarina, Marcellina, Bartolo, Don Basilio, and even Antonio and Don Curzio—are sharply delineated in the libretto and deftly characterized in the music.

With all its wealth of characterization, and its moments of serious emotion, *Figaro* is, above all, a comedy. It depicts a world ruled by reason rather than passion, one in which people discover their own failings and absurdities, and in which all complications are happily resolved by the final curtain. It is a world where only human forces are at work; there are no judgments of the characters beyond their opinions of each other, and nowhere is any divine or infernal presence suggested. The love that triumphs in this opera is wholly human; perhaps it is for this reason that many operagoers consider *The Marriage of Figaro* the most appealing of all Mozart's operas.

SYNOPSIS

Figaro, Count Almaviva's steward, is about to marry Susanna, the Countess's maid. Susanna informs Figaro that their master's kind attentions toward her are not as disinterested as they seem; in fact, he would like to spend the wedding night with her, in accordance with the medieval custom. Enraged, Figaro rushes off to consider retaliation. Marcellina, an old spinster who hopes to marry Figaro, and Bartolo, a former suitor of the Countess, are determined to prevent the wedding, but Susanna makes it clear that she is not to be intimidated. No sooner has Marcellina departed, than Cherubino, a young page, comes to lament his hopeless love for the Countess. He is surprised in Susanna's room by the Count and hides behind a chair listening delightedly to his master's amorous proposals to Susanna. At the arrival of the spiteful music master, Don Basilio, the Count, in turn, conceals himself, only to emerge in a jealous rage at Basilio's gossip about the Countess and Cherubino. Discovering the page's hiding place, the Count furiously orders him to join his regiment at Seville. The act ends with Figaro's mock-heroic farewell to Cherubino, who will now exchange his effete existence for the rigors of military life.

ACT TWO

The Countess has determined to assist Figaro and Susanna, hoping to regain her husband's wayward affections. Figaro discloses a plot to ridicule his master by arranging a meeting with Cherubino, dressed as a girl, and the Countess and Susanna begin to disguise the page. As the Count's voice is heard at the door, Susanna flees to her own room, while Cherubino hides in a closet. The Count demands to know who is locked behind the closet door. The Countess replies that it is Susanna, but she refuses to open the closet for her husband's inspection. While the Count goes off to get a crowbar, Susanna releases Cherubino and locks her-

6 *The Marriage of Figaro*

self into the closet in his place; the page escapes through a window. Upon returning, the Count discovers Susanna, and begs his wife's forgiveness for his suspicions. Figaro enters, anxious to begin the wedding ceremonies, but when Antonio, the gardener, appears with news that he has just seen a man jumping out of the Countess's window, the Count's suspicions are aroused anew. Figaro asserts that he himself was the unknown man. He is at first unable to cite the contents of a paper that Antonio has found under the window, but after adroit prompting by Susanna and the Countess, he correctly declares it to be the page's commission, which he claims had been given to him for sealing. The act ends in utter confusion, as Marcellina, Bartolo, and Don Basilio rush in, accusing Figaro of breach of promise, and demanding justice of the Count, to the disgust of Figaro, Susanna, and the Countess.

ACT THREE

The Countess and Susanna fabricate a new plot: Susanna is to make a rendezvous for that evening with the Count, but the Countess, dressed in Susanna's clothes, will go in her place. Meanwhile, Don Curzio, the Count's lawyer, has decided matters in Marcellina's favor—Figaro must either marry her or pay a sum of money that he owes her. In the explanations that follow it is discovered that Figaro is the long-lost son of Marcellina and Bartolo, who decide, somewhat belatedly, to get married that very day. Susanna misunderstands when she first sees the new-found mother and son embracing, but all is eventually explained, and the two couples go off to prepare for a double wedding. As soon as they are gone, Cherubino reappears with Susanna's cousin, Barbarina, who is taking him home to dress him as a girl, so that he can unobtrusively take part in the wedding festivities. Still deploring her husband's infidelities, the Countess returns to dictate a letter to Susanna, designating the place of meeting with the Count for that evening; Susanna is to give it to him with instructions to return the pin with which it is sealed. Cherubino is unmasked by Antonio as he presents a bouquet of flowers to the Countess, but Barbarina obtains his pardon by relating another of the Count's indiscretions. The wedding ceremonies finally begin, as Susanna manages to deliver her note to the Count. The act ends in general rejoicing, and a chorus in praise of the Count's benevolence.

ACT FOUR

That night, in the gardens of the castle, Barbarina laments the loss of the pin that the Count has asked her to return to Susanna, and innocently arouses Figaro's suspicions of his bride. Marcellina warns Susanna, as Figaro, after a diatribe on the infidelity of women, hides in the bushes to await his "rival." Discovering Figaro's hiding place, but pretending not to have seen him, Susanna taunts him by singing of the "lover" whom she awaits; then she conceals herself in the bushes at the opposite side of the garden. Cherubino comes to meet Barbarina and sees the Countess, disguised as Susanna. His attempts at flirtation are interrupted by the Count, who also mistakes his wife for Susanna, and behaves accordingly, finally sending her to wait for him in a summerhouse. Figaro's musings on his bride's betrayal are interrupted by Susanna, posing as her mistress. Figaro soon recognizes her, but continues the deception, pretending to be madly in love with the Countess. Susanna reveals herself; the lovers are reconciled and stage a violent love scene for the benefit of the Count, who happens to be passing at that moment. At the Count's shouts of indignation, all the characters emerge from various hiding places. When the real Countess unmasks herself, the disconcerted Count is forced to beg his wife's pardon, which is generously granted to him.

CHARACTERS

COUNT ALMAVIVA   *Baritone*

COUNTESS ALMAVIVA (ROSINA), *his wife*   *Soprano*

FIGARO, *the* COUNT'S *steward*   *Baritone or Bass-baritone*

SUSANNA, *the* COUNTESS'S *maid;*
  betrothed to FIGARO   *Soprano*

CHERUBINO, *a young page*   *Soprano or Mezzo-soprano*

DON BASILIO, *the* COUNT'S *music master*   *Tenor*

DOCTOR BARTOLO, *a physician from Seville;*
  formerly the COUNTESS'S *guardian*   *Bass*

MARCELLINA, *his housekeeper; formerly the*
  COUNTESS'S *governess*   *Soprano or Mezzo-soprano*

ANTONIO, *the* COUNT'S *gardener;* SUSANNA'S *uncle*   *Bass*

BARBARINA, *his daughter*   *Soprano*

DON CURZIO, *a lawyer*   *Tenor*

TWO PEASANT GIRLS   *Soprano and Mezzo-soprano*

CHORUS *of peasants*

The action takes place during one day, in and around the
COUNT'S *castle, near Seville, during the mid-eighteenth cen-*
tury.

ATTO PRIMO

Camera quasi smobiliata. FIGARO *prende la misura d' un letto;* SUSANNA *prova il suo cappello di nozze.*

1. Duettino

FIGARO: Cinque—dieci—venti—
Trenta—trenta sei—quarantatre.

SUSANNA: Ora sì, ch'io son contenta,
Sembra fatto in ver per me.

FIGARO: Cinque.

SUSANNA: Guarda un po', mio caro Figaro!

FIGARO: Dieci. Venti.

SUSANNA: Guarda adesso il mio cappello!

FIGARO: Quarantatre.

SUSANNA: Guarda un po', mio caro Figaro.
Guarda adesso il mio cappello!

FIGARO: Si, mio core, or è più bello.
Sembra fatto in ver per te.

SUSANNA: Guarda un po'.

FIGARO: Sì, mio core.

SUSANNA: Ora sì, ch'io son contenta.

FIGARO: Sì, mio core.

SUSANNA: Ah! il mattino alle nozze vicino,
Quant'è dolce al mio tenero sposo
Questo bel cappellino vezzoso
Che Susanna ella stessa si fè!

FIGARO: Ah! il mattino alle nozze vicino,
Quant'è dolce al tuo tenero sposo
Questo bel capellino vezzoso
Che Susanna ella stessa si fè!

Recitativo

SUSANNA: Cosa stai misurando, caro il mio Figaretto?

FIGARO: Io guardo se quel letto, che ci destina il Conte, farà buona figura in questo loco.

SUSANNA: In questa stanza?

FIGARO: Certo, a noi la cede generoso il padrone.

A half-furnished room. FIGARO *is measuring a bed;* SUSANNA *is trying on her wedding hat.*

1. Duettino

FIGARO: Five — ten — twenty — thirty — thirty-six — forty-three.

SUSANNA: Now I'm so very happy! It seems to be really made for me.

FIGARO: Five.

SUSANNA: Look at me, my dear Figaro!

FIGARO: Ten. Twenty.

SUSANNA: Now look at my hat!

FIGARO: Forty-three.

SUSANNA: Look at me, my dear Figaro. Now look at my hat!

FIGARO: Yes, my darling, now it's even prettier. It seems to be really made for you.

SUSANNA: Look at me.

FIGARO: Yes, my darling.

SUSANNA: Now I'm so very happy.

FIGARO: Yes, my darling.

SUSANNA: Ah, with our wedding day so near, how my dear fiancé loves this pretty, charming little hat that Susanna has made for herself.

FIGARO: Ah, with our wedding day so near, how my dear fiancée loves this pretty, charming little hat that Susanna has made for herself.

Recitative

SUSANNA: What are you measuring there, my dear little Figaro?

FIGARO: I'm seeing whether this bed, which our generous master has given us, will look well in this corner.

SUSANNA: In this room?

FIGARO: Surely; the Count has generously given it to us.

SUSANNA: Io per me te la dono.

FIGARO: E la ragione?

SUSANNA (*toccandosi la fronte*): La ragione l'ho qui.

FIGARO (*facendo lo stesso*): Perchè non puoi far, che passi un po' qui!

SUSANNA: Perchè non voglio. Sei tu mio servo, o no?

FIGARO: Ma non capisco perchè tanto ti spiacia, la più comoda stanza del palazzo.

SUSANNA: Perch'io son la Susanna, e tu sei pazzo.

FIGARO: Grazie, non tanti elogi; guarda un poco, se potria meglio stare in altro loco.

2. Duetto

Se a caso madama la notte ti chiama—
Din, din, din, din—
In due passi da quella puoi gir.
Vien poi l'occasione
Che vuolmi il padrone—
Don, don, don, don—
In tre salti lo vado a servir.

SUSANNA: Così se il mattino il caro Contino—
Din, din, don, don,
E ti manda tre miglia lontan—
Din, din, don, don—
A mia porta il diavol lo porta—
Ed ecco in tre salti—

FIGARO: Susanna pian, pian.

SUSANNA: Ed ecco—

FIGARO: Pian, pian—

SUSANNA: In tre salti—

FIGARO: Pian, pian—

SUSANNA: Din, din—

FIGARO: Pian, pian—

SUSANNA: Don, don!—

FIGARO: Pian, pian—

SUSANNA: Ascolta!

FIGARO: Fa presto!

SUSANNA: And I give my part of it back to you.

FIGARO: And your reason?

SUSANNA (*pointing to her forehead*): I have the reason here.

FIGARO (*pointing to his own forehead*): And why can't you transmit it *here?*

SUSANNA: Because I don't want to. Are you my slave or not?

FIGARO: But I don't understand why you're objecting to the most convenient room in the castle.

SUSANNA: Because I'm Susanna, and you're stupid!

FIGARO: Thank you; not so much flattery; look and see if you can find us a better place!

2. Duet

If the Countess, by chance, should call you at night— ding, ding!—just two steps from here and you'd be with her. And then, if the Count, should want *me*—dong, dong!—in three jumps I could be at his side.

SUSANNA: And so, if one morning, the dear little Count— ding, ding!—sends you three miles away—ding, ding— dong, dong!—the devil would bring him to my door—and then, in three jumps—

FIGARO: Be calm, Susanna!

SUSANNA: And then—

FIGARO: Be calm—

SUSANNA: In three jumps—

FIGARO: Be calm—

SUSANNA: Ding, ding!—

FIGARO: Be calm—

SUSANNA: Dong, dong!—

FIGARO: Be calm—

SUSANNA: Listen, now!

FIGARO: Tell me quickly.

SUSANNA: Se udir brami il resto,
Discaccia i sospetti, che torto mi fan.
FIGARO: Udir bramo il resto,
I dubbi, i sospetti gelare me fan.
SUSANNA: Discaccia i sospetti, che torto mi fan.
FIGARO: I dubbi, i sospetti gelare mi fan.

Recitativo
SUSANNA: Or bene, ascolta e taci.
FIGARO: Parla, che c'è di nuovo?
SUSANNA: Il signor Conte, stanco d'andar cacciando le straniere bellezze forestiere, vuole ancor nel castello ritentar la sua sorte; n'è già di sua Consorte, bada bene, appetito gli viene.
FIGARO: E di chi dunque?
SUSANNA: Della tua Susannetta.
FIGARO: Di te?
SUSANNA: Di me medesma, ed ha speranza ch'al nobil suo progetto utilissima sia tal vicinanza.
FIGARO: Bravo! tiriamo avanti.
SUSANNA: Queste le grazie son, questa la cura ch'egli prende di te, della tua sposa.
FIGARO: O guarda un po', che carità pelosa!
SUSANNA: Chetati, or viene il meglio; Don Basilio, mio maestro di canto, e suo factotum, nel darmi la lezione me ripete ogni dì questa canzone.

FIGARO: Chi! Basilio! Oh birbante!
SUSANNA: E tu credevi, che fosse la mia dote merto del tuo bel muso?
FIGARO: Me n'era lusingato.
SUSANNA: Ei la destina per ottener da me certe mezz'ore che il diritto feudale—
FIGARO: Come! ne' i feudi suoi non l'ha il Conte abolito?
SUSANNA: Ebben, ora è pentito, e par che tenti rescattarlo da me.
FIGARO: Bravo! mi piace; che caro signor Conte; Ci vogliamo divertir, trovato avete—
(*Suona un campanella.*)
Chi suona? La Contessa.

SUSANNA: If you want me to go on, discard your nasty suspicions! They only wrong me.

FIGARO: I want to hear the rest of it, but my doubts and suspicions make my blood run cold!

SUSANNA: Discard your suspicions! They only wrong me.

FIGARO: My doubts and suspicions make my blood run cold!

Recitative

SUSANNA: Very well, now listen and be quiet!

FIGARO: Tell me. What has happened?

SUSANNA: The Count is tired of pursuing foreign beauties, and he would like to try his luck again in his own castle; but it's not his wife, you see, who has aroused his passions.

FIGARO: Who is it, then?

SUSANNA: Your own Susanna.

FIGARO: You?

SUSANNA: My own little self, and he hopes that our proximity will further his plans.

FIGARO: Delightful! We're making progress!

SUSANNA: That's his great generosity! That's why he's so considerate of you and your fiancée.

FIGARO: Look at that! What hypocrisy!

SUSANNA: One moment; now comes the best of all. Don Basilio, my singing teacher, is the Count's willing helper, and during my lessons, he incessantly pleads the Count's cause.

FIGARO: Who—Basilio? That scoundrel!

SUSANNA: And you believed that my dowry was given for *your* good looks?

FIGARO: So I flattered myself!

SUSANNA: He intended the money to win from me certain privileges that the feudal rights—

FIGARO: What! Didn't he abolish his feudal rights?

SUSANNA: Well, now he's sorry, and it seems that he'll try to restore them through me.

FIGARO: Wonderful! I'm flattered! What a generous master! He wants some amusement, and he's found—
(*A bell rings.*)
Who's ringing? The Countess.

SUSANNA: Addio, addio, Figaro bello.
FIGARO: Coraggio, mio tesoro!
SUSANNA: E tu, cervello! (*Parte.*)

3. Aria

FIGARO: Bravo, signor padrone!
Ora incomincio a capire il mistero,
E a veder schietto
Tutto il vostro progetto.
A Londra, è vero?
Voi ministro, io corriero,
E la Susanna—
Segreta ambasciatrice.
Non sarà, Figaro il dice.
Se vuol ballare, signor Contino,
Il chitarrino le suonerò, sì.
Se vuol venire nella mia scuola,
La capriola le insegnerò, sì.
Saprò—ma piano, piano—
Meglio ogni arcano
Dissimulando scoprir potrò.
L'arte schermendo,
L'arte adoprando,
Di qua pungendo, di là scherzando,
Tutte le macchine rovescierò.
(*Parte. Entrano* BARTOLO *e* MARCELLINA.)

Recitativo

BARTOLO: Ed aspettaste il giorno fissato per le nozze, a parlarmi di questo?

MARCELLINA: Io non mi perdo, dottor mio, di coraggio, per romper de' sponsali più avanzati di questo, bastò spesso un pretesto; ed egli ha meco, oltre questo contratto certi impegni—so io—basta! Conviene la Susanna atterrir, convien con arte impuntigliarla a refiutari il conte; egli per vendicarsi prenderà il mio partito, e Figaro così fia mio marito.

BARTOLO: Bene, io tutto farò. Senza riserva, tutto a me palesate. (*a parte*) Avrei pur gusto di dar in moglie la mia serva antica, a chi mi fece un dì rapir l'amica.

4. Aria

La vendetta, oh, la vendetta
E un piacer serbato ai saggi.

SUSANNA: I must go now, Figaro darling!

FIGARO: Be brave, my love!

SUSANNA: And you, be clever! (*Exits.*)

3. *Aria*

FIGARO: So that's your game, my Lord! Now I'm beginning to understand the mystery, and to see your plans all too clearly. So we're going to London? You as minister, I as courier, and my Susanna—as secret ambassadress. You'll never succeed—Figaro has spoken! If my friend the Count wishes to dance, I'll be the one to play the guitar. If he wishes to come to my school, I'll teach him the steps. I'll know his plans—be calm now!—it's better to uncover a secret by stealth! I'll use art to conceal art; I'll fight or cajole, and I'll bring all his plots to ruin. (*He goes off.* BARTOLO *and* MARCELLINA *enter.*)

Recitative

BARTOLO: And you waited until the wedding day to mention this to me?

MARCELLINA: I would have courage, my dear Doctor, to break off a marriage even further advanced than this one is; a pretext is often enough; and I have one. In addition to this contract, I have with me certain pledges—enough! We must intimidate Susanna and make her resist the Count's proposals. To avenge himself, he'll take my part, and so Figaro will be forced to marry me!

BARTOLO: Good! I'll do everything, without reservations. But tell me all about it. (*aside*) How I would love to marry off Marcellina, my old servant, to the man who helped the Count to steal my Rosina from me.

4. *Aria*

Revenge! Ah, revenge is the satisfaction reserved for the

L'obliar l'onte, gli oltraggi
E bassezza, è ognor viltà.
Coll'astuzia, coll'arguzia
Col giudizio, col criterio
Si potrebbe, il fatto è serio;
Ma credete si farà.
Se tutto il codice
Dovessi volgere
Se tutto l'indice
Dovessi leggere,
Con un equivoco, con un sinomimo,
Qualche garbuglio si troverà.
Tutta Siviglio conosce Bartolo,
Il birbo Figaro vinto sarà. (*Parte.*)

Recitativo

MARCELLINA: Tutto ancor non ho perso; mi resta la speranza.
(SUSANNA *entra.*)
Ma Susanna si avanza; io vo' provarmi—fingiam di non vederla. (*come fra se, ma forte*) E quella buona perla la vorrebbe sposar.

SUSANNA (*a parte*): Di me favella.

MARCELLINA: Ma da Figaro alfine non può meglio sperarsi—*l'argent fait tout.*

SUSANNA: Che lingua! Manco male ch'ognun sa quanto vale.

MARCELLINA: Brava! Questo è giudizio! Con quegl'occhi modesti, con quell'aria pietosa! E poi—

SUSANNA: Meglio è partir.

MARCELLINA: Che cara sposa!
(*Tutti i due vogliono partire;* MARCELLINA *ironicamente invita* SUSANNA *a precedarla.*)

5. Duetto

Via resti servita, madama brillante.

SUSANNA: Non sono sì ardita, madama piccante.

MARCELLINA: No, prima a lei tocca.

SUSANNA: No, no, tocca a lei.

MARCELLINA e SUSANNA: Io so i dover miei,
Non fo' inciviltà.

MARCELLINA: La sposa novella!

wise. To forget a shame or an insult is a weakness; I call it vile. With subtlety and craft, with wisdom and discrimination, believe me, it can be done, although it's very difficult. If I have to overturn all the codes of law, if I must read all the statutes, I'll find some loophole, some contradiction that will confuse them. All of Seville respects Doctor Bartolo! That rascal Figaro will be beaten at last! (*Exits.*)

Recitative

MARCELLINA: All is not lost; some hope remains to me. (SUSANNA *enters.*) But Susanna is approaching; let's see what I can do— I'll ignore her completely. (*as if to herself, but loudly*) And that's the pearl of virtue that he'd like to marry!

SUSANNA (*aside*): She speaks of me.

MARCELLINA: After all, from Figaro's taste, one can't expect much—money is all that matters!

SUSANNA: How bitter! I'm glad that everyone knows her for what she is!

MARCELLINA: Well, this is wisdom! Such modest eyes! What a pious air! And yet—

SUSANNA: I'd better go.

MARCELLINA: What a sweet bride!

(*Both are about to leave;* MARCELLINA *ironically invites* SUSANNA *to go first.*)

5. *Duet*

I'm your servant, most brilliant of brides!

SUSANNA: I'm not so presumptuous, most learned lady!

MARCELLINA: You must precede me.

SUSANNA: No, no, after you.

MARCELLINA *and* SUSANNA: I've learned my manners; I'm never impolite!

MARCELLINA: The innocent little bride!

SUSANNA: La dama d'onore!

MARCELLINA: Del Conte la bella!

SUSANNA: Di Spagna l'amore!

MARCELLINA: I meriti!

SUSANNA: L'abito!

MARCELLINA: Il posto!

SUSANNA: L'età!

MARCELLINA: Perbacco, precipito
Se ancor resto qua.

SUSANNA: Sibilla decrepita,
Da rider mi fa!

MARCELLINA: Via resti servita.

SUSANNA: Non sono sì ardita.

(MARCELLINA *parte.*)

Recitativo

Va là, vecchia pedante, dottoressa arrogante, perchè hai letti due libri, e seccata madama in gioventù!
(*Entra* CHERUBINO *dalla finestra.*)

CHERUBINO: Susannetta, sei tu?

SUSANNA: Son io, cosa volete?

CHERUBINO: Ah, cor mio, che accidente!

SUSANNA: Cor vostro? Cosa avvenne?

CHERUBINO: Il Conte ieri, perchè trovommi sol con Barbarina, il congedo mi diede; e se la Constessina, la mia bella comare, grazia non m'intercede, io vado via, io non ti vedo più, Susanna mia.

SUSANNA: Non vedete più me? Bravo! Ma dunque non più per la Contessa secretamente il vostro cor sospira?

CHERUBINO: Ah, che troppo rispetto ella m'ispira! Felice te, che puoi vederla quando vuoi, che la vesti il mattino, che la sera la spogli, che le metti gli spilloni—i merletti— ah! se in tuo loco— Cos'hai lì? Dimmi un poco.

SUSANNA: Ah, il vago nastro e la notturna cuffia di comare sì bella.

SUSANNA: The respected old lady!

MARCELLINA: The Count's sweetheart!

SUSANNA: The sweetheart of all Spain!

MARCELLINA: Your virtue!

SUSANNA: Your manners!

MARCELLINA: Your position!

SUSANNA: Your age!

MARCELLINA: By God, I'll slap her if I stay here any longer!

SUSANNA: Decrepit old hag! She makes me laugh!

MARCELLINA: I'm your servant.

SUSANNA: I'm not so presumptuous.
(MARCELLINA *exits*.)

Recitative

Go ahead, you pedantic old woman! How can you be so
arrogant just because you've read two books and were
governess to my lady when she was a child?
(CHERUBINO *enters though a window*.)

CHERUBINO: Susanetta, is it you?

SUSANNA: It's I; what do you want?

CHERUBINO: Ah, my darling, what trouble!

SUSANNA: Your darling? What has happened?

CHERUBINO: Yesterday the Count, because he found me
alone with Barbarina, dismissed me from his service;
and if the lovely Countess, my beautiful godmother, won't
intercede for me, I'll have to go away, and then I won't see
you again, my dear Susanna.

SUSANNA: You won't see me again! How lovely! But then
it's no longer the Countess for whom you sigh in secret?

CHERUBINO: Ah, she inspires me with too much respect. Oh,
lucky you, who can see her when you want to, who dress
her each morning, and undress her every evening, who
fasten her pins and laces—oh, if only I were in your place
— What are you holding? Let me see it!

SUSANNA: Ah, this lovely ribbon belongs to the nightcap
of your beautiful godmother.

CHERUBINO: Deh, dammelo, sorella, per pietà.
(*Piglia il nastro.*)

SUSANNA: Presto quel nastro!
CHERUBINO: Oh caro, oh bello, oh fortunato nastro! Io non tel renderò che colla vita.
SUSANNA: Cos'è quest'insolenza?
CHERUBINO: Eh via, sta cheta. In ricompensa, poi, questa mia canzonetta io ti vo' dare.
SUSANNA: E che ne debbo fare?
CHERUBINO: Leggila alla padrona, leggila tu medesima, leggila a Barbarina, a Marcellina. Leggila ad ogni donna del palazzo!
SUSANNA: Povero Cherubin, siete voi pazzo?

6. *Aria*

CHERUBINO: Non so più cosa son, cosa faccio.
Or di foco, ora sono di ghiaccio.
Ogni donna cangiar di colore.
Ogni donna mi fa palpitar.
Solo ai nomi d'amore di diletto,
Mi si turba, mi s'altera il petto,
E a parlare mi sforza d'amore,
Un desio ch'io non posso spiegar.
Parlo d'amor vegliando,
Parlo d'amor sognando,
All'acqua, all'ombra, ai monti,
Ai fiori, all'erbe, ai fonti,
All'eco, all'aria ai venti,
Che il suon d'vani accenti
Portano via con se.
Parlo d'amor—
E se non ho chi m'oda,
Parlo d'amor con me.
(*Una voce di fuori.*)

   Recitativo

Ah, son perduto—il Conte![1]
SUSANNA: Oh, me meschina!
(*Entra* IL CONTE; CHERUBINO *si nasconde in dietro d'una poltrona.*)
IL CONTE: Susanna, come sembri agitata e confusa.

---

[1]In the Dover edition of the full score the words "il Conte!" are omitted, and Susanna's next line is "Che timor . . . il Conte . . . misera me!"

CHERUBINO: Please give it to me, dear Susanna, for pity's sake.

(*He snatches the ribbon from her.*)

SUSANNA: Give back that ribbon!

CHERUBINO: Oh, dear, beautiful, fortunate ribbon! I'll give it up only with my life!

SUSANNA: How can you be so horrid?

CHERUBINO: Now, now, be calm; instead I'll give you this little love song of mine.

SUSANNA: And what must I do with it?

CHERUBINO: Read it to my lady, read it to yourself, read it to Barbarina, to Marcellina. Read it to every woman in the castle!

SUSANNA: Poor Cherubino, you're quite insane!

6. *Aria*

CHERUBINO: I know no longer what I am, or what I'm doing. First I'm like fire, then I'm like ice. Every woman makes me blush and tremble. At the very mention of love I'm troubled and excited, and when I hear of the power of love, I feel a desire I can't explain. Waking and sleeping I speak of love—to water, to shadows, to hills, to flowers, to grass, to fountains, to the echo, to the air, to the winds, so that they may carry away the burden of my vain longings. I speak of love— And if no one will listen, I'll speak of love to myself!

(*He hears a noise.*)

Recitative

Ah, I'm lost! It's the Count!

SUSANNA: Oh, I'm afraid![1]

(*The* COUNT *comes in;* CHERUBINO *hides behind an armchair.*)

COUNT: Susanna, you seem confused and agitated.

---

[1]To conform to the Dover edition of the full score this line reads "What's wrong? . . . the Count! . . . woe is me!"

SUSANNA: Signor, io chiedo scusa, ma, se mai qui sorpresa —per carità, partite!

IL CONTE: Un momento e ti lascio. Odi.

SUSANNA: Non odo nulla.

IL CONTE: Due parole. Tu sai che ambasciatore a Londra il Re mi dichiarò. Di condur meco Figaro destinai.

SUSANNA: Signor, se osassi—

IL CONTE: Parla, mia cara, e con quel dritto ch'oggi prendi su me, finchè tu vivi chiedi, imponi, prescrivi.

SUSANNA: Lasciatemi, Signor; dritti non prendo, non ne vo', non ne intendo. Oh, me infelice!

IL CONTE: Ah, no, Susanna, io ti vo' far felice! Tu ben sai quant'io t'amo; a te Basilio tutto già disse. Or senti, se per pochi momenti meco in giardin, sull'imbrunir del giorno— Ah, per questo favore io pagherei.

DON BASILIO (*fuori*): E uscito poco fa.

IL CONTE: Chi parla?

SUSANNA: O Dei!

IL CONTE: Esci, ed alcun non entri.

SUSANNA: Ch'io vi lasci qui solo?

DON BASILIO (*fuori*): Da madama sarà, vado a cercarlo.

IL CONTE: Qui dietro mi porrò.

SUSANNA: Non vi celate.

IL CONTE: Taci—e cerca ch'ei parta.

SUSANNA: Ohimè! che fate?

(IL CONTE *si nasconde dietro della poltrona; non vede* CHERUBINO *chi si pose nella poltrona, e* SUSANNA *lo copre presto con un mantello. Entra* DON BASILIO).

DON BASILIO: Susanna, il ciel vi salvi! Avreste a caso veduto il Conte?

SUSANNA: E cosa deve far meco il Conte? Animo, uscite.

DON BASILIO: Aspettate, sentite! Figaro di lui cerca.

SUSANNA: My Lord, I ask your pardon, but if we were ever found here—for heaven's sake, please leave me!

COUNT: I'll leave you in a moment. Listen.

SUSANNA: I won't listen.

COUNT: Two words. You know that the King has appointed me as envoy to London, and that I expect to take Figaro with me.

SUSANNA: My Lord, if I dared to tell you—

COUNT: Tell me, tell me, my dear, and with the power you have over me now and as long as you live, ask me, order me, command me!

SUSANNA: Please let me go, my Lord; I don't claim this power, I don't wish it, I don't understand it. Oh, I'm so unhappy!

COUNT: Ah, no, Susanna, I want to make you happy. You know well how much I love you; Basilio has told you everything already. Listen; if for a few moments at twilight you'll join me in the garden—I'll reward you for that favor.

DON BASILIO (outside): He left a few minutes ago.

COUNT: Who's there?

SUSANNA: O heavens!

COUNT: Go out and stop him.

SUSANNA: And leave you alone here?

DON BASILIO (outside): He must be with the Countess. I'll go look for him there.

COUNT: I'll hide behind this chair.

SUSANNA: Not there!

COUNT: Quiet—and get him out of here!

SUSANNA: Oh, dear— What are you doing?

(The COUNT hides behind the armchair; CHERUBINO, unseen by the COUNT, jumps into the chair, and SUSANNA quickly covers him with a cloak. DON BASILIO enters.)

DON BASILIO: Susanna, heaven save you! Have you by any chance seen the Count?

SUSANNA: And what has the Count to do with me? You're rude; go away!

DON BASILIO: Wait, listen! Figaro is looking for him.

SUSANNA: Oh cielo! Ei cerca chi, dopo voi, più l'odia.

IL CONTE (*a parte*): Vediam come mi serve.

DON BASILIO: Io non ho mai nella moral sentito, ch'uno ch'ami la moglie odii il marito. Per dir che il Conte v'ama—

SUSANNA: Sortite, vil ministro dell'altrui sfrenatezza; io non ho d'uopo della vostra morale, del Conte, del suo amor!

DON BASILIO: Non c'è alcun male. Ha ciascun i suoi gusti. Io me credea che preferir doveste per amante, come fan tutte quante un signor liberal, prudente e saggio, a un giovinastro, a un paggio.

SUSANNA: A Cherubino?

DON BASILIO: A Cherubino, Cherubin d'amore, ch'oggi sul far del giorno passeggiava qui intorno per entrar.

SUSANNA: Uomo maligno, un impostura è questa!

DON BASILIO: E un maligno con voi chi ha gli occhi in testa? E quella canzonetta, ditemi in confidenza—Io sono amico ed altrui nulla dico—è per voi, o per madama?

SUSANNA (*a parte*): Chi diavol glie l'ha detto?

DON BASILIO: A proposito, figlia, instruitelo meglio. Egli la guarda a tavola sì spesso, e con tanta immodestia—che s'il Conte s'accorge—e su tal punto, sapete egli è un bestia.

SUSANNA: Scellerato! E perchè andate voi tai menzogne spargendo?

DON BASILIO: Io? Che ingiustizia! Quel che compró io vendo, a quel che tutti dicono io non aggiungo un pelo. (IL CONTE *si alza da dietro la poltrona.*)

IL CONTE: Come! Che dicon tutti?

DON BASILIO (*a parte*): Oh bella!

SUSANNA (*a parte*): Oh cielo!

7. *Terzetto*

IL CONTE: Cosa sento! Tosto andate
E scacciate il seduttor.

DON BASILIO: In mal punto son qui giunto;
Perdonate, o mio signor.

SUSANNA: In that case, he's looking for the one man who hates him more than you do.

COUNT (*aside*): Let's see how he serves me.

DON BASILIO: I've never read in any moral tract that one who loves the wife must hate the husband. In fact, since the Count loves you—

SUSANNA: Get out of here, you horrible panderer! I have no need of your morals, of the Count, or of his love!

DON BASILIO: I meant no harm. Everyone has his own tastes. But I believed you would prefer for a lover, as most women do, a lord who is liberal, prudent, and wise to a little boy, a page.

SUSANNA: To Cherubino?

DON BASILIO: To Cherubino, the cherub of love, who was wandering about outside this room at daybreak, hoping to get in.

SUSANNA: You're a wicked man, and that's a lie!

DON BASILIO: Is everyone with eyes in his head wicked in your opinion? And that love song, tell me in confidence— I'm a friend and won't say anything to anyone— Is it for you or for the Countess?

SUSANNA (*aside*): What devil could have told him?

DON BASILIO: Next time, my dear girl, you might teach him better. At the table he looks at her so often and with such immodesty—if the Count should notice—you know, when jealous, he's like a beast.

SUSANNA: Villain! Why do you go about spreading such lies?

DON BASILIO: I? How unjust! I say what I hear, without adding a word to the common gossip.

(*The* COUNT *rises from behind the armchair.*)

COUNT: What gossip?

DON BASILIO (*aside*): Delightful!

SUSANNA (*aside*): O heavens!

7. Trio

COUNT: What are you saying? That seducer Cherubino must be banished at once!

DON BASILIO: I came here at an awkward moment; pardon me, my Lord.

SUSANNA: Che ruina! Me meschina!
Son oppressa dal terror!

IL CONTE: Tosto andate e scacciate il seduttor!

DON BASILIO: In mal punto son qui giunto.

SUSANNA: Che ruina!

DON BASILIO *ed* IL CONTE: Ah! già svien la poverina.
Come, oh Dio, le batte il cor.

DON BASILIO: Pian, pianin, su questo seggio.

SUSANNA: Dove sono? Cosa veggio?
Che insolenza—andate fuor!

DON BASILIO *ed* IL CONTE: Siamo quì per aiutarvi(ti),
È sicuro il vostro onor.
Non turbati, o mio tesor.

DON BASILIO: Ah, del paggio quel ch'ho detto
Era solo un mio sospetto.

SUSANNA: E un'insidia, una perfidia,
Non credete all'impostor.

IL CONTE: Parta, parta il damerino.

SUSANNA *e* DON BASILIO: Poverino!

IL CONTE: Poverino! Poverino!
Ma da me sorpreso ancor!

SUSANNA: Come?

DON BASILIO: Che?

SUSANNA: Che?

IL CONTE: Da tua cugina, l'uscio ier trovai
Rinchiuso: picchio, m'apre
Barbarina paurosa fuor dell'uso.
Io, dal muso insospettito,
Guardo, cerco in ogni sito,
Ed alzando piano pianino
Il tappeto al tavolino,
(*Dimostra col mantello sulla poltrona.*)
Vedo il paggio.
Ah, cosa veggio?

SUSANNA: Ah, crude stelle!

DON BASILIO: Ah, meglio ancora!

IL CONTE: Onestissima signora!

SUSANNA: Accader non può di peggio.

IL CONTE: Or capisco come va!

SUSANNA: What a scandal! It's too much for me to bear!

COUNT: He must go at once!

DON BASILIO: I came here at an awkward moment.

SUSANNA: What a scandal!

DON BASILIO *and* COUNT: The poor girl is fainting. O God, how her heart is beating!

DON BASILIO: Let's put her gently in this armchair.

SUSANNA: Where am I? What are you doing? What insolence—go away!

DON BASILIO *and* COUNT: We are here to help you; your honor is safe. Don't worry, my darling.

DON BASILIO: What I told you about the page was only my own suspicion.

SUSANNA: It's a lie; don't believe this impostor!

COUNT: That damned page is going to leave the castle!

SUSANNA *and* DON BASILIO: Poor boy!

COUNT: Poor boy! Poor boy! But this isn't the first time that I've caught him!

SUSANNA: How?

DON BASILIO: What?

SUSANNA: Where?

COUNT: At your cousin's house—yesterday I found the door locked. I knocked and Barbarina opened, but she was very nervous. A suspicion crossed my mind; I looked, searching in every place, and drawing the tablecloth very gently from the table (*demonstrating with the cloak on the chair*) I saw Cherubino. Ah, what do I see?

SUSANNA: Good Lord!

DON BASILIO: Ah, better still!

COUNT: Most honest lady!

SUSANNA: Nothing worse could happen.

COUNT: Now I understand what's going on!

DON BASILIO: Così fan tutte
Le belle.
SUSANNA: Giusti Dei—
Che mai sarà?
DON BASILIO: Non c'è alcuna novità!
SUSANNA: Accader non—
Può di peggio—
Ah, no, ah, no!
DON BASILIO: Così fan tutte le belle.
Non c'è alcuna novità.
Ah, del paggio quel ch'ho detto,
Era solo un mio sospetto.
SUSANNA: Accader non può di peggio.
IL CONTE: Onestissima signora—
DON BASILIO: Così fan tutte le belle.

Recitativo

IL CONTE: Basilio, in traccia tosto di Figaro volate; io vo'
ch'ei veda.
SUSANNA: Ed io che senta; andate.
IL CONTE: Restate. (*a parte a* SUSANNA) Che baldanza! e
quale scusa, se la colpa è evidente?
SUSANNA: Non ha d'uopo di scusa un'innocente.
IL CONTE: Ma costui quando venne?
SUSANNA: Egli era meco, quando voi qui giungeste, e mi
chiedea d'impegnar la padrona a intercedergli grazia. Il
vostro arrivo in scompiglio lo pose, ed allor in quel loco si
nascose.
IL CONTE: Ma s'io stesso m'assisi, quando in camera entrai!

CHERUBINO: Ed allora di dietro io mi celai.
IL CONTE: E quando io là mi posi?
CHERUBINO: Allor io pian mi volsi e qui m'ascosi.

IL CONTE (*a* SUSANNA): Oh cielo! Dunque ha sentito quello
che io ti dicea!
CHERUBINO: Feci per non sentir quanto potea.
IL CONTE: Oh perfidia!
DON BASILIO: Frenatevi—vien gente.

DON BASILIO: That's how all the women do it.

SUSANNA: Good God—how will it ever end?

DON BASILIO: It's nothing new!
SUSANNA: Nothing worse could happen— Ah, no, ah, no!

DON BASILIO: That's how all the women do it. It's nothing new. Ha, what I said about the page was only my own suspicion.

SUSANNA: Nothing worse could happen.
COUNT: Most honest lady—
DON BASILIO: That's how all the women do it.

Recitative

COUNT: Basilio, go and find Figaro at once; I want to see him.
SUSANNA: And *I* want him to hear this; go on!
COUNT: Wait. (*aside to* SUSANNA) What boldness! What excuse can you have when your sin is so evident?
SUSANNA: I am innocent and have no need of an excuse.
COUNT: How long has this boy been here?
SUSANNA: He was with me when you came, and he was asking me to beg Madame to intercede with you for his pardon. Your arrival completely confused him, so he hid himself in that armchair.
COUNT: But I, myself, sat in that chair when I entered the room!
CHERUBINO: And then I hid myself behind it.
COUNT: But when I placed myself there?
CHERUBINO: Then I quietly turned around and hid myself in the chair.
COUNT (*to* SUSANNA): Good God! Then he heard what I said to you!
CHERUBINO: I did whatever I could not to hear.
COUNT: I'm sure you did!
DON BASILIO: Restrain yourself—someone is coming.

IL CONTE (*a* CHERUBINO): E voi restate qui, picciol serpente.
(*Entra un* CORO *dei contadini, con* FIGARO, *un velo in mano.*)

8. Coro

CORO: Giovani liete, fiori spargete,
Davanti al nobile nostro Signor,
Il suo gran core vi serba intatto
D'un più bel fiore l'almo candor.

Recitativo

IL CONTE: Cos'è questa commedia?

FIGARO (*a parte a* SUSANNA): Eccoci in danza, secondami, cor mio.

SUSANNA (*a parte a* FIGARO): Non ci ho speranza.

FIGARO: Signor, non disdegnate questo del nostro affetto meritato tributo; or che aboliste un diritto si ingrato a chi ben ama.

IL CONTE: Quel dritto or non v'è più; cosa si brama?

FIGARO: Della vostra saggezza il primo frutto oggi noi coglierem: le nostre nozze si son già stabilite; or a voi tocca costei che un vostro dono illibata serbò, coprir di questa, simbolo d'onestà, candida vesta.

IL CONTE (*a parte*): Diabolica astuzia, ma fingere convien. (*forte*) Son grato, amici, ad un senso si onesto, ma non merto per questo, nè tributi, nè lodi, e un dritto ingiusto ne' miei feudi abolendo a natura, al dover lor dritti io rendo.

TUTTI: Evviva, evviva, evviva!

SUSANNA: Che virtù!

FIGARO: Che giustizia!

IL CONTE: A voi prometto compier la cerimonia, chiedo sol breve indugio; io voglio in faccia de' miei più fidi, e con più ricca pompa rendervi appien felici. (*a parte*) Marcellina si trovi. (*ai contadini*) Andate, amici.

CORO: Giovani liete—
(*Il* CORO *parte.*)

FIGARO: Evviva!

SUSANNA: Evviva!

DON BASILIO: Evviva!

COUNT (*to* CHERUBINO): And you stay here, you little serpent!
(CHORUS *of peasants enters, followed by* FIGARO, *who has a veil in his hand.*)

8. *Chorus*

CHORUS: Happy young people, scatter flowers before our noble Count! His great kindness preserves the purity of a bride for the one she loves.

Recitative

COUNT: What is this comedy?

FIGARO (*aside to* SUSANNA): We're making progress; follow my lead, my dear.

SUSANNA (*aside to* FIGARO): There's no hope.

FIGARO: My Lord, don't spurn this merited tribute of our affection now that you've abolished a custom so repellent to those who really love each other.

COUNT: The custom is abolished. What more do you want?

FIGARO: We would like to reap the first fruit of your generosity: our wedding is already planned; now you must place this symbol of honor on my bride's head; this chaste wedding veil.

COUNT (*aside*): Devilish cunning! but I'll pretend to agree. (*aloud*) I'm grateful, friends, for such a warm reception, but I don't deserve these tributes and praises; it's an unjust custom that I abolished; I yield my right to nature and duty.

ALL: Hurrah, hurrah, hurrah!

SUSANNA: What virtue!

FIGARO: What wisdom!

COUNT: I promise that I'll complete the ceremony. I ask only a little time; I wish to gather my vassals and to unite you with richer pomp and ceremony. (*aside*) Marcellina will be there! (*to the peasants*) Leave me now, my friends.

CHORUS: Happy young people—
(CHORUS *exits.*)

FIGARO: Hurrah!

SUSANNA: Hurrah!

DON BASILIO: Hurrah!

FIGARO (*a* CHERUBINO): E voi non applaudite?
SUSANNA: E afflitto, poveretto, perchè il padron lo scaccia dal castello.
FIGARO: Ah, in un giorno sì bello!
SUSANNA: In un giorno di nozze!
FIGARO (*al* CONTE): Quando ognuno v'ammira!
CHERUBINO: Perdono, mio Signor!
IL CONTE: Nol meritate.
SUSANNA: Egli è ancora fanciullo.
IL CONTE: Men di quel che tu credi.
CHERUBINO: E ver, mancai; ma dal mio labbro alfine—
IL CONTE: Ben, bene; io vi perdono; anzi farò di più: vacante è un posto d'uffizial nel reggimento mio; io scelgo voi, partite tosto, addio.
SUSANNA *e* FIGARO: Ah, fin domani sol.
IL CONTE: No, parta tosto.
CHERUBINO: A ubbidirvi, Signor, son già disposto.
IL CONTE: Via, per l'ultima volta la Susanna abbracciate. (*a parte*) Inaspettato è il colpo.
(*Partono* IL CONTE *e* DON BASILIO.)
FIGARO: Ehi, capitano, a me pure la mano. (*a parte a* CHERUBINO) Io vo' parlarti pria che tu parta. (*forte*) Addio piccolo Cherubino! Come cangia in un punto il tuo destino!

9. Aria

Non più andrai, farfallone amoroso,
Notte e giorno d'intorno girando;
Delle belle turbando il riposo,
Narcisetto, Adoncino d'amor!
Non più avrai questi bei pennacchini,
Quel cappello leggero e galante,
Quella chioma, quell'aria brillante,
Quel vermiglio donnesco color!
Fra guerrieri, poffar Bacco!
Gran mustacchi, stretto sacco,
Schioppo in spalla, sciabola al fianco,
Collo dritto, muso franco,
O un gran casco o un gran turbante,
Molto onor, poco contante!
Ed in vece del fandango,

FIGARO (*to* CHERUBINO): Why don't you cheer him?

SUSANNA: He's upset, poor little thing, because the Count has banished him from the castle.

FIGARO: Ah, on such a beautiful day!

SUSANNA: On the day of a wedding!

FIGARO (*to the* COUNT): When everyone will admire you!

CHERUBINO: My Lord, forgive me!

COUNT: You don't deserve it.

SUSANNA: He's only a child.

COUNT: You'd be surprised!

CHERUBINO: Even a child can repeat what he hears—

COUNT: Very well, I forgive you. I'll do even more than that. There's an officer's post vacant in my regiment. I appoint you to it; go at once; good-by!

SUSANNA *and* FIGARO: Let him stay here today!

COUNT: No; he must go at once.

CHERUBINO: I'm ready to obey you immediately, my Lord.

COUNT: Come, for the last time kiss Susanna. (*aside*) My strategy has succeeded.

(*The* COUNT *and* DON BASILIO *exit.*)

FIGARO: Well, Captain, shake my hand. (*aside to* CHERUBINO) I want to speak to you alone before you go. (*aloud*) Good-by, my little Cherubino. How your destiny has changed in a moment!

9. Aria

No longer, you amorous butterfly, will you enjoy your customary boudoir excursions! No longer will you disturb the sleep of beautiful women, you Narcissus, you Adonis of love! You won't flaunt your beautiful feathers—your light and gallant cap, your curls, your brilliant air, those feminine pink cheeks! You'll live among soldiers, by Jove —with huge mustaches and a narrow bag, a gun on your shoulder and a sword at your side, a stiff neck and a frank expression, a heavy helmet or a large turban, much honor, but little pay! And instead of dancing, you'll be marching

Una marcia per il fango,
Per montagne, per valloni,
Colle nevi e i sollioni,
Al concerto di tromboni,
Di bombarde, di cannoni,
Che le palle in tutti i tuoni,
All'orecchio fan fischiar.
Cherubino all vittoria,
Alla gloria militar!

through the mud—over mountains, through valleys, in the snow and scorching sun, to the sound of trumpets, and bombardments, and cannons, and bullets thundering past your ear! Cherubino, on to glory, on to military fame!

ATTO SECONDO

La stanza della CONTESSA. LA CONTESSA *è sola.*

10. *Aria*

LA CONTESSA: Porgi amor, qualche ristoro,
Al mio duolo, a' miei sospir!
O mi rendi il mio tesoro,
O mi lascia almen morir!

Recitativo

Vieni, cara Susanna finiscimi l'istoria.
(*Entra* SUSANNA.)

SUSANNA: E già finita.

LA CONTESSA: Dunque volla sedurti?

SUSANNA: Oh, il signor Conte non fa tai complimenti colle donne mie pari; egli venne a contratto di danari.

LA CONTESSA: Ah! il crudel più non m'ama.

SUSANNA: E come poi è geloso di voi?

LA CONTESSA: Come lo sono i moderni mariti, per sistema infedeli, per genio capricciosi, e per orgoglio poi tutti gelosi. Ma se Figaro t'ama, ei sol potria.
(*Entra* FIGARO, *cantando.*)

FIGARO: La la la la la la—

SUSANNA: Eccolo. Vieni, amico, madama impaziente.

FIGARO: A voi non tocca stare in pena per questo, alfin di che si tratta? Al signor Conte piace la sposa mia; indi segretamente ricuperar vorria il diritto feudale; possibil è la cosa e naturale.

LA CONTESSA: Possibil?

SUSANNA: Natural?

FIGARO: Naturalissima e, se Susanna vuol, possibilissima.

SUSANNA: Finiscila una volta.

FIGARO: Ho già finito. Quindi prese il partito di sceglier me

The COUNTESS'S *boudoir. The* COUNTESS *is alone.*

10. Aria

COUNTESS: Is there no consolation, O God of Love, in return for my sorrows and my sighs? Either restore my dearest one's affection to me, or let me find peace in death!

Recitative

Come, dear Susanna, and finish your story.

(SUSANNA *enters.*)

SUSANNA: It's already finished.

COUNTESS: Then he hopes to seduce you?

SUSANNA: Oh, my lord Count doesn't pay such a compliment to women of the lower classes; he offered me money.

COUNTESS: Then the cruel man doesn't love me any longer!

SUSANNA: In that case, why is he so jealous?

COUNTESS: That's the custom of modern husbands; they're unfaithful by philosophy, capricious by character, and jealous as a matter of pride. But if Figaro loves you, it's possible that he can help us.

(*Enter* FIGARO *singing.*)

FIGARO: La la la la la la—

SUSANNA: Here he is! Come, my dear; the Countess is impatient.

FIGARO: There's no reason to worry about this matter. After all, what is the problem? My fiancée pleases the Count; therefore, he secretly decides to restore his feudal rights—the thing is very possible and very natural.

COUNTESS: Possible?

SUSANNA: Natural?

FIGARO: Very natural. And, if Susanna wishes, very possible.

SUSANNA: That's enough. Let's end this conversation.

FIGARO: I've already finished. That's why the Count

corriero, e la Susanna consigliera segreta d'ambasciata; e
perch'ella ostinata ognor rifiuta il diploma d'onor che la
destina, minaccia di protegger Marcellina; questo è tutto
l'affare.

SUSANNA: Ed hai coraggio di trattar scherzando un negozio
sì serio?

FIGARO: Non vi basta, che scherzando io ci pensi? ecco il
progetto; per Basilio un biglietto io gli fò capitar, che
l'avvertisca di certo appuntamento, che per l'ora del ballo
a un amante voi deste.

LA CONTESSA: O ciel! Che sento! Ad un uom sì geloso—

FIGARO: Ancora meglio, così potrem più presto imbaraz-
zarlo, confonderlo, imbrogliarlo, rovesciargli i progetti,
empierlo di sospetti, e porgli in testa, che la moderna festa
ch'ei di fare a me tenta, altri a lui faccia; onde qui perda
il tempo, ivi la traccia, così, quasi ex abrupto, e senza
ch'abbia fatto per frastornarci alcun disegno vien l'ora
delle nozze, in faccia a lei non fia, ch'osi d'opporsi ai voti
miei.

SUSANNA: E ver, ma in di lui vece s'opporrà Marcellina.

FIGARO: Aspetta, al Conte farai subito dir, che verso sera
attendati in giardino; il picciol Cherubino, per mio consiglio
non ancor partito, da femmina vestito, faremo che in sua
vece ivi sen vada; questa è l'unica strada, onde Monsù,
sorpreso da Madama sia costretto a far poi quel che si
brama.

LA CONTESSA (*a* SUSANNA): Che ti par?

SUSANNA: Non c'è mal.

LA CONTESSA: Nel nostro caso?

SUSANNA: Quand'egli è persuaso—

LA CONTESSA: E dove? E il tempo?

FIGARO: Ito è il Conte alla caccia, e per qualch'ora non
sarà di ritorno; io vado, e tosto Cherubino vi mando, lascio
a voi la cura di vestirlo.

LA CONTESSA: E poi?

FIGARO: E poi? Se vuol ballare, Signor Contino, il chitarrino Le suonerò, sì. Le suonerò! (*Parte.*)

decided to appoint me as courier, and to consult Susanna as secret ambassadress. And because she has obstinately refused this honor, he threatens to assist Marcellina; that's the whole of the story.

SUSANNA: Have you the courage to joke about such a serious matter?

FIGARO: You should be glad that I can joke about it. Here's my plan! I'll send a note by Basilio to inform the Count of a certain rendezvous that you made this evening with a lover.

COUNTESS: O heavens! What are you saying? With such a jealous husband—

FIGARO: All the better. We'll be able to embarrass him, confound him, confuse him, overturn all his plans, fill him with suspicions, and fix it in his mind that the trick he's trying to play on me may be played on him by others. While he's losing his time and his composure, our wedding hour will come before he can oppose it.

SUSANNA: That's true, but Marcellina will oppose us in his place.

FIGARO: Wait—tell the Count that you'll wait for him in the garden toward evening. Little Cherubino—I told him not to leave yet—dressed in women's clothes, can meet him there instead of you. That's the only way that my lord, surprised by my lady, will be forced to agree to everything that we ask for.

COUNTESS (*to* SUSANNA): What do you think?

SUSANNA: It's not bad.

COUNTESS: In our situation?

SUSANNA: When Figaro's persuaded—

COUNTESS: Where? And at what time?

FIGARO: The Count has gone hunting, and won't return for several hours. I'm going to send Cherubino here at once. I leave to you the task of dressing him.

COUNTESS: And then?

FIGARO: And then? If my friend, the Count, wishes to dance, I'll be the one to play the guitar, yes! I'll be the one to play the guitar! (*Exits.*)

LA CONTESSA: Quanto duolmi, Susanna, che questo giovinotto abbia del Conte le stravaganze udito! Ah! tu non sai —ma per qual causa mai da me stessa ei non venne? Dov'è la canzonetta?

SUSANNA: Eccola, appunto facciam che ce la canti, Zitto; vien gente—
(*Va alla porta.*)
È desso: avanti, signor ufficiale!
(*Entra* CHERUBINO.)

CHERUBINO: Ah non chiamarmi con nome sì fatale! Ei mi rammenta che con abbandonar degg'io comare tanto buona—

SUSANNA: E tanto bella!

CHERUBINO: Ah, sì, certo!

SUSANNA: Ah, sì, certo! Ipocritone, via presto la canzone, che stamane a me deste, a madama cantate.

LA CONTESSA: Chi n'è l'autor?

SUSANNA: Guardate, egli ha due braccia di rossor sulla faccia.

LA CONTESSA: Prendi la mia chitarra e l'accompagna.

CHERUBINO: Io sono sì tremante— Ma se Madama vuole—

SUSANNA: Lo vuole, sì, lo vuol, manco parole.

11. Aria

CHERUBINO: Voi che sapete che cosa è amor,
Donne, vedete s'io l'ho nel cor.
Quello ch'io provo vi ridirò.
E per me nuovo, capir nol so.
Sento un affetto pien di desir,
Ch'ora è diletto, ch'ora è martir.
Gelo, e poi sento l'alma avvampar
E in un momento torno a gelar;
Ricerco un bene fuori di me,
Non so ch'il tiene, non so cos'è,
Sospiro e gemo senza voler,
Palpito e tremo senza saper.
Non trovo pace notte nè dì,
Ma pur mi piace languir così.

COUNTESS: It makes me so unhappy, Susanna, that that young boy heard all the Count's indiscretions. Ah, you don't yet understand—but why didn't Cherubino come to me himself, instead of asking you to intercede for him? Where is that song that he gave you?

SUSANNA: Here it is. Now we'll make him sing it to us. Wait! someone's coming—
(*She goes to the door.*)
It's he! Come in, come in, exalted officer!
(CHERUBINO *enters.*)

CHERUBINO: Don't call me that fatal name! It reminds me that I must leave such a kind godmother—

SUSANNA: So kind and so pretty!

CHERUBINO: Oh, yes, lovely!

SUSANNA: Oh, yes, lovely! You flatterer! Now, quickly, sing the song that you gave me this morning for Madame.

COUNTESS: Who is the author?

SUSANNA: Look at him! His cheeks are like two bunches of roses!

COUNTESS: Take my guitar and accompany him.

CHERUBINO: I'm trembling with embarrassment—but if Madame wishes it—

SUSANNA: Of course she does—quickly, now, sing it!

11. Aria

CHERUBINO: Ladies, you who know the nature of love, search for it in my heart! I will tell you about my emotions; since they are new to me, I can't understand them. I feel longing full of desire that first is pleasure and then becomes pain. I freeze, and then I feel my soul aflame, and in the next moment, I turn cold again. I'm drawn by something beyond myself—I don't know how to grasp it; I don't know what it may be. Without wishing to, I sigh and groan; without knowing why, I shake and tremble. I find no rest night or day, but somehow I enjoy suffering like this.

Recitativo

LA CONTESSA: Bravo, che bella voce, io non sapea che cantaste sì bene.

SUSANNA: Oh, in verità egli fa tutto ben quello ch'ei fa. Presto a noi, bel soldato; Figaro v'informò—

CHERUBINO: Tutto me disse.

SUSANNA: Lasciatemi veder; andrà benissimo: siam d'uguale statura—giù quel manto.

LA CONTESSA: Che fai?

SUSANNA: Niente paura.

LA CONTESSA: E se qualcuno entrasse?

SUSANNA: Entri, che mal facciamo? La porta chiuderò, ma come poi acconciargli i capelli?

LA CONTESSA: Una mi cuffia prendi mel gabinetto, presto! (SUSANNA *parte.*) Che carta è quella?

CHERUBINO: La patente.

LA CONTESSA: Che sollecita gente!

CHERUBINO: L'ebbi or da Basilio.

LA CONTESSA: Della fretta obliato hanno il sigillo! (SUSANNA *ritorna.*)

SUSANNA: Il sigillo di che?

LA CONTESSA: Della patente.

SUSANNA: Cospetto! Che premura! Ecco la cuffia.

LA CONTESSA: Spicciati; va bene; miserabili noi se il Conte viene!

12. Aria

SUSANNA: Venite inginocchiatvei,
Restate fermo lì.
Pian piano or via giratevi.
Bravo! va ben così.
La faccia ora volgetemi.
Olà, quegli occhi a me.
Drittissimo guardatemi,
Madama qui non è!
La faccia ora volgetemi—
Restate fermo lì,

Recitative

COUNTESS: Bravo! What a beautiful voice! I didn't know that you sang so well.

SUSANNA: Oh, really he does everything well when he tries. Quickly, come here, handsome soldier. Figaro has told you—

CHERUBINO: Everything!

SUSANNA: Let me see. It will do nicely; we're just the same size— Take your cloak off.

COUNTESS: What are you doing?

SUSANNA: Nothing to fear.

COUNTESS: And if anyone should come in?

SUSANNA: Let him come in; what harm are we doing? I'll lock the door. But how shall we cover his hair?

COUNTESS: Take one of my bonnets out of my closet— quickly!

(SUSANNA *goes out.*)

What paper is this?

CHERUBINO: My commission.

COUNTESS: They certainly hurried the matter.

CHERUBINO: I got it just now from Basilio.

COUNTESS: In their haste they've forgotten the seal.

(SUSANNA *comes back.*)

SUSANNA: The seal on what?

COUNTESS: On the commission.

SUSANNA: Good heavens! How stupid! Here is the bonnet.

COUNTESS: Put it on—that's nice. How dreadful it would be if the Count returned now!

12. Aria

SUSANNA: Come, get down on your knees. Stay there without moving—stay there! Now you may turn yourself, slowly. Bravo! that's very good! Now turn your face in my direction. Heavens, what eyes you're making at me! Straight, now—look at me, the Countess isn't there! Now turn your face—stay there without moving; now you may turn; look at me, bravo! This collar should be higher; the eyes a bit lowered, the hands folded on your breast. Let's see how he walks, when he gets up— Look at the little rascal! How pretty he is! What a roguish glance! What

Or via giratevi,
Guardatemi, bravo!
Più alto quel colletto.
Quel ciglio un po' più basso,
Le mani sotto il petto,
Vedremo poscia il passo,
Quando sarete in piè.
Mirate il bricconcello,
Mirate quanto è bello,
Che furba guardatura,
Che vezzo, che figura.
Se l'amano le femmine,
Hanno certo il lor perchè!

Recitativo

LA CONTESSA: Quante buffonerie!

SUSANNA: Ma se ne sono io medesma gelosa! Ehi serpentello volete tralasciar d'esser sì bello?

LA CONTESSA: Finiam le ragazzate, or quelle maniche oltre il gomito gli alza, onde più agiatamente l'abito gli si adatti.

SUSANNA: Ecco.

LA CONTESSA: Più indietro, così. Che nastro è quello?

SUSANNA: È quel ch'esso involommi.

LA CONTESSA: E questo sangue?

CHERUBINO: Quel sangue io non so come, poco pria sdrucciolanda in un sasso, la pelle io mi sgraffiai e la piaga col nastro io mi fasciai.

SUSANNA: Mostrate—non è mal; cospetto! Ha il braccio più candido del mio! Qualche ragazza—

LA CONTESSA: E segui a far la pazza? Va nel mio gabinetto e prendi un poco d'inglese taffetà ch'è sullo scrigno.
(SUSANNA *parte*.)
In quanto al nastro in ver per il colore mi spiacea di privarmene.
(SUSANNA *ritorna*.)

SUSANNA: Tenete, e da legargli il braccio?

LA CONTESSA: Un altro nastro prendi insiem col mio vestito.
(SUSANNA *parte*.)

CHERUBINO: Ah, più presto m'avria quello guarito!

charm, and what a figure! If women love him, they certainly have their reasons!

Recitative

COUNTESS: What ridiculous nonsense!

SUSANNA: But I'm jealous of him myself! Oh, you little
serpent, why are you so beautiful?

COUNTESS: That's enough of this childishness! Now roll up
his sleeves above his elbow, then his dress will fit him
better.

SUSANNA: Like this?

COUNTESS: Further; this way. What is this ribbon?

SUSANNA: It's the one that he snatched from me.

COUNTESS: And this blood?

CHERUBINO: This blood—I don't know; just before, I fell
and scratched myself, and I bound the wound with this
ribbon.

SUSANNA: Show me—it's not bad. Good heavens, his arm is
whiter than my own—just like a girl's!

COUNTESS: Stop wasting time. Go into my closet and find
some plaster that's on the dresser.

(SUSANNA *goes out.*)

As for the ribbon, really, I wouldn't like to lose it—the
color is very pretty.

(SUSANNA *returns.*)

SUSANNA: Take this; it's for his arm.

COUNTESS: We need another ribbon; bring it with the dress.

(SUSANNA *goes out.*)

CHERUBINO: Ah, the first one would have cured me much
more quickly!

LA CONTESSA: Perchè? Questo è migliore.

CHERUBINO: Allor che un nastro legò la chimoa ovver toccò la pelle d'oggetto—

LA CONTESSA: Forestiero, è buon per le ferite, non è vero? Guardate qualità ch'io non sapea!

CHERUBINO: Madama scherza, ed io frattanto parto.

LA CONTESSA: Poverin! Che sventura!

CHERUBINO: Oh me infelice!

LA CONTESSA: Or piange.

CHERUBINO: O ciel! perchè morir non lice! Forse vicino all'ultimo momento, questa bocca oseria—

LA CONTESSA: Siate saggio, cos'è questa follia?
(*Si picchia alla porta.*)
Chi picchia alla mia porta?

IL CONTE (*di fuori*): Perchè chiusa?

LA CONTESSA: Il mio sposo! oh Dei! son morta. Voi qui, senza mantello, in questo stato. Un ricevuto foglio, la sua gran gelosia!

IL CONTE (*di fuori*): Cosa indugiate?

LA CONTESSA: Son sola, ah sì, son sola!

IL CONTE (*di fuori*): E a chi parlate?

LA CONTESSA: A voi, certo, a voi stesso.

CHERUBINO: Dopo quel ch'è successo—il suo furore—non trovo altro consiglio.
(CHERUBINO *corre nel gabinetto e serra la porta.*)

LA CONTESSA: Ah, mi difenda il cielo in tal periglio!
(*Apre la porta della sua stanza. Entra* IL CONTE.)

IL CONTE: Che novità! Non fu mai vostra usanza di rinchiudervi in stanza.

LA CONTESSA: E ver, ma io—io stava quì mettendo—

IL CONTE: Via mettendo—

LA CONTESSA: Certe robe, era meco la Susanna, che in sua camera è andata.

IL CONTE: Ad ogni modo voi non siete tranquilla. Guardate questo foglio!

LA CONTESSA (*a parte*): Numi! E il foglio Figaro gli scrisse.
(*V'è uno strepito nel gabinetto.*)

COUNTESS: Why? This one is wider.

CHERUBINO: But if a ribbon has bound the hair or touched the skin of someone—

COUNTESS: With whom you're casually acquainted, it's good for wounds, isn't that true? It must have qualities that I didn't know of!

CHERUBINO: Madame is joking, and yet I must go away!

COUNTESS: Poor boy! What misfortune!

CHERUBINO: Oh, I'm unhappy!

COUNTESS: You're crying!

CHERUBINO: O God! Why don't you allow me to die? Perhaps at my last gasp, my lips would dare to tell you—

COUNTESS: Get up—this is ridiculous!
(*There is a knocking at the door.*)
Who's knocking at my door?

COUNT (*outside*): Why are you locked in?

COUNTESS: My husband! O God—I'm dying! You're here, without your cloak, in this condition. That letter he received—his dreadful jealousy!

COUNT (*outside*): What are you doing?

COUNTESS: I'm alone here—oh, yes, I'm alone!

COUNT (*outside*): And to whom were you speaking?

COUNTESS: To you; certainly, to you.

CHERUBINO: After all that has happened; his anger— I can't think what to do!
(CHERUBINO *runs into a closet and locks the door.*)

COUNTESS: May heaven defend me in this peril!
(*She unlocks outer door. The* COUNT *enters.*)

COUNT: What a novelty! It was never your custom to lock yourself into your room!

COUNTESS: That's true, but I—I was here arranging—

COUNT: Arranging? Go on!

COUNTESS: Some dresses; Susanna was with me, but she has gone into her room.

COUNT: At any rate, you're upset. Look at this letter.

COUNTESS (*aside*): Heavens! It's the note that Figaro wrote to him.
(*There is a noise in the closet.*)

IL CONTE: Cos'è codesto strepito? In gabinetto qualche cosa è caduta!

LA CONTESSA: Io non intesi niente.

IL CONTE: Convien che abbiate i gran pensieri in mente.

LA CONTESSA: Di che?

IL CONTE: Là v'è qualcuno.

LA CONTESSA: Chi volete che sia?

IL CONTE: Lo chiedo a voi, io vengo in questo punto.

LA CONTESSA: Ah, sì, Susanna appunto—

IL CONTE: Che passò mi diceste alla sua stanza.

LA CONTESSA: Alla sua stanza, o quì, non vidi bene.

IL CONTE: Susanna, e donde viene che siete si turbata?

LA CONTESSA: Per la mia cameriera?

IL CONTE: Io non so nulla, ma turbata senz'altro.

LA CONTESSA: Ah quella serva più che non turba me, turba voi stesso.

IL CONTE: È vero, è vero! e lo vedrete adesso.

(SUSANNA *entra, inosservata, dalla sua stanza, e si nasconde dietro un paravento.*)

13. *Terzetto*
Susanna, or via sortite,
Sortite, così vo'!

LA CONTESSA: Fermatevi!

SUSANNA (*a parte*): Cos'è, codesta lite?

LA CONTESSA: Sentite!
Sortire ella non può.

SUSANNA (*a parte*): Il paggio dove andò?

IL CONTE: E chi vietarlo or osa? chi?

LA CONTESSA: Lo vieta l'onestà.
Un abito da sposa provando ella si sta.

IL CONTE: Chiarissima è la cosa—

LA CONTESSA: Brutissima è la cosa—

IL CONTE: L'amante qui sarà—

SUSANNA (*a parte*): Capisco qualche cosa,
Veggiamo come va.

LA CONTESSA: Brutissima è la cosa,
Chi sa cosa sarà.

COUNT: What's that noise? Something fell down in your closet!

COUNTESS: I didn't hear anything.

COUNT: In that case, you must be thinking great thoughts!

COUNTESS: Of what?

COUNT: There's someone there.

COUNTESS: Who could it possibly be?

COUNT: I'm asking you that; *I've* just come in.

COUNTESS: Oh, yes—Susanna, of course—

COUNT: But you said that she went into her room.

COUNTESS: To her room or to that one; I didn't watch her.

COUNT: If it was Susanna, why are you so nervous?

COUNTESS: On my maid's account?

COUNT: I know nothing about that, but you're definitely upset.

COUNTESS: You're far more upset by that girl than I am.

COUNT: That's true, that's true, and I'll prove it immediately!

(SUSANNA *comes in, unobserved, from another room, and hides behind a screen.*)

13. Trio

Susanna, come out at once! Come out—I order you to!

COUNTESS: Stay in there!

SUSANNA (*aside*): What is this quarrel about?

COUNTESS: Listen! She isn't able to come out.

SUSANNA (*aside*): Where has Cherubino gone?

COUNT: And who is forbidding her to come out? Who?

COUNTESS: Her modesty forbids her. She is trying on her wedding dress.

COUNT: The matter is most clear—

COUNTESS: The matter is very sordid—

COUNT: Her lover must be there—

SUSANNA (*aside*): I'm beginning to understand. Let's see what will happen.

COUNTESS: The matter is very sordid. Who knows what may happen!

IL CONTE: Chiarissima è la cosa,
L'amante qui sarà.
Dunque parlate almeno,
Susanna, se qui siete.
LA CONTESSA: Nemmen, nemmen, nemmeno, io v'ordino
Tacete, tacete, tacete!
IL CONTE: Consorte mia—
Guidizio!
SUSANNA: O cielo!
Un precipizio!
Un scandalo, un disordine,
Qui certo nascerà!
LA CONTESSA: Consorte mio, guidizio!
LA CONTESSA ed IL CONTE: Un scandalo, un disordine,
Schiviam per carità!

Recitativo

IL CONTE: Dunque voi non aprite?
LA CONTESSA: E perchè deggio le mie camere aprir?
IL CONTE: Ebben lasciate, l'aprirem senza chiave. Ehi,
gente!
LA CONTESSA: Come? Porreste a repentaglio d'una dama
l'onore?
IL CONTE: È vero, io sbaglio, posso senza rumore, senza
scandalo alcun di nostra gente, andar io stesso prender
l'occorrente. Attendete pur qui—ma perchè in tutto sia il
mio dubbio distrutto, anco le porte io prima chiuderò.

LA CONTESSA: Che imprudenza!
IL CONTE: Voi la condiscendenza di venir meco avrete;
Madama, eccovi il braccio, andiamo!
LA CONTESSA: Andiamo!
IL CONTE: Susanna starà qui finchè torniamo.
(*Partono* IL CONTE *e* LA CONTESSA. SUSANNA *corre al
gabinetto.*)

14. Duetto

SUSANNA: Aprite, presto aprite, è la Susanna!
Sortite, andate via di quà!
CHERUBINO: Ohimè, che scena orribile!
Che gran fatalità!

COUNT: The matter is most clear. Her lover must be there. Then, at least speak, Susanna, if you are there.

COUNTESS: No, no! I command you to be silent!

COUNT: My lady—I warn you!

SUSANNA: O heavens! What danger! A scandal, a disaster, will certainly occur!

COUNTESS: My Lord, I warn you!
COUNTESS *and* COUNT: For pity's sake, let's avoid a scandal!

Recitative

COUNT: Then you won't open the closet?
COUNTESS: And why should I?
COUNT: Well then, don't; I'll open it without keys. Servants!
COUNTESS: What? Can you rob a lady of her honor?

COUNT: That's true; I was mistaken. I can do it without noise or scandal, without disturbing any of the servants. I'll go myself to get what I need. You'll wait for me here —but, to dispel all my doubt, first I'll lock the closet door, and the door of this room.
COUNTESS: How unreasonable!
COUNT: You'll have the kindness to accompany me; Madame, here is my arm; let's go.
COUNTESS: Very well, then.
COUNT: Susanna will stay here until we return.
(COUNT *and* COUNTESS *exit.* SUSANNA *runs to the closet.*)

14. Duet

SUSANNA: Open the door quickly! It's Susanna. Come out, you must escape from this room!
CHERUBINO: Oh, what a horrible scene! What a dreadful fate!

SUSANNA: Di quà —di là—
Le porte son serrate—
SUSANNA e CHERUBINO: Le porte son serrate,
Che mai sarà?
CHERUBINO: Qui perdersi non giova.
SUSANNA: V'uccide, se vi trova.
CHERUBINO: Veggiamo un po' qui fuori:
Dà proprio nel giardino.
SUSANNA: Fermate Cherubino, fermate, per pietà!
CHERUBINO: Qui perdersi non giova.
SUSANNA: Fermate, Cherubino!
CHERUBINO: M'uccide, se mi trova.
SUSANNA: Tropp'alto per un salto.
CHERUBINO: Lasciami—
SUSANNA: Fermate, per pietà!
CHERUBINO: Lasciami!
Pria di nuocerle nel foco volerei.
Abbraccio te per lei. Addio!
(*Abbraccia* SUSANNA.)
Così si fa!
(*Salta dalla finestra.*)
SUSANNA: Ei va a perire, O Dei! Fermate, per pietà!
Fermate, fermate!
(*Corre alla finestra, e guarda* CHERUBINO.)

Recitativo

Oh, guarda il demonietto fugge! (*ridendo*) È
già un miglio lontano; ma non perdiamci
invano; entriam nel gabinetto; venga poi
lo smargiasso, io qui l'aspetto!
(*Va nel gabinetto, e chiude la porta. Entrano* IL CONTE *e*
LA CONTESSA.)
IL CONTE: Tutto è come io lasciai; volete dunque aprir voi
stessa, o deggio?
LA CONTESSA: Ahimè, fermate, e ascoltatemi un poco. Mi
credete capace di mancar al dover?
IL CONTE: Come vi piace, entro quel gabinetto che v'è
chiuso vedrò!
LA CONTESSA: Sì, lo vedrete, ma uditemi tranquillo.
IL CONTE: Non è dunque Susanna?

SUSANNA: You must get out! The doors are all locked—

SUSANNA *and* CHERUBINO: The doors are all locked. What shall we do?

CHERUBINO: I'm lost if I stay here.

SUSANNA: He'll kill you if he finds you!

CHERUBINO: Perhaps I can use the window; it opens on the garden.

SUSANNA: Stop it, Cherubino, stop, for heaven's sake!

CHERUBINO: I'm lost if I stay here.

SUSANNA: Stop it, Cherubino!

CHERUBINO: He'll kill me if he finds me here.

SUSANNA: It's too high for you to jump.

CHERUBINO: Let me go—

SUSANNA: Stop, for heaven's sake!

CHERUBINO: Let me go! Rather than hurt her, I would leap through fire—I embrace you for her sake. Farewell!
(*He kisses* SUSANNA.)
Here I go!
(*He jumps out of the window.*)

SUSANNA: He'll be killed. O God! Stop, for heaven's sake! Stop, stop!
(*She rushes to the window and looks out after* CHERUBINO.)

Recitative

Oh, look at that little demon—how he's running! (*laughing*) He's already a mile away! But I must hurry; I'll take his place in the closet. When that bully, the Count, comes back here, I'll be waiting for him!
(*She goes into the closet, closing the door. The* COUNT *and* COUNTESS *enter.*)

COUNT: Everything's as I left it. Would you like to open the door, or must I?

COUNTESS: Oh, no, wait a moment, and listen to me. Do you think I would betray you?

COUNT: That's the point in question. I'm going to the closet, to find out who is locked in there!

COUNTESS: Yes, you will find him, but listen to me calmly.

COUNT: Then it isn't Susanna?

LA CONTESSA: No, ma invece è un oggetto, che ragion di sospetto non vi deve lasciar: per questa sera una burla innocente di farsi disponeva, ed io vi giuro che l'onor, l'onestà—

IL CONTE: Chi è dunque? Dite—l'ucciderò!

LA CONTESSA: Sentite—(*a parte*) Ah, non ho cor!

IL CONTE: Parlate.

LA CONTESSA: È un fanciullo.

IL CONTE: Un fanciul?

LA CONTESSA: Sì, Cherubino.

IL CONTE: E mi farà il destino ritrovar questo paggio in ogni loco! Come— Non è partito? Scellerati: ecco i dubbi spiegati, ecco l'imbroglio, ecco il raggiro onde m'avverte il foglio!

15. Finale

Esci ormai, garzon malnato!
Sciagurato, non tardar!

LA CONTESSA: Ah! signore, quel furore
Per lui fammi il cor tremar!

IL CONTE: E d'opporvi ancor osate?

LA CONTESSA: No, sentite.

IL CONTE: Via, parlate.

LA CONTESSA: Giuro al ciel ch'ogni sospetto
E lo stato in che il trovate,
Sciolto il collo, nudo il petto—

IL CONTE: Sciolto il collo! nudo il petto!
Seguitate!

LA CONTESSA: Per vestir femmineo spoglie—

IL CONTE: Ah, comprendo, indegna moglie,
Mi vo' tosto vendicar!

LA CONTESSA: Mi fa torto quel trasporto!
M'oltraggiate a dubitar!

IL CONTE: Qua la chiave!

LA CONTESSA: Egli è innocente!
Voi sapete.

IL CONTE: Non so niente!
Va lontan dagli occhi miei.
Un'infida, un'empia sei,
E mi cerchi d'infamar.

COUNTESS: No; but it's someone who couldn't give you reason for suspicion. We had planned an innocent joke for this evening—that's why he was here. And I swear to you that my honor—

COUNT: Who is in there? Tell me—I'll kill him!

COUNTESS: Listen—(*aside*) Ah, I haven't the courage!

COUNT: Speak.

COUNTESS: It's a young boy.

COUNT: A young boy?

COUNTESS: Yes, Cherubino.

COUNT: Is it my destiny to find that page wherever I go? What—he hasn't left for Seville yet? Rascals! Now my doubts are confirmed—that's the trick of which the letter warned me!

15. Finale

Come out here at once, you damned page!

COUNTESS: Ah, my Lord, what fury! You make me tremble for his safety!

COUNT: And you still dare to defy me?

COUNTESS: No—listen to me!

COUNT: Well, speak quickly.

COUNTESS: I swear to heaven that your suspicions are false and that the state you'll find him in—collar undone, chest naked—

COUNT: Collar undone! Chest naked! As I expected!

COUNTESS: He's dressed in women's clothes—

COUNT: Ah, I understand now, unworthy wife; I'll avenge myself at once!

COUNTESS: Your anger wrongs me! Your doubts are outrageous!

COUNT: Give me the key!

COUNTESS: He's innocent and you know it!

COUNT: I know nothing of the sort! Get out of my sight! You're unfaithful and evil, and you've conspired to disgrace me!

LA CONTESSA: Vado, sì, ma—

IL CONTE: Non ascolto.

LA CONTESSA: Ma—

IL CONTE: Non ascolto.

LA CONTESSA: Non son rea!

IL CONTE: Vel leggo in volto!
Mora, mora!

LA CONTESSA: Ah! la cieca gelosia.
Qualche eccesso gli fa far.

IL CONTE: Mora, mora e più non sia
Ria cagion del mio penar!
(*Spada in mano*, IL CONTE *apre la porta, e trova* SUSANNA.)
Susanna!

LA CONTESSA: Susanna!

SUSANNA: Signore!
Cos'è quel stupore?
Il brando prendete,
Il paggio uccidete,
Quel paggio malnato,
Vedetelo quà.

IL CONTE (*a parte*): Che scola!

LA CONTESSA (*a parte*): Che storia è mai questa?

IL CONTE: La testa girando mi va.

SUSANNA (*a parte*): Confusa han la testa, non san come va.

LA CONTESSA: Susanna v'è là—

IL CONTE: Sei sola?

SUSANNA: Guardate! quì ascoso sarà.

IL CONTE: Guardate!

SUSANNA *ed* IL CONTE: Guardiamo! quì ascoso sarà.
(IL CONTE *va nel gabinetto, e poi ritorna.*)

LA CONTESSA (*a parte a* SUSANNA): Susanna, son morta,
Il fiato mi manca.

SUSANNA (*a parte alla* CONTESSA): Più lieta, più franca,
Il salvo è di già.

COUNTESS: Yes, I'll go, but—

COUNT: I won't listen!

COUNTESS: But—

COUNT: I won't listen!

COUNTESS: I'm not guilty!

COUNT: I can read guilt in your face! I'll kill him, and then I'll be avenged.

COUNTESS: Ah! His jealousy is blind. It makes him go too far.

COUNT: I'll kill him, and then I'll be avenged on the deceitful cause of my suffering!

(*He draws his sword, opens the door—and finds* SUSANNA.)
Susanna!

COUNTESS: Susanna!

SUSANNA: My Lord! Why do you look so amazed? Are you brandishing your sword to kill that disobedient page? In that event, you see him right here!

COUNT (*aside*): What a shock!

COUNTESS (*aside*): How could this happen?

COUNT: My head is whirling.

SUSANNA (*aside*): They're both so confused they don't know what has happened.

COUNTESS: Susanna was there—

COUNT: You were alone there?

SUSANNA: You might look! Someone may still be hidden.

COUNT: I'll look.

SUSANNA *and* COUNT: Let's look. Someone might still be there.
(*The* COUNT *goes to the closet and then returns.*)

COUNTESS (*aside to* SUSANNA): Susanna, I'm dying; my breath is failing me.

SUSANNA (*aside to* COUNTESS): Be happy; be cheerful. He's safe by now.

IL CONTE: Che sbaglio mai presi.
Appena lo credo.
Se a torto v'offesi,
Perdono vi chiedo,
Ma far burla simile
È poi crudeltà.

SUSANNA e LA CONTESSA: Le vostre follie
Non mertan pietà.

IL CONTE (*alla* CONTESSA): Io v'amo!

LA CONTESSA: Nol dite!

IL CONTE: Vel giuro!

LA CONTESSA: Mentite!
Son l'empia, l'infida,
Che ognora v'inganna.

IL CONTE: Quell'ira, Susanna,
M'aita a calmar.

SUSANNA: Così si condanna
Chi può sospettar.

LA CONTESSA: Adunque la fede
D'un anima amante
Sì fiera mercede
Doveva sperar?

IL CONTE: Quell'ira, Susanna—

SUSANNA: Così si condanna,
Chi può sospettar. (*alla* CONTESSA)
Signora!

IL CONTE: Rosina!

LA CONTESSA: Crudele!
Più quella non sono.
Ma il misero oggetto
Del vostro abbandono
Che avete diletto
Di far disperar.

IL CONTE: Confuso, pentito,
Son troppo punito.

SUSANNA: Confuso, pentito,
È troppo punito.

LA CONTESSA: Crudele! crudele! soffrir sì gran torto.
Quest'alma non sa.

IL CONTE: Abbiate pietà, abbiate pietà!

SUSANNA: Abbiate pietà, abbiate pietà!

COUNT: What a mistake! I still don't believe it. If I wrongly offended you, I ask your pardon. But you'll admit that it's very cruel to joke in that way!

SUSANNA *and* COUNTESS: Your arrogance doesn't deserve pity.

COUNT (*to* COUNTESS): I love you!

COUNTESS: Don't speak of it!

COUNT: I swear it!

COUNTESS: You're lying! I'm evil and unfaithful, and always deceiving you!

COUNT: Susanna, help me to calm her anger!

SUSANNA: How a jealous man condemns himself!

COUNTESS: I see that my fidelity has been fittingly rewarded.

COUNT: Susanna, help me—

SUSANNA: How a jealous man condemns himself! (*to* COUNTESS) My Lady!

COUNT: Rosina!

COUNTESS: Cruel man! I'm not Rosina any more, but the miserable, abandoned object of your scorn.

COUNT: I'm confused and repentant; I've been punished already.

SUSANNA: He's confused and repentant; he's been punished already.

COUNTESS: Cruel man; my heart cannot endure such great wrongs!

COUNT: Have mercy on me!

SUSANNA: Have mercy on him!

IL CONTE: Ma il paggio rinchiuso?
LA CONTESSA: Fu sol per provarvi.
IL CONTE: Ma i tremiti, i palpiti?
LA CONTESSA: Fu sol per burlarvi.
IL CONTE: Ma un foglio sì barbaro?
SUSANNA e LA CONTESSA: Di Figaro è il foglio,
E a voi per Basilio.
IL CONTE: Ah, perfidi! Io voglio—
SUSANNA e LA CONTESSA: Perdono non merta
Chi agli altri nol dà.
IL CONTE: Ebben se vi piace,
Comune è la pace.
Rosina inflessibile
Con me non sarà.
LA CONTESSA: Ah, quanto Susanna,
Son dolce di core!
Di donne al furore
Chi può crederà?
SUSANNA: Cogli uomin, signora,
Girate, volgete,
Vedrete che ognora
Si cade poi là.
IL CONTE (*alla* CONTESSA): Guardatemi!
LA CONTESSA: Ingrato!
IL CONTE: Guardatemi, ho torto,
E mi pento.
SUSANNA: Da questo momento,
Quest'alma a conoscerla
Apprender potrà.
LA CONTESSA: Da questo momento,
Quest'alma a conoscermi
Apprender potrà.
IL CONTE: Da questo momento,
Quest'alma a conoscervi
Apprender potrà.
(*Entra* FIGARO.)
FIGARO: Signori, di fuori,
Son già i suonatori.
Le trombe sentite,
I pifferi udite;
Tra canti, tra balli

COUNT: But the page was locked in?

COUNTESS: It was only to test you.

COUNT: But your trembling, your nervousness?

COUNTESS: It was only to tease you.

COUNT: And that barbarous letter?

SUSANNA *and* COUNTESS: Figaro wrote it and sent it to you through Basilio.

COUNT: Ah, traitors! I'll—I'll—

SUSANNA *and* COUNTESS: You'll never be forgiven if you cannot forgive!

COUNT: Well then, if you're satisfied, we are all at peace; Rosina would never be adamant with me.

COUNTESS: Ah! How tender my heart must be, Susanna! After this, who will ever believe in women's anger?

SUSANNA: With men, my Lady, you may maneuver as much as you please, but you'll never get the better of them.

COUNT (*to* COUNTESS): Look at me!

COUNTESS: You're ungrateful!

COUNT: Look at me; I was wrong, and now I'm sorry.

SUSANNA: From this moment, perhaps he'll value his wife at her true worth.

COUNTESS: From this moment, perhaps he'll value me at my true worth.

COUNT: From this moment, perhaps I'll value my wife at her true worth.

(FIGARO *enters.*)

FIGARO: My Lord, the musicians are already outside. Hear the trumpets! Listen to the flutes! With all your servants dancing and singing, let's hurry to celebrate our wedding.

De' vostri vassalli,
Corriamo, voliamo le nozze a compir.
IL CONTE: Pian, piano, men fretta!
FIGARO: La turba m'aspetta!
IL CONTE: Pian, piano, men fretta,
Un dubbio toglietemi
In pria di partir.
SUSANNA, LA CONTESSA, FIGARO: La cosa è scabrosa—
Com'han da finir?
IL CONTE: Con arte le carte convien scoprir.
Conoscete, Signor Figaro,
Questo foglio chi vergò?
FIGARO: Nol conosco.
SUSANNA: Nol conosci?
FIGARO: No!
LA CONTESSA: Nol conosci?
FIGARO: No!
IL CONTE: Nol conosci?
FIGARO: No!
SUSANNA, LA CONTESSA, IL CONTE: Nol conosci?
FIGARO: No! No! No!
SUSANNA: E nol desti a Don Basilio?
LA CONTESSA: Per recarlo—
IL CONTE: Tu c'intendi?
FIGARO: Oibò, oibò!
SUSANNA: E non sai del damerino—
LA CONTESSA: Che stasera nel giardino—
IL CONTE: Già capisci?
FIGARO: Io no lo so.
IL CONTE: Cerchi invan difesa e scusa,
Il tuo ceffo già t'accusa,
Vedo ben che vuoi mentir.
FIGARO: Mente il ceffo, io già non mento.
SUSANNA *e* LA CONTESSA: Il talento aguzzi invano.
Palesato abbiam l'arcano—
Non v'e nulla da ridir.
IL CONTE: Che rispondi?
FIGARO: Niente, niente!

COUNT: One moment; there's no hurry!

FIGARO: The people are waiting!

COUNT: There's no hurry; just resolve one of my doubts before we go.

SUSANNA, COUNTESS, FIGARO: The matter is very delicate—How will it end?

COUNT: Now is the time to present those papers. Do you know, Mr. Figaro, where this letter came from?

FIGARO: I know nothing about it.

SUSANNA: You don't know it?

FIGARO: No!

COUNTESS: You don't know it?

FIGARO: No!

COUNT: You don't know it?

FIGARO: No!

SUSANNA, COUNTESS, COUNT: You don't know it?

FIGARO: No! No! No!

SUSANNA: Wasn't it for Don Basilio?

COUNTESS: To give him—

COUNT: Now do you understand?

FIGARO: No. Not at all!

SUSANNA: And you don't know about the little rascal—

COUNTESS: Who this evening, in the garden—

COUNT: Now you remember?

FIGARO: Not a word.

COUNT: You're trying in vain to defend and excuse yourself; your face already accuses you, and I can easily tell that you are lying.

FIGARO: My face may lie, then, but I don't know.

SUSANNA *and* COUNTESS: Your elusiveness is in vain. We've told all the secrets—there's nothing to repeat.

COUNT: What is your answer?

FIGARO: Nothing, nothing!

IL CONTE: Dunque accordi?

FIGARO: Non accordo!

SUSANNA: Eh, via, chetati, balordo—

SUSANNA e LA CONTESSA: Eh, via, chetati, balordo,
La burletta ha da finir.

FIGARO: Per finirla lietamente
E all'usanza teatrale,
Un'azion matrimoniale
Le faremo ora seguir.

SUSANNA, LA CONTESSA, FIGARO: Deh signor, nol contrastate,
Consolate i miei (lor) desir.

SUSANNA e LA CONTESSA: Deh signor, nol contrastate—

IL CONTE (*a parte*): Marcellina!
Marcellina! Quante tardi a comparir!

(ANTONIO, *ubriaco, entra; porta dei garofani.*)

ANTONIO: Ah, Signor! Signor!

IL CONTE: Cosa è stato?

ANTONIO: Che insolenza!
Ch'il fece? Chi fu?

SUSANNA, LA CONTESSA, IL CONTE, FIGARO: Cosa dici?
Cos'hai, cosa è nato?

ANTONIO: Ascoltate!

SUSANNA, LA CONTESSA, IL CONTE, FIGARO: Via parla di sù!

ANTONIO: Dal balcone che guarda in giardino,
Mille cose ogni dì gittar veggio,
E poc'anzi può darsi di peggio,
Vidi un uom, signor mio, gittar giù.

IL CONTE: Dal balcone?

ANTONIO: Vedete i garofani!

IL CONTE: In giardino?

ANTONIO: Sì!

SUSANNA e LA CONTESSA: Figaro, all'erta!

IL CONTE: Cosa sento?

SUSANNA, LA CONTESSA, FIGARO: Costui ci sconcerta,
Quel briacone che viene a far quì?

IL CONTE: Dunque un uom! Ma dov'è gito?

ANTONIO: Ratto, ratto il birbone è fuggito;
Ed ad un tratto di vista m'usci.

SUSANNA (*a* FIGARO): Sai che il paggio!

COUNT: Then you admit it?

FIGARO: I don't admit it.

SUSANNA: Don't be stupid, Figaro—

SUSANNA *and* COUNTESS: Don't be stupid, Figaro, this joke must come to an end.

FIGARO: To end it happily, according to theatrical custom, please give us your consent to get married without further delay.

SUSANNA, COUNTESS, FIGARO: Then, my Lord, don't resist us—grant us our wishes.

SUSANNA *and* COUNTESS: Then, my Lord, don't resist us—

COUNT (*aside*): Marcellina! Marcellina! How late you are.

(ANTONIO, *rather drunk, enters with a flowerpot.*)

ANTONIO: Ah, my Lord!

COUNT: What has happened?

ANTONIO: How outrageous! Who has done it? Who was it?

SUSANNA, COUNTESS, COUNT, FIGARO: What are you saying? What's the matter? What has happened?

ANTONIO: Listen!

SUSANNA, COUNTESS, COUNT, FIGARO: Well, tell us, at once!

ANTONIO: Every day a thousand things are thrown down from that balcony over there, but today it was even worse —they threw out a man, my Lord!

COUNT: From the balcony?

ANTONIO: Look at the carnations!

COUNT: Into the garden?

ANTONIO: Yes!

SUSANNA *and* COUNTESS: Figaro, listen!

COUNT: Are you certain?

SUSANNA, COUNTESS, FIGARO: This drunkard will ruin us. Why has he come here?

COUNT: But the man—where did he go?

ANTONIO: Quickly, the rascal vanished; as soon as I saw him, he escaped.

SUSANNA (*to* FIGARO): It was the page!

FIGARO (*a* SUSANNA): So tutto lo vidi! (*ridendo*)
Ah ah ah ah!

IL CONTE: Taci là!

FIGARO: Ah ah ah ah!

ANTONIO: Cosa ridi?

FIGARO (*ad* ANTONIO): Tu sei cotto dal sorger del dì.

IL CONTE: Or ripetimi: un uom
Dal balcone?

ANTONIO: Dal balcone—

IL CONTE: In giardino?

ANTONIO: In giardino.

SUSANNA, LA CONTESSA, FIGARO: Ma signore, se in lui parla
il vino.

IL CONTE (*ad* ANTONIO): Segui pure, nè in volto vedesti?

ANTONIO: No nol vidi.

SUSANNA: Olà! Figaro—

SUSANNA *e* LA CONTESSA: Olà! Figaro ascolta!

IL CONTE: No?

ANTONIO: Nol vidi.

FIGARO (*ad* ANTONIO): Via piangione, sta zitto una volta!
Per tre soldi far tanto tumulto!
Giacchè il fatto non può stare occulto,
Sono io stesso saltato di lì.

IL CONTE: Chi? Voi stesso?

SUSANNA *e* LA CONTESSA: Che testa, che ingegno!

FIGARO: Che stupor!

ANTONIO: Chi? Voi stesso?

FIGARO: Che stupor! Che stupor!

IL CONTE: Già creder nol posso.

ANTONIO: Come mai diventasti sì grosso?
Dopo il salto non fosti così.

FIGARO: A chi salta succede così.

ANTONIO: Ch'il direbbe!

SUSANNA *e* LA CONTESSA: Ed insiste quel pazzo?

IL CONTE (*ad* ANTONIO): Tu che dici?

ANTONIO: A me parve il ragazzo.

IL CONTE: Cherubin?

FIGARO (*to* SUSANNA): I know it; I saw him. (*laughing*)
Ha ha ha!

COUNT: Quiet there!

FIGARO: Ha ha ha ha!

ANTONIO: What are you laughing at?

FIGARO (*to* ANTONIO): You're drunk from dawn to midnight!

COUNT: Now repeat your story: a man jumped from the balcony?

ANTONIO: From the balcony—

COUNT: Into the garden?

ANTONIO: Into the garden.

SUSANNA, COUNTESS, FIGARO: But, my Lord, it's the wine that's speaking in him!

COUNT (*to* ANTONIO): Now continue. Did you see his face?

ANTONIO: No, I didn't see it.

SUSANNA: There! Figaro—

SUSANNA *and* COUNTESS: There! Figaro, listen!

COUNT: No?

ANTONIO: I didn't see it.

FIGARO (*to* ANTONIO): When will you stop your complaining! Such a disturbance over nothing! Now, to clarify matters, I'll admit that I, myself, jumped from that balcony.

COUNT: You?

SUSANNA *and* COUNTESS: What a brain! How clever!

FIGARO: What a surprise!

ANTONIO: It was you?

FIGARO: What a surprise, what a surprise!

COUNT: I still can't believe it.

ANTONIO: Then how have you grown so tall? When you jumped you were much smaller.

FIGARO: That's what happens to one after one jumps.

ANTONIO: Is that true?

SUSANNA *and* COUNTESS: That idiot is persistent.

COUNT (*to* ANTONIO): What do you say?

ANTONIO: He looked to me like a boy.

COUNT: Cherubino?

SUSANNA *e* LA CONTESSA: Maledetto, maledetto!

FIGARO: Esso appunto, da Siviglia
A cavallo qui giunto,
Da Siviglia ov'ei forse sarà.

ANTONIO: Questo no, chè il cavallo
Io no vidi saltare di là.

IL CONTE: Che pazienza!

SUSANNA *e* LA CONTESSA: Come mai—
Giusto ciel, finirà!

IL CONTE: Finiam questo ballo. (*a* FIGARO)
Dunque tu?

FIGARO: Saltai giù.

IL CONTE: Ma perchè?

FIGARO: Il timor.

IL CONTE: Che timor?

FIGARO: Là rinchiuso,
Aspettando quel caro visetto,
Tippe, tappe un susurro fuor d'uso,
Voi gridaste, lo scritto biglietto,
Saltai giù dal terrore confuso,
E stravolto n'ho un nervo del piè.

ANTONIO: Vostra dunque saran queste
Carte che perdeste.

IL CONTE: Olà, porgile a me.

FIGARO: Sono in trappola.

SUSANNA *e* LA CONTESSA: Figaro, all'erta.

IL CONTE: Dite un po', questo foglio cos'è?

FIGARO: Tosto, tosto, n'ho tante, aspettate.

ANTONIO: Sarà forse il sommario dei debiti?

FIGARO: No, la lista degli osti.

IL CONTE: Parlate! (*ad* ANTONIO) E tu lascialo.

SUSANNA *e* LA CONTESSA: Lascialo e parti.

FIGARO: Lasciami e parti.

ANTONIO: Parto sì, ma se torno a trovarti—

FIGARO: Vanne, non temo di te!
(ANTONIO *parte.*)

IL CONTE: Dunque?

LA CONTESSA (*a parte a* SUSANNA): Oh ciel, la patente del
paggio!

SUSANNA *and* COUNTESS: Oh, good heavens!

FIGARO: He, of course. Perhaps he returned from Seville on horseback—for he was on his way there, you know.

ANTONIO: No, no, I didn't see a horse jumping out of the window.

COUNT: I must have patience!

SUSANNA *and* COUNTESS: Great heavens—However will this end?

COUNT: Let's finish this nonsense. (*to* FIGARO) Then it was you?

FIGARO: I jumped out.

COUNT: But why?

FIGARO: I was afraid.

COUNT: Afraid of what?

FIGARO: I was locked in the closet, waiting to see my sweet little Susanna; suddenly I heard loud noises—you were shouting—I thought of the letter that I had written. I jumped out, confused with terror, and strained a muscle in my foot.

ANTONIO: Then this paper that was lost in the garden must be yours?

COUNT: Give it to me.

FIGARO: Now I'm trapped!

SUSANNA *and* COUNTESS: Figaro, listen.

COUNT: Give me some idea of what this paper concerns.

FIGARO: At once—I have so many; only wait a moment.

ANTONIO: Perhaps it's a list of his debts.

FIGARO: No, a list of the wedding guests.

COUNT: Speak out! (*to* ANTONIO) And you leave him alone.

SUSANNA *and* COUNTESS: Leave him alone and go.

FIGARO: Leave me alone and go.

ANTONIO: I'll go, yes, but the next time I find you—

FIGARO: Go on, I'm not afraid of you!

(ANTONIO *exits.*)

COUNT: Well, then?

COUNTESS (*aside to* SUSANNA): O Lord! The page's commission!

IL CONTE: Dunque?

SUSANNA (*a parte a* FIGARO): Giusti Dei, la patente!

IL CONTE: Coraggio!

FIGARO: O che testa! Quest'è la patente
Che poc'anzi il fanciullo mi diè.

IL CONTE: Per che fare?

FIGARO: Vi manca—

IL CONTE: Vi manca?

LA CONTESSA (*a parte a* SUSANNA): Il suggello.

SUSANNA (*a parte a* FIGARO): Il suggello.

IL CONTE: Rispondi!

FIGARO: E l'usanza—

IL CONTE: Su via ti confondi?

FIGARO: E l'usanza di porvi il suggello.

IL CONTE: Questo birbo mi toglie
Il cervello.
Tutto, tutto è un mistero per me!

SUSANNA *e* LA CONTESSA: Si mi salvo da questa tempesta,
Più non havvi naufragio per me!

FIGARO: Sbuffa invano e la terra calpesta!
Poverino, ne sa, men di me.
(*Entrano* MARCELLINA, DON BASILIO *e* BARTOLO.)

MARCELLINA, DON BASILIO, BARTOLO: Voi signor, che giusto
siete,
Ci dovete or ascoltar.

SUSANNA, LA CONTESSA, FIGARO: Son venuti a sconcertarmi.
Qual rimedio a ritrovar?

IL CONTE: Son venuti a vendicarmi.
Io mi sento a consolar.

FIGARO: Son tre stolidi, tre pazzi,
Cosa mai vengono a far?

IL CONTE: Pian, pianin senza schiamazzi,
Dica ognun quel che gli par.

MARCELLINA: Un impegno nuziale
Ha costui con me contratto,
E pretendo che il contratto
Deva meco effettuar.

COUNT: Well, then?

SUSANNA (*aside to* FIGARO): Good heavens! The commission!

COUNT: Go on.

FIGARO: Oh, how stupid of me! That's the commission that the boy gave me a while ago.

COUNT: For what purpose?

FIGARO: It lacked—

COUNT: It lacked?

COUNTESS (*aside to* SUSANNA): The seal.

SUSANNA (*aside to* FIGARO): The seal.

COUNT: Answer me!

FIGARO: It's usual—

COUNT: Go on, are you confused?

FIGARO: It's usual to seal a commission.

COUNT: This rascal will drive me insane! A seal! All this is a mystery to me!

SUSANNA *and* COUNTESS: If I survive this storm, there can be no other shipwreck for me.

FIGARO: Let him rant and shake the earth! He knows less about this affair than I do!

(MARCELLINA, DON BASILIO, *and* BARTOLO *enter*.)

MARCELLINA, DON BASILIO, BARTOLO: My Lord, justice demands that you give us another hearing.

SUSANNA, COUNTESS, FIGARO: They have come to make trouble. What can we do to combat their malice?

COUNT: They have come to avenge me. I will soon be consoled.

FIGARO: They're three stupid idiots! Whatever are they doing here?

COUNT: Be quiet; without commotion, everyone will get his chance to speak.

MARCELLINA: Figaro contracted a marriage with me, and I claim that he must keep to his bargain!

SUSANNA, LA CONTESSA, FIGARO: Come? Come?
IL CONTE: Olà, silenzio, silenzio, silenzio!
Io son qui per giudicar.
BARTOLO: Io da lei scelto avvocato,
Vengo a far le sue difese,
Le legittime pretese,
Io vi vengo a palesar.
SUSANNA, LA CONTESSA, FIGARO: È un birbante!
IL CONTE: Olà, silenzio!
Io son quì per giudicar.
DON BASILIO: Io, com'uomo al mondo cognito,
Vengo quì per testimonio
Del promesso matrimonio
Con prestanza de danar.
SUSANNA, LA CONTESSA, FIGARO: Son tre matti!
IL CONTE: Olà, silenzio!
Lo vedremo, il contratto leggeremo,
Tutto in ordin deve andar.
SUSANNA, LA CONTESSA, FIGARO: Son confusa (confuso),
son stordita (stordito)!
MARCELLINA, DON BASILIO, IL CONTE, BARTOLO: Che bel
colpo! che bel caso!
SUSANNA, LA CONTESSA, FIGARO: Disperata (Disperato),
sbalordita (sbalordito).
MARCELLINA, DON BASILIO, IL CONTE, BARTOLO: È cresciuto
a tutti il naso.
SUSANNA, LA CONTESSA, FIGARO: Certo un diavol dell'inferno
Quì li ha fatti capitar!
MARCELLINA, DON BASILIO, IL CONTE, BARTOLO: Qualche
nume a noi propizio
Quì ci ha fatti capitar.

SUSANNA, COUNTESS, FIGARO: What? What's this?

COUNT: Now, then, silence! I'm here to be the judge.

BARTOLO: I'm this lady's chosen lawyer; I'm here to defend her, and I want to state that in my opinion her claim is strictly legal.

SUSANNA, COUNTESS, FIGARO: He's a scoundrel!

COUNT: Now then, silence! I'm here to be the judge.

DON BASILIO: I, a man known to the world, am here to witness that he promised her marriage, after which she lent him money.

SUSANNA, COUNTESS, FIGARO: They're all crazy.

COUNT: Now then, silence! we'll read the contract first; everything must proceed in order.

SUSANNA, COUNTESS, FIGARO: I'm confused and stupefied!

MARCELLINA, DON BASILIO, COUNT, BARTOLO: What a stroke! What a lovely case!

SUSANNA, COUNTESS, FIGARO: We're shaken and in despair.

MARCELLINA, DON BASILIO, COUNT, BARTOLO: We'll make them pay through the nose.

SUSANNA, COUNTESS, FIGARO: Surely an infernal devil is plotting against us.

MARCELLINA, DON BASILIO, COUNT, BARTOLO: A friendly fate has helped our cause!

ATTO TERZO

Una sala nel palazzo. IL CONTE *è solo.*

Recitativo

IL CONTE: Che imbarazzo è mai questo! Un foglio anonimo,
la cameriera in gabinetto chiusa, la padrona confusa, un
uom che salta dal balcone in giardino, un'altro appresso,
che dice esser quel desso; non so cosa pensar, potrebbe
forse qualcun de' miei vassalli, a simil razza è comune
l'ardir! Ma la Contessa, ah, che un dubbio l'offende! Ella
rispetta troppo sè stessa, e l'onor mio—l'onor! Dove, diamin, l'ha posto umano errore!
(LA CONTESSA *entra con* SUSANNA. *Restano a parte, e
parlano inascoltate dal* CONTE.)
LA CONTESSA: Via, fatti core, digli che ti attenda in giardino.

IL CONTE (*fra se*): Saprò, se Cherubino era giunto a
Siviglia, a tale oggetto ho mandato Basilio.
SUSANNA (*alla* CONTESSA): O cielo! e Figaro?
LA CONTESSA: A lui non dei dir nulla, in vece tua voglio
andarci io medesma.
IL CONTE: Avanti sera dovrebbe ritornar.
SUSANNA: O Dio! non oso.
LA CONTESSA: Pensa ch'è in tua mano il mio riposo.
IL CONTE: E Susanna? Chi sa ch'ella tradito abbia il segreto
mio—Oh, se ha parlato, gli fo sposar la vecchia.
(SUSANNA *viene avanti, e ascolta agl'ultime parole del*
CONTE. LA CONTESSA *parte.*)

SUSANNA (*fra se*): Marcellina! (*al* CONTE) Signor!

IL CONTE: Cosa bramate?
SUSANNA: Mi par che siete in collera!
IL CONTE: Volete qualche cosa?
SUSANNA: Signor, la vostra sposa ha i soliti vapori e vi
chiede il fiaschetto degli odori.

A hall in the castle. The COUNT *is alone.*

Recitative

COUNT: What confusion! An anonymous letter; the maid locked in the closet; the mistress unnerved; one man jumps down from the balcony into the garden; another claims that it was *he.* I don't know what to think— On the other hand, it might have been one of my servants. People like that are too bold for their own good. But the Countess? No; to doubt her is to insult her. She has too much self-respect. But, my honor? What has human error done to my honor? (*The* COUNTESS *enters with* SUSANNA. *They remain in the background and converse unheard by the* COUNT.)

COUNTESS: Come along; take courage. Tell him to wait for you in the garden.

COUNT (*to himself*): I've sent Basilio to find out whether Cherubino has really gone to Seville.

SUSANNA (*to the* COUNTESS): O heavens! And Figaro?

COUNTESS: Don't tell him anything about it. Instead of you, I'll go there myself.

COUNT: He should be back before evening.

SUSANNA: O God! I don't dare!

COUNTESS: Remember that you're doing it for me.

COUNT: And Susanna? Who knows whether she's betrayed my secret? Oh, if she has told them, I'll make Figaro marry the old woman!

(SUSANNA *comes forward and overhears the* COUNT'S *last words, as the* COUNTESS *exits.*)

SUSANNA (*to herself*): Marcellina! (*to the* COUNT) My Lord!

COUNT: What do you want?

SUSANNA: It seems that you are angry.

COUNT: Do you want something?

SUSANNA: My Lord, your wife is indisposed, and would like a flask of smelling salts.

IL CONTE: Prendete.

SUSANNA: Or vel riporto.

IL CONTE: Ah no, potete ritenerlo per voi.

SUSANNA: Per me? Questi non son mali da donne triviali.

IL CONTE: Un'amante che perde il caro sposo sul punto d'ottenerlo?

SUSANNA: Pagando Marcellina colla dote che voi mi prometteste—

IL CONTE: Ch'io vi promisi! Quando?

SUSANNA: Credea d'averlo inteso.

IL CONTE: Si, se voluto aveste intendermi voi stessa.

SUSANNA: E mio dovere, e quel di Sua Eccellenza è il mio volere.

16. Duetto

IL CONTE: Crudel! Perchè finora
Farmi languir così?

SUSANNA: Signor, la donna ognora
Tempo ha di dir così.

IL CONTE: Dunque in giardin verrai?

SUSANNA: Se piace a voi verrò.

IL CONTE: E non mi mancherai?

SUSANNA: No, non vi mancherò.

IL CONTE: Verrai?

SUSANNA: Si!

IL CONTE: Non mancherai?

SUSANNA (*preoccupata*): No!

IL CONTE: Non mancherai?

SUSANNA: No, non mancherò, no,
Non vi mancherò.

IL CONTE: Mi sento dal contento
Pieno di gioia il cor.

SUSANNA: Scusatemi se mento
Vi che intendete amor.

IL CONTE: Mi sento dal contento
Pieno di gioia il cor.
Dunque in giardin verrai—

SUSANNA: Se piace a voi verrò—

IL CONTE: Dunque verrai?

COUNT: Take it.

SUSANNA: I'll bring it back soon.

COUNT: Ah, no; you can keep it for yourself.

SUSANNA: Myself? Chambermaids don't have such illnesses.

COUNT: A chambermaid who is losing her dear husband on the point of marrying him?

SUSANNA: But I'll pay Marcellina with the dowry that you promised me—

COUNT: That I promised you? When?

SUSANNA: I believed that I understood you.

COUNT: Yes, if you yourself had wished to understand me.

SUSANNA: It is my duty, and your lordship's wishes are my own.

16. Duet

COUNT: Cruel one! Why have you made me suffer for so long?

SUSANNA: My Lord, a woman always takes her time to say yes.

COUNT: Then you'll meet me in the garden.

SUSANNA: If you wish it, I will.

COUNT: And you won't fail me?

SUSANNA: No, I won't fail you.

COUNT: You'll come?

SUSANNA: Yes!

COUNT: You won't fail.

SUSANNA (*preoccupied*): No!

COUNT: No?

SUSANNA: I won't fail you. I won't fail you.

COUNT: I'm so happy. My heart is full of joy!

SUSANNA: Forgive me if I lie, all of you who understand love.

COUNT: I'm so happy. My heart is full of joy. Then I will see you in the garden—

SUSANNA: If you wish it, I will—

COUNT: Then I will see you?

SUSANNA: No!

IL CONTE: No?

SUSANNA: Si, se piace a voi, verrò.

IL CONTE: Non mancherai?

SUSANNA: No!

IL CONTE: Dunque verrai?

SUSANNA: Si!

IL CONTE: Non mancherai?

SUSANNA: Si!

IL CONTE: Si?

SUSANNA: No, non vi mancherò.

Recitativo

IL CONTE: E perchè fosti meco stamattina si austera?

SUSANNA: Col paggio ch'ivi c'era?

IL CONTE: Ed a Basilio che per me ti parlò?

SUSANNA: Ma qual bisogno abbiam noi che un Basilio—

IL CONTE: È vero, e mi prometti poi se tu manchi, o cor mio— Ma la Contessa attenderà il fiaschetto.

SUSANNA: Eh, fu un pretesto, parlato io non avrei senza questo.

IL CONTE: Carissima!

SUSANNA: Vien gente.

IL CONTE (*fra se*): È mia senz'altro.

SUSANNA (*fra se*): Forbitevi la bocca, o signor scaltro.

(FIGARO *entra in dietro.*)

FIGARO: Ehi! Susanna, dove vai?

SUSANNA: Taci, senza avvocato hai già vinta la causa.

FIGARO: Cos'è nato?

(SUSANNA *e* FIGARO *partono.*)

IL CONTE: Hai già vinta la causa! Cosa sento! In qual laccio io cadea? Perfidi, io voglio di tal modo punirvi; a piacer mio la sentenza sarà. Ma s'ei pagasse la vecchia pretendente? Pagarla! in qual maniera? E poi v'è Antonio che all'incognito Figaro ricusa di dare una nipote in matrimonio. Coltivando l'orgoglio di questo mentecatto—tutto giova a un raggiro—il colpo è fatto.

SUSANNA: No!

COUNT: No?

SUSANNA: Yes; if you wish, I will.

COUNT: You won't fail?

SUSANNA: No!

COUNT: Then I'll see you?

SUSANNA: Yes!

COUNT: You won't fail?

SUSANNA: Yes!

COUNT: Yes?

SUSANNA: No, I won't fail you.

Recitative

COUNT: But why were you so prudish with me this morning?

SUSANNA: With the page there?

COUNT: And to Basilio, who spoke to me for you?

SUSANNA: But what need have we for a Basilio?

COUNT: That's true, that's true; and you must promise me —if you disappoint me, my darling— But the Countess is waiting for the smelling salts.

SUSANNA: It was a pretext. I couldn't have spoken to you without it.

COUNT: Dearest!

SUSANNA: Someone's coming!

COUNT (*to himself*): She's mine, without a doubt.

SUSANNA (*to herself*): Don't be too sure, Mr. Conceit!
(FIGARO *enters in the background.*)

FIGARO: Eh, Susanna, where are you going?

SUSANNA: Quiet! Without a lawyer, you've already won your case!

FIGARO: What has happened?
(SUSANNA *and* FIGARO *exit.*)

COUNT: Already won your case? What does that mean? In what net am I caught? Traitors! I'll punish them, and the sentence will depend on my own pleasure. But if he should pay off the old woman? Pay her? How can he? And then there's Antonio, who'll refuse to marry his niece to an orphan like Figaro. I'll flatter the pride of that drunkard; it will aid my plot. I have decided!

17. *Aria*

Vedrò mentr'io sospiro,
Felice un servo mio!
E un ben che invan desio
Ei posseder dovrà?
Vedrò per man d'amore
Unita a un vile oggetto
Che in me destò un affetto
Che per me poi non ha?
Ah, no! Lasciarti in pace
Non vo' questo contento,
Tu non nascesti, audace,
Per dare a me tormento,
E forse ancor per ridere
Di mia infelicità!
Già la speranza sola
Delle vendette mie
Quest'anima consola,
E giubilar mi fa.

(MARCELLINA, DON CURZIO, FIGARO e BARTOLO *entrano*.)

Recitativo

DON CURZIO: È decisa la lite, o pagarla, o sposarla. Ora ammutite.

MARCELLINA: Io respiro.

FIGARO: Ed io moro.

MARCELLINA: Alfin sposa io sarò d'un uom che adoro.

FIGARO: Eccellenza! m'appello—

IL CONTE: È giusta la sentenza, o pagar, o sposar—bravo, Don Curzio.

DON CURZIO: Bontà di Sua Eccellenza!

BARTOLO: Che superba sentenza!

FIGARO: In che superba?

BARTOLO: Siam tutti vendicati.

FIGARO: Io non la sposerò.

BARTOLO: La sposerai.

DON CURZIO: O pagarla, o sposarla; lei t'ha prestati due mille pezzi duri.

FIGARO: Son gentiluomo e senza l'assenso dei miei nobili parenti—

IL CONTE: Dove sono? Chi sono?

17. Aria

Shall I, while I am sighing, see a servant of mine so happy? And shall he possess that which I desire? Shall I see her lovingly united to a mere peasant, who has awakened an affection she does not have for me? Ah, no! Be assured that I won't suffer such misery. You audacious villain, you won't rise up to torment me and to laugh at my unhappiness! Only the thought of vengeance consoles my spirit and makes my heart rejoice.

(MARCELLINA, DON CURZIO, FIGARO, *and* BARTOLO *come in.*)

Recitative

DON CURZIO: The matter is decided! Either marry her or pay her. Now be quiet!

MARCELLINA: I live again!

FIGARO: I'm dying!

MARCELLINA: At last I'll be the wife of the man I love!

FIGARO: Your Lordship! I appeal—

COUNT: The sentence is just. Either marry her or pay her. Bravo, Don Curzio!

DON CURZIO: Your Lordship is too kind.

BARTOLO: What a superb sentence!

FIGARO: In what respect?

BARTOLO: We're all avenged.

FIGARO: I won't marry her.

BARTOLO: You will.

DON CURZIO: Marry her, or pay the two thousand pieces of gold she lent you.

FIGARO: I'm a gentleman, and without the consent of my noble relations—

COUNT: Where are they? Who are they?

FIGARO: Lasciate ancor cercarli, dopo dieci anni io spero di trovarli.

BARTOLO: Qualche bambin trovato?

FIGARO: No, perduto, dottor, anzi rubato.

IL CONTE: Come?

MARCELLINA: Cosa?

BARTOLO: La prova?

DON CURZIO: Il testimonio?

FIGARO: L'oro, le gemme e i ricamati panni, che ne' più teneri anni mi ritrovaron addosso i masnadieri, sono gli indizii veri di mia nascita illustre: e sopratutto questo al mio braccio impresso geroglifico—

MARCELLINA: Una spatola impressa al braccio destro?

FIGARO: E a voi ch'il disse?

MARCELLINA: Oh Dio! è desso!

FIGARO: E ver, son io!

DON CURZIO: Chi?

IL CONTE: Chi?

BARTOLO: Chi?

MARCELLINA: Raffaello!

BARTOLO: E i ladri ti rapir?

FIGARO: Presso un castello.

BARTOLO (*indicando* MARCELLINA): Ecco tua madre.

FIGARO: Balia?

BARTOLO: No, tua madre.

DON CURZIO *ed* IL CONTE: Sua madre?

FIGARO: Cosa sento?

MARCELLINA (*indicando* BARTOLO): Ecco tua padre.

18. Sestetto

Riconosci in questo amplesso
Una madre, amato figlio!

FIGARO: Padre mio, fate lo stesso,
Non mi fate più arrossir.

BARTOLO: Resistenza la coscienza
Far non lascia al tuo desir.

DON CURZIO: Ei suo padre—

FIGARO: Let me go looking for them. Within ten years I hope to find them.

BARTOLO: You're a foundling?

FIGARO: I was lost, Doctor, or rather stolen.

COUNT: How?

MARCELLINA: What?

BARTOLO: Is there proof?

DON CURZIO: Is there evidence?

FIGARO: The gold, jewels, and the embroidered clothes that the robbers found on me—they are the true indications of my illustrious birth—but above all, this symbol branded on my arm.

MARCELLINA: A spatula branded on your right arm?

FIGARO: And who told you about it?

MARCELLINA: O God! It's he!

FIGARO: Of course, it's I.

DON CURZIO: Who?

COUNT: Who?

BARTOLO: Who?

MARCELLINA: Raffaello!

BARTOLO: And the robbers kidnapped you?

FIGARO: Near a castle.

BARTOLO (*pointing to* MARCELLINA): Then there is your mother.

FIGARO: My nurse?

BARTOLO: No, your mother.

DON CURZIO *and* COUNT: His mother?

FIGARO: Are you insane?

MARCELLINA (*pointing to* BARTOLO): And this is your father!

18. Sextet

In this embrace, my dear son, you'll recognize your mother!

FIGARO: Father, spare my blushes, and embrace me also.

BARTOLO: My conscience won't let me oppose your wishes.

DON CURZIO: He's his father—

IL CONTE: Son smarrito—
DON CURZIO: Ella sua madre!
IL CONTE: Son stordito!
DON CURZIO: L'imeneo
Non può seguir!
IL CONTE: Meglio è assai di quà partir.
MARCELLINA: Figlio amato!
DON CURZIO: Ei suo padre—
Ella sua madre!
BARTOLO: Figlio amato!
IL CONTE: Son smarrito, son stordito!
FIGARO: Parenti amati!
(SUSANNA *entra con una borsa in mano.*)
SUSANNA: Alto, alto! Signor Conte,
Mille doppie son qui pronte,
A pagar vengo per Figaro,
Ed a porlo in libertà.
DON CURZIO *ed* IL CONTE: Non sappiam com'è la cosa—
Osservate un poco là!
MARCELLINA *e* BARTOLO: Figlio amato!
FIGARO: Parenti amati!
SUSANNA: Già d'accordo con la sposa?
Guisti Dei, che infedeltà!
Lascia, iniquo!
FIGARO: No, t'arresta!
Senti, o cara, senti, senti!
SUSANNA: Senti questa!
(*Lo batte al' orecchio.*)
MARCELLINA, FIGARO, BARTOLO: È un effetto di—
Buon core.
IL CONTE: Fremo, smanio dal furore—
Il destino a me la fa!
SUSANNA: Fremo, smanio dal furore—
Una vecchia a me la fa!
DON CURZIO: Freme smania dal furore—
Il destino gliela fa!
MARCELLINA: Lo sdegno calmate,
Mia cara figliuola.
Sua madre abbracciate
Che or vostra sarà.

COUNT: I'm amazed—
DON CURZIO: She's his mother!
COUNT: I'm stupefied!
DON CURZIO: The wedding cannot go on.

COUNT: I can't bear any more of this.
MARCELLINA: Beloved son!
DON CURZIO: He's his father— She's his mother!

BARTOLO: Beloved son!
COUNT: I'm amazed, I'm stupefied!
FIGARO: Beloved parents!
(SUSANNA *enters with purse in her hand.*)
SUSANNA: Wait a moment, your Lordship. I have a thousand gold pieces ready. I've come to pay for Figaro and to give him his liberty.

DON CURZIO *and* COUNT: Who knows what will happen— Let's observe it for a while!
MARCELLINA *and* BARTOLO: Beloved son!
FIGARO: Beloved parents!
SUSANNA: He's already agreed to marry her! Good heavens, what infidelity! Let me go, you villain!

FIGARO: No, wait a moment! Listen, dear! Listen!

SUSANNA: Listen to this!
(*She slaps him.*)
MARCELLINA, FIGARO, BARTOLO: That's proof of—her love.

COUNT: I'm boiling with rage— Fate is certainly against me!
SUSANNA: I'm boiling with rage— This old woman has got the better of me!
DON CURZIO: He's boiling with rage— Fate is certainly against him!
MARCELLINA: Calm your anger, my dear little daughter. Embrace Figaro's mother, who soon will be yours.

SUSANNA: Sua madre?

BARTOLO: Sua madre!

SUSANNA: Sua madre?

IL CONTE: Sua madre!

SUSANNA: Sua madre?

DON CURZIO: Sua madre!

SUSANNA: Sua madre?

MARCELLINA: Sua madre!

MARCELLINA, DON CURZIO, IL CONTE, BARTOLO: Sua madre!
Sua madre!

SUSANNA: Tua madre?

FIGARO: E quello è mio padre,
Che a te lo dirà.

SUSANNA: Suo padre?

MARCELLINA, DON CURZIO, IL CONTE, BARTOLO: Suo padre!

SUSANNA: Tuo padre?

FIGARO: E quella è mia madre
Che a te lo dirà.

DON CURZIO *ed* IL CONTE: Al fiero tormento—
Di questo momento,
Quest'anima appena resistar or sa.

SUSANNA, MARCELLINA, FIGARO, BARTOLO: Al dolce contento—
Di questo momento,
Quest'anima appena resistar or sa.
(IL CONTE *e* DON CURZIO *partono.*)

Recitativo

MARCELLINA (*a* BARTOLO): Eccovi, o caro amico, il dolce frutto del antico amor nostro.

BARTOLO: Or non parliamo di fatti sì rimoti; egli è mio figlio, mia consorte voi siete, e le nozze farem quando volete.

MARCELLINA: Oggi; e doppie saranno. (*a* FIGARO) Prendi questo—il biglietto del denar che a me devi, ed è tua dote.

SUSANNA (*a* FIGARO): Prendi ancor questa borsa.

BARTOLO: E questa ancora.

FIGARO: Bravi! gittate pur, ch'io piglio ognora.

SUSANNA: His mother?
BARTOLO: His mother!
SUSANNA: His mother?
COUNT: His mother!
SUSANNA: His mother?
DON CURZIO: His mother!
SUSANNA: His mother?
MARCELLINA: His mother!
MARCELLINA, DON CURZIO, COUNT, BARTOLO: His mother! His mother!
SUSANNA: Your mother?
FIGARO: And this is my father. He'll tell you so himself.

SUSANNA: His father?
MARCELLINA, DON CURZIO, COUNT, BARTOLO: His father!
SUSANNA: Your father?
FIGARO: And this is my mother. She'll tell you so herself.

DON CURZIO *and* COUNT: My soul can hardly endure the bitter torments of this moment.

SUSANNA, MARCELLINA, FIGARO, BARTOLO: My soul can hardly endure the sweet happiness of this moment.
(*The* COUNT *and* DON CURZIO *exit.*)

Recitative

MARCELLINA (*to* BARTOLO): My darling, there is the ripe fruit of our past love affair.

BARTOLO: Let's not speak of such remote matters. He's my son; you'll be my wife, and we'll get married whenever you wish it.

MARCELLINA: Today—a double wedding! (*to* FIGARO) Take this bill for the money you owe me; it's your dowry.

SUSANNA (*to* FIGARO): Take this purse too.

BARTOLO: And this one too.

FIGARO: Thank you; money is always welcome; I'll take it all.

SUSANNA: Voliamo ad informar d'ogni avventura Madama e nostro zio. Chi al par di me contenta!

FIGARO: Io!

BARTOLO: Io!

MARCELLINA: Io!

SUSANNA, MARCELLINA, FIGARO, BARTOLO: E schiatti il signor Conte al gusto mio!

(*Escono tutti, ridendo.* BARBARINA *entra, con* CHERUBINO.)

BARBARINA: Andiam, bel paggio; in casa mia tutte ritroverai le più belle ragazze del castello, di tutte sarai tu certo il più bello.

CHERUBINO: Ah! se il Conte mi trova! Misero me! Tu sai che partito ei mi crede per Siviglia.

BARBARINA: O ve', che meraviglia! e se ti trova non sarà cosa nuova, odi: vogliamo vestirti come noi. Tutte insiem andrem poi a presentar de' fiori a Madamina. Fidati, o Cherubin, di Barbarina.

(BARBARINA *e* CHERUBINO *escono. Entra* LA CONTESSA.)

19. Recitativo ed Aria

LA CONTESSA: E Susanna non vien! Sono ansiosa di saper come il Conte accolse la proposta. Alquanto ardito il progetto mi par— Ad uno sposo sì vivace e geloso— Ma che mal c'è? Cangiando i miei vestiti con quelli di Susanna, e i suoi co' miei al favor della notte— Oh cielo! a qual umil stato fatale io son ridotta da un consorte crudel! che dopo avermi con un misto inaudito d'infedeltà, di gelosia, di sdegno—prima amata, indi offesa, ed alfin tradita—fammi or cercar da una mia serva aita!

Dove sono i bei momenti
Di dolcezza e di piacer?
Dove andaron i giuramenti,
Di quel labbro menzogner?
Perchè mai, se in pianti e in pene
Per me tutto si cangiò,
La memoria di quel bene
Dal mio sen non trapassò?
La memoria di quel bene non trapassò?
Ah! se almen la mia costanza
Nel languire amando ognor
Mi portasse una speranza
Di cangiar l'ingrato cor!

(LA CONTESSA *parte.* IL CONTE *ed* ANTONIO *entrano.*)

SUSANNA: I want to tell Madame and my uncle about what has happened. Who is as happy as I am?

FIGARO: I am!

BARTOLO: I am!

MARCELLINA: I am!

SUSANNA, MARCELLINA, FIGARO, BARTOLO: The Count is disconcerted—what a delightful spectacle! (*They all exit, laughing.* BARBARINA *and* CHERUBINO *enter.*)

BARBARINA: Come on, handsome page! At my house you will meet the prettiest girls of the castle, but you will certainly be the most beautiful!

CHERUBINO: Ah! If the Count finds me, it will be terrible! You know that he believes I've gone to Seville.

BARBARINA: Oh, what a calamity! But if he finds you, it won't be anything new. Listen! We want to dress you like a girl. All together, we'll go to present the flowers to Madame. Trust me, Cherubino—trust Barbarina! (BARBARINA *and* CHERUBINO *exit. The* COUNTESS *enters.*)

19. Recitative and Aria

COUNTESS: Susanna is late! I'm anxious to know how the Count received the proposal. Our plan is dangerous—my husband is so impulsive and so jealous! But what real harm is in it? I'll change clothes with Susanna in the darkness of evening— O heaven! My cruel husband has reduced me to such horrible humiliation! He's behaved with an irrational mixture of infidelity, jealousy, and scorn; he loved me at first, then he offended me, and finally betrayed me. Now he's driven me to seek my maid's assistance!

Where have they vanished, those tender moments of sweet pleasure? What has become of the promises sworn by those unfaithful lips? Everything has changed to grief and pain for me. But why does that past sweetness still possess my memory? Ah, my constant heart, whose love survives my suffering, gives me some hope of regaining my husband's affection!

(*The* COUNTESS *exits. The* COUNT *and* ANTONIO *enter.*)

Recitativo

ANTONIO: Io vi dico, signor, che Cherubino è ancora nel castello e vedete per prova il suo cappello.

IL CONTE: Ma come, se a quest'ora esser giunto a Siviglia egli dovria?

ANTONIO: Scusate, oggi Siviglia è a casa mia. Là vestissi da donna, e là lasciati ha gli altri abiti suoi.

IL CONTE: Perfidi!

ANTONIO: Andiam, e li vedrete voi.

(IL CONTE *ed* ANTONIO *partono.* LA CONTESSA *e* SUSANNA *entrano.*)

LA CONTESSA: Cosa mi narri? E che ne disse il Conte?

SUSANNA: Gli si leggeva in fronte il dispetto e la rabbia.

LA CONTESSA: Piano, che meglio or lo porremo in gabbia! Dov'è l'appuntamento, che tu gli proponesti?

SUSANNA: In giardino.

LA CONTESSA: Fissiamogli un loco. Scrivi.

SUSANNA: Ch'io scriva, ma, signora—

LA CONTESSA: Eh, scrivi, dico, e tutto io prendo su me stessa: (*dettando*) Canzonetta sull'aria—

20. *Duetto*

SUSANNA (*scrive*): Sull'aria.

LA CONTESSA: Che soave zeffiretto—

SUSANNA: Zeffiretto—

LA CONTESSA: Questa sera spirerà—

SUSANNA: Questa sera spirerà—

LA CONTESSA: Sotto i pini del boschetto.

SUSANNA: Sotto i pini?

LA CONTESSA: Sotto i pini del boschetto.

SUSANNA: Sotto i pini del boschetto.

LA CONTESSA: Ei già il resto capirà!

SUSANNA: Certo, certo, il capirà!

Recitativo

Piegato è il foglio, or come si sigilla?

LA CONTESSA: Ecco, prendi una spilla, servirà di sigillo. Attendi, scrivi sul riverso del foglio: Rimandate il sigillo.

Recitative

ANTONIO: I'm telling you, my Lord, Cherubino is still in the castle, and here's his hat to prove it.

COUNT: But that's impossible—he should have arrived at Seville by this time.

ANTONIO: Excuse me; today Seville is my house. There they dressed him as a girl, and he's left all his clothes there.

COUNT: Traitors!

ANTONIO: Come with me, and you'll see for yourself. (*The* COUNT *and* ANTONIO *exit. The* COUNTESS *and* SUSANNA *enter.*)

COUNTESS: What are you telling me? And how did the Count react?

SUSANNA: One could read displeasure and anger in his face.

COUNTESS: Good! Now it will be easier to catch him in our trap. Where did you promise to meet him?

SUSANNA: In the garden.

COUNTESS: Let's specify a place. Write to him.

SUSANNA: I, write to him? But, my Lady—

COUNTESS: Go on; write, and I'll take all the consequences: (*dictating*) A little song to the breezes—

20. *Duet*

SUSANNA (*writing*): To the breezes—

COUNTESS: That gentle Zephyr—

SUSANNA: Zephyr—

COUNTESS: Will breathe this evening—

SUSANNA: Will breathe this evening—

COUNTESS: Among the pines in the grove—

SUSANNA: Among the pines?

COUNTESS: Among the pines in the grove.

SUSANNA: Among the pines in the grove.

COUNTESS: He'll understand the rest without being told.

SUSANNA: Certainly he'll understand!

Recitative

The letter is folded; how shall I seal it?

COUNTESS: Here, take a pin; it will serve as a seal. Listen, write on the back of the note: Return the seal!

SUSANNA: È più bizzarra di quel della patente.

LA CONTESSA: Presto, nascondi; io sento venir gente.
(*Entra il* CORO *delle contadine, poi* CHERUBINO, *travestito da ragazza, e* BARBARINA.)

21. *Coro*

CORO: Ricevete, o padroncina,
Queste rose e questi fior,
Che abbiam colti stamattina,
Per mostrarvi il nostro amor.
Siamo tante contadine,
E siam tutte poverine,
Ma quel poco che rechiamo
Ve lo diamo di buon cuor.

Recitativo

BARBARINA: Queste sono, madama, le ragazze del loco che il poco ch'han vi vengono ad offrire e vi chiedon perdon del loro ardire.

LA CONTESSA: O brave! vi ringrazio.

SUSANNA: Come sono vezzose!

LA CONTESSA: E chi è, narratemi, quell'amabil fanciulla ch'ha l'aria sì modesta?

BARBARINA: Ella è una mia cugina, e per le nozze è venuta stasera.

LA CONTESSA: Onoriamo la bella forestiera. Venite qui, datemi i vostri fiori. Come arrossì! Susanna, e non ti pare che somigli ad alcuno?

SUSANNA: Al naturale.
(*Entrano* IL CONTE *ed* ANTONIO.)

ANTONIO (*indicando* CHERUBINO): Eh cospettaccio! È questi l'uffiziale!

LA CONTESSA: Oh stelle!

SUSANNA: Malandrino!

IL CONTE (*alla* CONTESSA): Ebben, madama—

LA CONTESSA: Io sono, signor mio, irritata e sorpresa al par di voi.

IL CONTE: Ma stamane?

LA CONTESSA: Stamane, per l'odierna festa volevam travestirlo al modo stesso che l'han vestito adesso!

IL CONTE (*a* CHERUBINO): E perchè non partisti?

SUSANNA: This is even more complicated than the affair of Cherubino's commission!

COUNTESS: Quickly; hide it; I hear someone coming.

(*Enter* CHORUS *of peasants,* CHERUBINO, *disguised as a girl, and* BARBARINA.)

21. Chorus

CHORUS: O dear mistress, please accept these flowers which we gathered this morning to show our love for you. We're all country girls, and we're all poor, but we offer you these flowers from our hearts!

Recitative

BARBARINA: Here are the girls of the neighborhood, my Lady, who come to bring you the little that they have, and they ask your pardon for their presumption.

COUNTESS: It's lovely; I thank you.

SUSANNA: They all look so pretty!

COUNTESS: And tell me, who is that sweet girl with such a modest air?

BARBARINA: She's one of my cousins, and she came here last night for the wedding.

COUNTESS: Let's honor our pretty visitor. Come here and give me your flowers. How she blushes! Susanna, doesn't she seem to resemble someone?

SUSANNA: Absolutely!

(*The* COUNT *and* ANTONIO *enter.*)

ANTONIO (*pointing to* CHERUBINO): I knew it—that's the officer!

COUNTESS: O God!

SUSANNA: Stupid boy!

COUNT (*to the* COUNTESS): Well, Madame!

COUNTESS: My Lord, I'm just as surprised and irritated as you are.

COUNT: But, this morning?

COUNTESS: To prepare him for tonight, we dressed him this morning in the same way that they've dressed him now.

COUNT (*to* CHERUBINO): And why didn't you go to Seville?

CHERUBINO: Signor—

IL CONTE: Saprò punire la tua disubbidienza.

BARBARINA: Eccellenza! Eccellenza! Voi mi dite sì spesso qual volta m'abbracciate e mi baciate: "Barbarina, se m'ami, ti darò quel che brami!"

IL CONTE: Io dissi questo?

BARBARINA: Voi; or datemi, padrone, in sposo Cherubino; e v'amerò com'amo il mio gattino.

LA CONTESSA (*al* CONTE): Ebbene, or tocca a voi.

ANTONIO (*a* BARBARINA): Brava figliuola, hai buon maestro che ti fa la scola!

IL CONTE (*fra se*): Non so qual uom, qual demone, qual dio, rivolga tutto quanto a torto mio.

(*Entra* FIGARO.)

FIGARO: Signor, se trattenete tutte queste ragazze, addio feste, addio danza!

IL CONTE: E che? Vorresti ballar col piè stravolto?

FIGARO: Eh, non mi duol più molto. Andiam, belle fanciulle.

LA CONTESSA (*a* SUSANNA): Come si caverà dall'imbarazzo?

SUSANNA: Lasciate fare a lui.

IL CONTE: Per buona sorte i vasi eran di creta!

FIGARO: Senza fallo. (*alle contadine*) Andiamo dunque, andiamo.

ANTONIO: E intanto a cavallo di galoppo a Siviglia andava il paggio.

FIGARO: Di galoppo, o di passo, buon viaggio! (*alle contadine*) Venite, o belle giovani.

IL CONTE: E a te la sua patente era in tasca rimasta?

FIGARO: Certamente, che razza di domanda!

ANTONIO (*a* SUSANNA): Via, non gli far più motti, ei non t'intende (*presenta* CHERUBINO) ed ecco che pretende che sia un bugiardo il mio signor nipote!

FIGARO: Cherubino!

ANTONIO: Or ci sei!

FIGARO: Che diamin canta?

CHERUBINO: My Lord!

COUNT: I'll see that you're punished for your disobedience.

BARBARINA: My Lord, my Lord! You've told me so often, when you embraced and kissed me: "Barbarina, if you'll love me, I'll give you anything you wish!"

COUNT: Did I say that?

BARBARINA: Yes, you did. Now, my Lord, let me marry Cherubino, and I will love you as dearly as my little kitten!

COUNTESS (*to the* COUNT): I see that the problem is yours.

ANTONIO (*to* BARBARINA): Well done, my daughter; you have a teacher who instructs you well!

COUNT (*to himself*): I don't know what demon is turning everything to my disadvantage!

(FIGARO *enters.*)

FIGARO: My Lord, if you delay these girls there'll be no party or dancing!

COUNT: What? Do you plan to dance with a sprained ankle?

FIGARO: It doesn't hurt me any more. Follow me, my pretty girls!

COUNTESS (*to* SUSANNA): How will he get out of this predicament?

SUSANNA: Leave it to him!

COUNT: It's lucky that the flowerpots were of clay!

FIGARO: Without a doubt. (*to the girls*) Let's go then; let's go!

ANTONIO: And meanwhile the page was galloping toward Seville.

FIGARO: Galloping or trotting; I hope he got there! (*to the girls*) Come, pretty girls!

COUNT: And of course you had his commission in your pocket?

FIGARO: Certainly. What a question!

ANTONIO (*to* SUSANNA): Come, don't signal to him; he doesn't understand you. (*presenting* CHERUBINO) And here's the proof that my illustrious nephew is a liar!

FIGARO: Cherubino!

ANTONIO: Now you understand!

FIGARO: What story did he tell you?

IL CONTE: Non canta, no, ma dice ch'egli saltò stamane in sui garofani.

FIGARO: Ei lo dice—sarà—se ho saltato io, si può dare che anch'esso abbia fatto lo stesso.

IL CONTE: Anch'esso?

FIGARO: Perchè no? Io non impugno mai quel che non so.

22. Finale

Ecco la marcia, andiamo!
Ai vostri posti, o belle! Ai vostri posti!
Susanna, dammi il braccio!

SUSANNA: Eccolo!

(*Escono tutti. Restano* IL CONTE *e* LA CONTESSA.)

IL CONTE: Temerari!

LA CONTESSA: Io son di ghiaccio!

IL CONTE: Contessa!

LA CONTESSA: Or non parliamo.
Ecco quì le due nozze!
Riceverle dobbiam, alfin si tratta
D'una vostra protetta.
Seggiamo.

IL CONTE: Seggiamo! (*fra se*)
E meditiam vendetta.

(*La procezione nuziale entra.* DUE CONTADINE *portano il cappello e il velo di* SUSANNA.)

DUE CONTADINE: Amanti costanti
Seguaci d'onor,
Cantate, lodate
Sì saggio signor.
A un dritto cedendo
Che oltraggia, che offende,
Ei caste vi rende
Ai vostri amator.

(SUSANNA *dà il biglietto al* CONTE.)

TUTTI: Cantiamo, lodiamo sì saggio signor—
(*Si balla;* IL CONTE *legge il biglietto.*)

IL CONTE: Eh, già, solita usanza, le donne
Ficcan aghi in ogni loco—
Ah, ah, capisco il gioco!

FIGARO (*a* SUSANNA): Un biglietto amoroso che gli diè
Nel passar qualche galante, ed era

COUNT: No story—only that he jumped into the carnations this morning.

FIGARO: He said that! Perhaps it's true. If I jumped, it's possible that he could have done the same thing.

COUNT: He, also?

FIGARO: And why not? I never commit myself when I don't know the facts.

22. Finale

There's the march; let's go! To your places, pretty girls! To your places! Susanna, give me your arm!

SUSANNA: Here it is!

(*All exit, except the* COUNT *and* COUNTESS.)

COUNT: The rascals!

COUNTESS: I feel as cold as ice!

COUNT: My Lady!

COUNTESS: Let's not discuss it now. Here are the two couples! We must receive them. Anyway, one of the brides is a special protégée of yours. Let's sit down.

COUNT: Very well! (*to himself*) And I'll consider my vengeance!

(*The wedding procession enters.* TWO PEASANT GIRLS *carry* SUSANNA'S *bridal hat and veil.*)

TWO PEASANT GIRLS: Constant lovers, here you may follow the path of honor. Sing the praises of such a wise lord. He yields an offensive right and now returns you chaste to your lovers!

(SUSANNA *gives the* COUNT *the note.*)

ALL: We sing the praises of our wise lord—

(*Dancing begins; the* COUNT *reads the note.*)

COUNT: Oh, now it's the custom for women to stick pins in everything—Ha, ha! Now I understand the joke!

FIGARO (*to* SUSANNA): It's a loving note that a lady has given him in passing, and it was sealed with a pin, on which

Sigillato d'una spilla, ond'egli
Si punse il dito. Il Narciso or la
Cerca—oh! che stordito!
IL CONTE: Andate, amici! e sia per questa sera
Disposto l'apparato nuziale colla
Più ricca pompa! Io vo' che sia
Magnifica la festa, e canti, e
Fuochi, e gran cena, e gran ballo;
E ognuno impari, com'io tratto color
Che a me son cari.
TUTTI: Amanti costanti—

he pricked his finger. Now that Narcissus is looking for it
—oh, what stupidity!

COUNT: Go now, my friends. This evening all will be prepared to celebrate the weddings with due ceremony. It will
be a magnificent occasion, with singing, fireworks, a great
banquet and ball, so that everyone may learn how I treat
those who are dear to me.

ALL: Constant lovers—

ATTO QUARTO

I giardini del castello. Notte. BARBARINA *entra con una lanterna.*

23. Aria

BARBARINA: L'ho perduta! Me meschina!
Ah, chi sa dove sarà?
Non la trovo.
Meschinella! L'ho perduta!
E mia cugina, ed il padron,
Cosa dirà?
(*Entrano* MARCELLINA *e* FIGARO.)

Recitativo

FIGARO: Barbarina, cos'hai?

BARBARINA: L'ho perduta, cugino.

FIGARO: Cosa?

MARCELLINA: Cosa?

BARBARINA: La spilla che a me diede il padrone per recar a Susanna.

FIGARO: A Susanna, la spilla? e così, tenerella, il mestiero già sai di far tutto sì ben quel che tu fai?

BARBARINA: Cos'è? Vai meco in collera?

FIGARO: E non vedi ch'io scherzo? Osserva: (*prende una spilla da* MARCELLINA) Questa è la spilla che il Conte da recare ti diede alla Susanna, e servia di sigillo a un bigliettino; vedi s'io sono instrutto.

BARBARINA: E perchè il chiedi a me quando sai tutto?

FIGARO: Avea voglia d'udir come il padrone ti diè la commissione.

BARBARINA: Che miracoli! "Tieni, fanciulla, reca questa spilla alla bella Susanna, e dille: 'questo è il sigillo dei pini.' "

FIGARO: Ah! Ah! de' pini.

BARBARINA: E ver ch'ei soggiunse; "Guarda che alcun non veda." Ma tu già tacerai.

ACT FOUR

The gardens of the castle. Twilight. BARBARINA *enters, with a lantern.*

23. Aria

BARBARINA: I have lost it! Ah, who knows were it might be? I can't find it! Poor me—how miserable I am! I have lost it! And my cousin and the Count— What will they say? (MARCELLINA *and* FIGARO *enter.*)

Recitative

FIGARO: Barbarina, what's the matter?

BARBARINA: I've lost it, Cousin.

FIGARO: What?

MARCELLINA: What?

BARBARINA: The pin my master gave me to return to Susanna.

FIGARO: To Susanna? The pin? And that's how discreetly you accomplish such errands?

BARBARINA: Why are you angry with me?

FIGARO: Don't you see that I'm joking? Look: (*taking a pin from* MARCELLINA) this is the pin that the Count gave you to give back to Susanna. It served as a seal for a letter; you can see that I'm well informed.

BARBARINA: Then why are you asking me, if you know all about it?

FIGARO: I was curious to know how the Count gave you the commission.

BARBARINA: What a fuss you're making! "Wait, child, return this pin to your pretty cousin Susanna and tell her: 'This is the seal of the pine grove.' "

FIGARO: Aha! The pine grove!

BARBARINA: It's true that he continued, "Take care that no one sees you." But you certainly won't tell.

FIGARO: Sicuramente.

BARBARINA: A te già niente preme.

FIGARO: Oh niente, niente.

BARBARINA: Addio, mio bel cugino; vo da Susanna, e poi da Cherubino (*Parte.*)

FIGARO: Madre!

MARCELLINA: Figlio!

FIGARO: Son morto.

MARCELLINA: Calmati, figlio mio!

FIGARO: Son morto, dico.

MARCELLINA: Flemma, flemma, e poi flemma: il fatto è serio, e pensar ci convien. Ma guarda un poco che ancor non sai di chi si prenda gioco.

FIGARO: Ah! quella spilla, o madre, è quella stessa che poc'anzi ei raccolse.

MARCELLINA: È ver, ma questo al più ti porge un dritto di stare in guardia e vivere in sospetto, ma non sai se in effetto—

FIGARO: All'arte dunque! il loco del convegno so dov'è stabilito.

MARCELLINA: Dove vai, figlio mio?

FIGARO: A vendicar tutt'i mariti. Addio! (*Parte.*)

MARCELLINA: Presto avvertiam Susanna. Io la credo innocente—quella faccia, quell'aria di modestia—e caso ancora ch'ella non fosse—Ah, quando il cor non ciurma personale interesse, ogni donna è portata alla difesa del suo povero sesso, da quest'uomini ingrati a torto oppresso.

24. Aria

Il capro e la capretta
Son sempre in amistà.
L'agnello all'agnelletta
La guerra mai non fa.
Le più feroce belve,
Per selve e per campagne,
Lascian le lor compagne
In pace e libertà.
Sol noi povere femmine,
Che tanto amiam quest'uomini,
Trattate siam dai perfidi

FIGARO: Certainly.

BARBARINA: It doesn't concern you.

FIGARO: Oh, not at all.

BARBARINA: Good-by, my dear cousin; I'm going to see Susanna, and then to Cherubino! (*Exits.*)

FIGARO: Mother!

MARCELLINA: My son?

FIGARO: I'm dying!

MARCELLINA: Calm yourself, my dear son!

FIGARO: I'm dead, I tell you!

MARCELLINA: We must keep calm. The matter is serious and needs careful thought. But remember that you don't know yet who it is that's being made a fool of.

FIGARO: Ah, this pin, Mother, is the one his lordship picked up.

MARCELLINA: True, but that's only sufficient to put you on guard and make you suspicious. You can't really be sure that—

FIGARO: I must be clever, then! I know where the rendezvous is to be.

MARCELLINA: Where are you going?

FIGARO: To avenge all wronged husbands! Good-by! (*Exits.*)

MARCELLINA: I'll quickly warn Susanna. I believe she is innocent. She seems so sweet and modest—but still it's possible that she may be guilty. But when personal interests aren't at stake, every woman should defend her poor sex, so wrongly oppressed by ungrateful men!

24. Aria●

Among goats the sexes are always friendly. Male and female lambs don't quarrel. The most ferocious boar leaves his companions in peace and liberty in the forests and fields. Only we poor women, who love men so much, are treated by them with disdain, and even with cruelty!

(MARCELLINA *exits.* BARBARINA *enters.*)

● Usually omitted in performance.

Ognor con crudeltà!
(MARCELLINA *parte.* BARBARINA *entra.*)

Recitativo

BARBARINA: Nel padiglione a manca, ei così disse—è questo,
è questo. E poi, se non venisse?
(*Vedendo* FIGARO.)
Son morta!
(*Esce* BARBARINA. FIGARO *entra.*)
FIGARO: È Barbarina! Chi va là?
(DON BASILIO *e* BARTOLO *entrano.*)
DON BASILIO: Son quelli che invitasti a venir.
BARTOLO: Che brutto ceffo! Sembri un cospirator! Che
diamin sono quegli infausti apparati?
FIGARO: Lo vedrete fra poco. In questo stesso loco celebre-
rem la festa della mia sposa onesta e del feudal signor.
(*Parte.*)
DON BASILIO: Hai i diavoli nel corpo!
BARTOLO: Ma che guadagni?
DON BASILIO: Nulla. Susanna piace al Conte; ella d'accordo
gli diè un appuntamento ch'a Figaro non piace.
(DON BASILIO *e* BARTOLO *si nascondono.* FIGARO *rientra,*
porta una lanterna.)
FIGARO: Tutto è disposto; l'ora dovrebbe esser vicina; io
sento gente—è dessa! non è alcun. Buia è la notte, ed io
comincia omai a fare il scimunito mestiere di marito. Ingrata! Nel momento della mia cerimonia ei godeva leg-
gendo, e nel vederlo io rideva di me senza saperlo. Ah,
Susanna! Quanta pena mi costi! Con quell'ingenua faccia,
con quegli occhi innocenti, chi creduto l'avria? Ah! che il
fidarsi a donna è ognor follia.

26. *Aria*

Aprite un po' quegli occhi,
Uomini incauti e sciocchi;
Guardate queste femmine,
Guardate cosa son!
Queste chiamate Dee
Dagli ingannati sensi,
A cui tributa incensi
La debole ragion.
Son streghe che incantano per farci penar,

Recitative

BARBARINA: In the pavilion on the left, that's what he said. It's this one! But if he shouldn't come. (*She catches sight of* FIGARO.) Oh, I'm afraid!

(BARBARINA *exits.* FIGARO *enters.*)

FIGARO: That was Barbarina! Who goes there?

(DON BASILIO *and* BARTOLO *enter.*)

DON BASILIO: It's those whom you invited.

BARTOLO: What an ugly expression! You look like a conspirator. What the devil are these weapons for?

FIGARO: You'll see in a minute. Hide yourselves, and don't come out until I whistle. (*Exits.*)

DON BASILIO: He's possessed by the devil.

BARTOLO: Why is he so upset?

DON BASILIO: It's nothing. Susanna pleased the Count by giving him an appointment, and that doesn't please Figaro. (DON BASILIO *and* BARTOLO *hide.* FIGARO *re-enters, carrying a lantern.*)

FIGARO: Everything is ready; the time should be near. I hear people—it's she! No, it's no one. The night is dark. Already I'm beginning to play the foolish role of a deceived husband. Ungrateful! At the very moment of the ceremony he was reading that letter, and I laughed to see it—I laughed at myself without knowing it. O Susanna, Susanna! How much pain you've cost me. With that innocent face, those candid eyes, who would have believed it? Ah, whoever trusts in woman is gravely misguided!

26. *Aria*

Open your eyes a little, you foolish deluded men; look at these women; see them for what they are! These creatures, deceiving your senses, seem to you like goddesses, and your weak reason burns incense to them in tribute. They're witches enchanting us to bring us pain; they're sirens singing to make us drown; they're owls who attract us to pull out our feathers; comets that burn to extinguish our lights. They're roses with thorns; they're charming foxes; they're sweet bears; evil doves; mistresses of deceit; friends of

Sirene che cantano per farci affogar,
Civette che allettano per trarci le piume,
Comete che brillano per toglierci il lume.
Son rose spinose,
Son volpi vezzose,
Son orse benigne,
Colombe maligne,
Maestre d'inganni,
Amiche d'affanni,
Che fingono, mentono,
Amore non senton,
Non senton pietà.
No, no, no, no!
Il resto nol dico,
Già ognuno lo sa.

(FIGARO *si nasconda negli alberi.* Entrano SUSANNA, LA CON-
TESSA *e* MARCELLINA.)

Recitativo

SUSANNA: Signora! ella mi disse che Figaro verravvi.

MARCELLINA: Anzi è venuto, abbassa un po' la voce.

SUSANNA: Dunque un ci ascolta, e l'altro dee venir a cer-
carmi. Incominciam!

MARCELLINA: Io voglio qui celarmi.
(MARCELLINA *va nel padiglione.*)

SUSANNA (*alla* CONTESSA): Madama, voi tremate; avreste
freddo?

LA CONTESSA: Parmi umida la notte; io mi ritiro.

FIGARO (*fra se*): Eccoci della crisi al grande istante.

SUSANNA: Io sotto questi pini, se madama il permette, resto
a prendere il fresco una mezz'ora.

FIGARO (*fra se*): Il fresco! il fresco!

LA CONTESSA: Restaci in buon'ora. (*Parte.*)

SUSANNA (*fra se*): Il birbo è in sentinella; divertiamoci
anche noi. Diamogli la mercè de' dubbi suoi! (*forte*)
Giunse alfin il momento che godrò senza affanno in braccio
all'idol mio. Timide cure, uscite dal mio petto, a turbar
non venite il mio diletto! Oh come par che all'amoroso

trouble, pretending to love us, but it's all a lie. They don't feel pity. No, no, no, no! I won't tell you the rest; already you know it too well!

(FIGARO *hides behind the bushes.* SUSANNA, *the* COUNTESS, *and* MARCELLINA *enter.*)

Recitative

SUSANNA: My Lady! Marcellina told me that Figaro would come here.

MARCELLINA: Rather, he's here already; lower your voice a little.

SUSANNA: Then one man is listening, and the other will come to look for me. Let's begin!

MARCELLINA: I'll hide here.

(MARCELLINA *exits into pavilion.*)

SUSANNA (*to* COUNTESS): Madame, you're trembling. Are you cold?

COUNTESS: The night seems humid. I'll go in now.

FIGARO (*to himself*): Here we are at the great moment of crisis!

SUSANNA: I'll stay under these pine trees if Madame will permit me, to enjoy the cool breezes for half an hour.

FIGARO (*to himself*): The breezes! The breezes!

COUNTESS: Stay here if you like. (*Exits.*)

SUSANNA (*to herself*): The rascal is playing sentinel. I'll have my joke on him as well. I'll reward him in kind for his cruel suspicions! (*aloud*) At last the moment has come when I may freely enjoy myself in the arms of my lover. Timid fears, leave my breast, and don't disturb my pleas-

foco l'amenità del loco, la terra e il ciel risponda, come la notte i furti miei seconda!

27. *Aria*

Deh vieni, non tardar, o gioia bella,
Vieni ove amore per goder t'appella,
Finchè non splende in ciel notturna face,
Finchè l'aria è ancor bruna, e il mondo tace.
Qui mormora il ruscel, qui scherza l'aura.
Che col dolce sussurro il cor ristaura,
Qui ridono i fioretti e l'erba è fresca,
Ai piaceri d'amor qui tutto adesca.
Vieni, ben mio, tra queste piante ascose,
Vieni, vieni! ti vo' la fronte incoronar di rose.
(*Si nasconde nei siepi e si metta il mantello della* CONTESSA.)

Recitativo

FIGARO: Perfida! e in quella forma meco mentia, non so s'io veglio o dormo.
(*Entra* CHERUBINO.)
CHERUBINO: La, la, la, la, la, la, la lera!
(LA CONTESSA *entra, nel mantello della* SUSANNA.)
LA CONTESSA: Il picciol paggio.
CHERUBINO: Io sento gente—entriamo ove entrò Barbarina. Oh, vedo qui una donna!
LA CONTESSA: Ahimè, meschina!
CHERUBINO: M'inganno! a quel cappello che nell'ombra vegg'io parmi Susanna.
LA CONTESSA: E se il Conte ora vien—sorte tiranna!

28. *Finale*

CHERUBINO: Pian, pianin, le andrò più presso,
Tempo perso non sarà.
LA CONTESSA: Ah! se il conte arriva adesso,
Qualche imbroglio accaderà.
CHERUBINO: Susanetta! Non risponde?
Colla mano il volto asconde,
Or la burlo in verità!
LA CONTESSA: Arditello, sfacciatello!
Ite presto via di qua!

ure! Oh, how it seems that this charming place, the earth, and the sky respond to my amorous desires! How even the darkness befriends my wishes!

27. Aria

Then come, do not be late, my darling! Come where love calls you to enjoy yourself, while there's no moon in the sky, while the air remains dark and the world is silent. Here the brook is murmuring and the breeze is playing, refreshing the heart with its sweet whisper. Here the flowers are smiling, the grass is fresh, and everything favors the pleasures of love. Join me, my darling, among these secluded trees! Come, come! I want to crown your forehead with roses!

(*She hides in the bushes opposite* FIGARO *and puts on the* COUNTESS'S *cloak.*)

Recitative

FIGARO: Traitress! And she lied like that to me! I don't know whether I'm awake or dreaming.

(CHERUBINO *enters.*)

CHERUBINO: La, la, la, la, la, la, la, la!

(*The* COUNTESS *enters, wearing* SUSANNA'S *cloak.*)

COUNTESS: It's the little page.

CHERUBINO: I hear someone. I'll go to meet Barbarina. Oh, is that she over there?

COUNTESS: How awkward!

CHERUBINO: I was wrong; from that cap I see in the darkness, it seems to be Susanna.

COUNTESS: Oh, if my husband should come now, fate would be cruel!

28. Finale

CHERUBINO: Softly, softly, I'll approach her; it won't be lost time.

COUNTESS: Ah, if the Count should suddenly appear, how horrible it would be!

CHERUBINO: Susanetta! You don't answer? Why do you hide your face with your hand? Now I'll really tease her!

COUNTESS: You're audacious and bold! Leave me alone at once!

CHERUBINO: Smorfiosa, maliziosa,
Già so perchè sei qua.
(*Entra* IL CONTE, *in dietro.*)
COUNT: Ecco quì la mia Susanna!
SUSANNA *e* FIGARO: Ecco quì l'uccellatore!
CHERUBINO: Non far meco la tiranna!
SUSANNA, IL CONTE, FIGARO: Ah! nel sen mi batte il cor!
Un'altr'uom con lei si sta!
LA CONTESSA: Via, partite, o chiamo gente!
CHERUBINO: Dammi un bacio, oh, non fai niente!
SUSANNA, IL CONTE, FIGARO: Alla voce è quegli il paggio!
LA CONTESSA: Anche un bacio!
Che coraggio!
CHERUBINO: E perchè far io non posso
Quel che il conte ognor farà?
Oh veh, che smorfie!
Sai ch'io fui dietro il sofà!
SUSANNA, IL CONTE, FIGARO: Temerario!
SUSANNA, LA CONTESSA, IL CONTE, FIGARO: Se il ribaldo
ancor sta saldo,
La faccenda guasterà.
CHERUBINO: Prendi intanto!
(IL CONTE *va tra* CHERUBINO *e* LA CONTESSA.)
LA CONTESSA: O cielo! il Conte!
CHERUBINO: O cielo! il Conte!
FIGARO (*fra se*): Vo' veder cosa fan là.

IL CONTE: Perchè voi non ripetete,
Ricevete questo qua!
(*Da uno schiaffo a* CHERUBINO.)
SUSANNA, LA CONTESSA, IL CONTE, FIGARO: Ah! ci ha fatto
un bel guadagno
Colla sua temerità!
(CHERUBINO *esce nel padiglione.*)
IL CONTE: Partito è alfin l'audace;
Accostati, ben mio.
LA CONTESSA (*finge la voce di* SUSANNA): Giacchè così vi
piace,
Eccomi qui, signor!

CHERUBINO: You're affected and nasty! I already know why you're here.

(*The* COUNT *enters in the background.*)

COUNT: There's my Susanna.

SUSANNA *and* FIGARO: Here comes the mighty hunter!

CHERUBINO: Don't play the fine lady with me.

SUSANNA, COUNT, FIGARO: Ah! My heart is pounding. Another man is there with her!

COUNTESS: Go; leave me, or I'll call for help!

CHERUBINO: Give me a kiss, or you won't escape!

SUSANNA, COUNT, FIGARO: The voice is Cherubino's!

COUNTESS: A kiss too! What boldness!

CHERUBINO: And why can't I follow the Count's example? Heavens, what affectation! You knew that I was behind that chair!

SUSANNA, COUNT, FIGARO: What boldness!

SUSANNA, COUNTESS, COUNT, FIGARO: If this young fool remains here any longer, he'll spoil all our plans!

CHERUBINO: Take this, meanwhile!

(*The* COUNT *steps between* CHERUBINO *and the* COUNTESS.)

COUNTESS: O heavens, the Count!

CHERUBINO: O heavens, the Count!

FIGARO (*to himself*): I want to see what they're doing over there.

COUNT: So that you don't repeat your mistake, take this from me!

(*He slaps* CHERUBINO.)

SUSANNA, COUNTESS, COUNT, FIGARO: Ah, he's caused a charming situation with his boldness and curiosity!

(CHERUBINO *exits into the pavilion.*)

COUNT: The rascal has gone at last. Come nearer, my darling.

COUNTESS (*imitating* SUSANNA): Here I am, my Lord, if it pleases you!

FIGARO (*fra se*): Che compiacente femmina,
Che sposa di buon cor!

IL CONTE: Porgimi la manina.

LA CONTESSA: Io ve la do.

IL CONTE: Carina!

FIGARO: Carina!

IL CONTE: Che dita tenerelle! che delicata pelle!
Mi pizzica, mi stuzzica,
M'empie d'un nuovo ardor!

SUSANNA, LA CONTESSA, FIGARO: La cieca prevenzione
Delude la ragione
Inganna i sensi ognor.

IL CONTE: Oltre la dote, o cara,
Ricevi ancor un brillante
Che a te porge un amante
In pegno del suo amor!

LA CONTESSA: Tutto Susanna piglia
Dal suo benefattor.

SUSANNA, IL CONTE, FIGARO: Va tutto a maraviglia,
Ma il meglio manca ancor.

LA CONTESSA: Signor, d'accese fiaccole
Io veggio il balenar.

IL CONTE: Entriam, mia bella Venere,
Andiamoci a celar!

SUSANNA e FIGARO: Mariti scimuniti
Venite ad imparar.

LA CONTESSA: Al buio, signor mio?

IL CONTE: È quello che voglio;
Tu sai che là per leggere
Io non desio entrar!

SUSANNA e LA CONTESSA: I furbi sono in trappola,
Comincia ben l'affar.

FIGARO: La perfida lo seguita,
E vano il dubitar.

IL CONTE: Chi passa?

FIGARO (*forte*): Passa gente.

LA CONTESSA: È Figaro! Men vo!

IL CONTE: Andate, andate! Io poi verrò.

(IL CONTE e LA CONTESSA *escono da parte.*)

FIGARO (*to himself*): How very obliging! What a sweet bride!

COUNT: Give me your little hand.

COUNTESS: Here it is.

COUNT: My darling!

FIGARO: His darling!

COUNT: What tender fingers! What delicate skin! It stirs me; it teases me and fills me with new desire!

SUSANNA, COUNTESS, FIGARO: His blind infatuation robs him of reason. His senses are still deceived.

COUNT: Besides the dowry, my darling, receive also this jewel that carries the pledge of my love.

COUNTESS: Susanna gladly accepts her benefactor's gifts.

SUSANNA, COUNT, FIGARO: The plot is going beautifully, but the best is still to come.

COUNTESS: My Lord, I see lighted torches in the distance.

COUNT: Let's go in, my beautiful Venus: let's hide ourselves!

SUSANNA *and* FIGARO: Misguided husbands come here to learn!

COUNTESS: In the dark, my Lord?

COUNT: That's just what I want. You know we're not going there in order to read.

SUSANNA *and* COUNTESS: The scoundrel is in a trap; the affair progresses well.

FIGARO: The faithless creature is following him; now all doubts are in vain.

COUNT: Who's passing?

FIGARO (*aloud*): People are passing.

COUNTESS: It's Figaro! I'd better go!

COUNT: Go ahead, then! I'll follow you soon.

(COUNT *and* COUNTESS *exit, separately*.)

FIGARO: Tutto è tranquillo e placido;
Entrò la bella Venere;
Col vago Marte prendere,
Nuovo Vulcan del secolo,
In rete la potrò!

SUSANNA (*finge la voce della* CONTESSA): Ehi, Figaro!
Tacete!

FIGARO: Oh questa è la Contessa!
A tempo vi giungete;
Vedrete là voi stessa,
Il Conte e la mia sposa.
Di propria man la cosa
Toccar io vi farò.

SUSANNA: Parlate un po' più basso!
Di qua non muovo il passo,
Ma vendicar mi vo'.

FIGARO (*fra se riconosce la voce di* SUSANNA): Susanna!
(*forte*)
Vendicarsi?

SUSANNA: Si!

FIGARO: Come potria farsi?

SUSANNA: L'iniquo io vo' sorprendere;
Poi so quel che farò.

FIGARO (*a parte*): La volpe vuol sorprendermi
E secondarla vo'. (*forte*)
Ah, se madama il vuole!

SUSANNA: Su via, manco parole!

FIGARO: Ah madama!

SUSANNA: Su via, manco parole!

FIGARO: Eccomi ai vostri piedi;
Ho pieno il cor di foco!
Esaminate il loco,
Pensate al traditor!

SUSANNA (*fra se*): Come la man mi pizzica!

FIGARO (*fra se*): Come il polmon mi s'altera!

SUSANNA (*fra se*): Che smania! Che furor!

FIGARO (*fra se*): Che smania! Che calor!

SUSANNA (*finge la voce della* CONTESSA): E senz'alcun
affetto?

FIGARO: Everything is calm and placid. The beautiful Venus has gone off with the charming Mars, but I, like Vulcan, will catch them in a net!

SUSANNA (*imitating the* COUNTESS): O Figaro! Be quiet!

FIGARO: Oh, that's the Countess! You've come just in time; you'll see there, with your own eyes, the Count and my bride going into the pavilion.

SUSANNA: Speak a little more softly. I won't move a step from here, yet I'll have my revenge.

FIGARO (*to himself, recognizing* SUSANNA'S *voice*): Susanna! (*aloud*) You'll have revenge?

SUSANNA: Yes!

FIGARO: How will you arrange it?

SUSANNA: The wretch will be surprised by me, then I'll know what to do!

FIGARO (*aside*): The vixen means to surprise me, and I'll play along with her scheme. (*aloud*) Ah, if Madame wishes it!

SUSANNA: Go on; I'm speechless!

FIGARO: Ah, my Lady.

SUSANNA: Go on; I'm speechless!

FIGARO: Here I am at your feet; my heart is consumed by fire! Look at this secluded place, and recall your husband's treachery!

SUSANNA (*to herself*): How my hand itches to slap him!

FIGARO (*to himself*): How my heart enjoys this relief!

SUSANNA (*to herself*): What rage, what fury I feel!

FIGARO (*to himself*): What rage, what vehemence!

SUSANNA (*imitating the* COUNTESS): But without any affection?

FIGARO: Suppliscavi il rispetto.
Non perdiam tempo in vano;
Datemi un po' la mano,
Datemi un po' la mano!

SUSANNA (*nella sua propria voce*): Servitevi, signor!
(*Lui da uno schiaffo.*)

FIGARO: Che schiaffo!

SUSANNA: E questo, e questo, e ancora questo,
E questo, e poi quest'altro.
E questo, signor scaltro!

FIGARO: O schiaffi graziosissimi!
O mio felice amor!

SUSANNA: Impara, impara, o perfido!
A fare il seduttor!

FIGARO: Pace, pace, mio dolce tesoro!
Io conobbi la voce che adoro,
E che impressa ognor serbo nel cor.

SUSANNA: La mia voce?

FIGARO: La voce che adoro.

SUSANNA e FIGARO: Pace, pace, mio dolce tesoro;
Pace, pace, mio tenero amor!
(IL CONTE *ritorna.*)

IL CONTE: Non la trovo e girai tutto il bosco.

SUSANNA e FIGARO: Quest'è il Conte, alla voce il conosco.

IL CONTE: Ehi, Susanna! Sei sorda? Sei muta?

SUSANNA: Bella, bella! Non l'ha conosciuta!

FIGARO: Chi?

SUSANNA: Madama!

FIGARO: Madama?

SUSANNA: Madama!

SUSANNA e FIGARO: La commedia, idol mio, terminiamo;
Consoliamo il bizzarro amator!

FIGARO: Sì, madama, voi siete il ben mio!
Un ristoro al mio cor concedete.

IL CONTE: La mia sposa? ah! senz'arme son io!

SUSANNA: Io son qui, faccio quel che volete.

IL CONTE: Ah, ribaldi, ribaldi!

FIGARO: I'll substitute respect. Let's not waste time in vain discussion; give me your hand for a moment. Give me your hand!

SUSANNA (*in her own voice*): It's at your service, Sir!
(*She slaps him.*)
FIGARO: What a blow!
SUSANNA: Take this one! And this one, and this, and then another! And this one, and still another one! And this, you scheming rascal!
FIGARO: Oh, most welcome blows! Oh, my happy love!

SUSANNA: I'll teach you, traitor, to play the seducer!

FIGARO: Peace, peace, my sweet treasure! I know the voice that I love—it is impressed upon my heart.

SUSANNA: My voice?
FIGARO: The voice I adore.
SUSANNA *and* FIGARO: Peace, peace, my sweet treasure! Peace, peace, my tender love!
(*The* COUNT *returns.*)
COUNT: I can't find her, and I've walked all through the woods!
SUSANNA *and* FIGARO: That's the Count; I know his voice.
COUNT: Oh, Susanna! Are you deaf? Can't you hear me?
SUSANNA: Lovely, lovely; he didn't recognize her!
FIGARO: Who?
SUSANNA: The Countess!
FIGARO: The Countess?
SUSANNA: The Countess!
SUSANNA *and* FIGARO: Let's conclude the comedy, my darling. Let's console this unhappy lover!
FIGARO: Yes, my Lady, you are my beloved! Won't you grant some refreshment to my heart?
COUNT: It's my wife! And I'm here without my sword!
SUSANNA: I'm here to do whatever you wish!
COUNT: Ah, disgusting, disgusting!

SUSANNA e FIGARO: Ah, corriamo, corriamo, mio bene,
E le pene compensi il piacer.
(IL CONTE *prende il braccio di* FIGARO.)
IL CONTE: Gente, gente, all'armi, all'armi!
FIGARO: Il padrone!
IL CONTE: Gente, gente! aiuto, aiuto!
FIGARO: Son perduto!
(SUSANNA *va nel padiglione. Entrano* DON BASILIO, DON
CURZIO, BARTOLO *ed* ANTONIO.)
DON BASILIO, DON CURZIO, BARTOLO, ANTONIO: Cos'av-
venne? Cos'avvenne?
IL CONTE: Il scellerato
M'ha tradito, m'ha infamato,
E con chi state a veder!
FIGARO: Son storditi, sbalorditi!
DON BASILIO, DON CURZIO, BARTOLO, ANTONIO: Son stordito,
sbalordito!
FIGARO: O che scena, che piacer!
DON BASILIO, DON CURZIO, BARTOLO, ANTONIO: Non mi par
che cio sia ver!
IL CONTE: Invan resistete,
Uscite, madama!
Il premio ora avete
Di vostra onestà!
(CHERUBINO *esce dal padiglione.*)
Il paggio!
ANTONIO (*prendendo* BARBARINA): Mia figlia!
FIGARO (*prendendo* MARCELLINA): Mia madre!
(SUSANNA *esce.*)
FIGARO, DON BASILIO, DON CURZIO, BARTOLO, ANTONIO:
Madama!
IL CONTE: Scoperta è la trama,
La perfida è qua!
SUSANNA (*s'inginocchia*): Perdono, perdono!
IL CONTE: No, no, non sperarlo!
FIGARO: Perdono, perdono!
IL CONTE: No, no, non vo' darlo.
TUTTI: Perdono!

SUSANNA *and* FIGARO: Let's run away, my darling, and joy will repay us for our pain!
(*The* COUNT *seizes* FIGARO'S *arm.*)
COUNT: Help, help, bring weapons!
FIGARO: My master!
COUNT: Everyone, come and bear witness!
FIGARO: I'm lost!
(SUSANNA *exits into the pavilion.* DON BASILIO, DON CURZIO, BARTOLO, *and* ANTONIO *enter.*)
DON BASILIO, DON CURZIO, BARTOLO, ANTONIO: What has happened?
COUNT: This villain has betrayed me, disgraced me, and you'll see with whom!

FIGARO: I'm stupefied and bewildered!
DON BASILIO, DON CURZIO, BARTOLO, ANTONIO: We're stupefied and bewildered!
FIGARO: What a scene! What a comedy!
DON BASILIO, DON CURZIO, BARTOLO, ANTONIO: It doesn't seem that this can be true!
COUNT: Resistance is vain; come out, my Lady! Now you'll receive the reward for your fidelity.
(CHERUBINO *comes out of the pavilion.*)
The page!

ANTONIO (*bringing out* BARBARINA): My daughter!
FIGARO (*bringing out* MARCELLINA): My mother!
(SUSANNA *comes out.*)

FIGARO, DON BASILIO, DON CURZIO, BARTOLO, ANTONIO: The Countess!
COUNT: The plot is discovered; the traitress is here.

SUSANNA (*kneeling*): Forgive me, forgive me!
COUNT: No, there's no hope!
FIGARO: Forgive me, forgive me!
COUNT: I'll never forgive you.
ALL: Forgive her!

IL CONTE: No.
No, no, no, no, no, no!
(LA CONTESSA *emerge dal padiglione aposito.*)
LA CONTESSA: Almeno io per loro perdono otterrò.
IL CONTE, DON BASILIO, DON CURZIO, BARTOLO, ANTONIO:
Oh cielo, che veggio!
Deliro! Vaneggio!
Che creder non so!
IL CONTE (*s'ingaroccia*): Contessa, perdono! Perdono, perdono!
LA CONTESSA: Più docil'io sono e dico di sì.

TUTTI: Ah tutti contenti saremo così!
Questo giorno di tormenti,
Di capricci e di follia,
In contenti e in allegria
Solo amor può terminar.
Sposi! Amici! Al ballo! Al gioco!
Alle mine date foco!
Ed al suon di lieta marcia,
Corriam tutti a festeggiar!

COUNT: No. No, no, no, no, no, no!

(*The* COUNTESS *comes out of the opposite pavilion.*)

COUNTESS: Perhaps I can obtain pardon for them.

COUNT, DON BASILIO, DON CURZIO, BARTOLO, ANTONIO: What is this? It's delirious! It's a mirage! I don't know what to believe!

COUNT (*kneeling*): My Lady, forgive me, forgive me!

COUNTESS: My kindness prevails, and I consent to forgive you.

ALL: Everyone will be happy now. This day of torments, of caprices and follies, is finished—only love can end it in happiness and gaiety. Lovers and friends! Dance and be gay! Let joy light your faces! And to the music of a happy march, let us hurry off to celebrate!

DON
GIOVANNI

An opera
in two acts

Music by
Wolfgang Amadeus Mozart
(K. 527)

Words by
Lorenzo da Ponte

INTRODUCTION

Don Giovanni was first performed at Prague in October 1787, a little more than a year after the premiere of *The Marriage of Figaro.* Although its merit has never been questioned, its essential quality is elusive—is it a comedy, a tragedy, or both? And so to this day, it has remained an enigma to both critics and operagoers. Mozart and Da Ponte may have intended this: they entitled the work a *dramma giocoso,* instead of using one of the prevailing terms, *opera buffa* or *opera seria.*

Although *Don Giovanni* includes an extraordinary range of effects, moods, and emotions, the story of the opera is simple; but the libretto, unlike that of *Così fan tutte,* has seeming inconsistencies. Donna Anna's first explanation of her seduction by Don Giovanni is absurd. She claims that she mistook the intruder for Don Ottavio, her fiancé, but what would Don Ottavio be doing at midnight in the room of a well-brought-up young lady? Her story seems to be an incoherent combination of nightmare and wish, and this mixture of dream and reality pervades the opera. While the comic impulse of *Don Giovanni* moves toward a parody of social realities, its tragic impulse intimates the darkness of human desire and fate.

The story moves from Donna Anna's tragic cries of vengeance after her father's murder, to the semicomic scene ending in Leporello's "Catalogue" aria, to the wholly comic episode of Don Giovanni's flirtation with Zerlina. But the comedy never brings complete pleasure or relief. In seeming to avoid the opera's tragic impulse, Mozart makes that impulse more obscure and more ominous.

Although the opera is dominated by Don Giovanni, it is not so much what happens to him that concerns us, but rather his effect on everyone around him. He is more than simply a character; he represents a force: the principle of sensuality. His "morality" consists of pursuing his desires and of seeking new experience; the morality of the other characters demands that they resist his power. Every character in the opera questions himself, except for Don Giovanni; there is nothing inward about him; he is all thrust and motion, energy and appetite. And though he is callous and inhuman we identify ourselves with him; we feel a surge of elation when Don Giovanni defies the Statue and refuses to repent. Nevertheless, in action we would never choose to take his place, for we lack the courage to suffer his fate; we are among the bystanders—we gossip, we moralize, yet we cannot take our eyes from the awesome spectacle of Don Giovanni's downfall.

At least three of the characters do not seem really comfortable with the morality that prevails at the end of the opera—Donna Anna and Don Ottavio delay their wedding, and Donna Elvira plans to enter a convent to forget her sorrows. They and the comic characters, however, rationalize Don Giovanni's loss and attempt to exorcize him in a self-righteous sextet. For Zerlina and Masetto a measure of domestic happiness is probable—the world will go on. And Leporello, though he will find a new master, will forever be made restless by his memories—the best part of his life is over. And so, structurally and dramatically, the final sextet is necessary to the resolution of the opera.

Don Giovanni represents vitality directed toward self-gratification. Although he is Anarchy in opposition to Morality, his irrepressible good spirits are infectious; everyone in the opera is fascinated by him. But Don Giovanni's fate is not simply to be punished by eternal flames; he also suffers the endless dissatisfaction and final emptiness of self-love. There is peace perhaps in loving a single woman, but the pursuit of womankind allows no repose. For Don Giovanni the beginning and the ending of love are one; love is a game that he must ceaselessly begin, and a lie that he must unceasingly attempt to end. His love perpetuates itself only through unfulfillment, and release from this love is to be found only in death.

Leporello is the most human character in the opera. Although he envies Don Giovanni, and although he will even attempt, however ludicrously, to imitate him, he also shows fear and repugnance for Don Giovanni. He constantly threatens desertion, but his continued fidelity is assured by Don Giovanni's fascination, as well as by his bribery. Not even Don Giovanni's death can free Leporello from his vulgar appetites and dreams; he is the bridge between the formal morality of Don Ottavio and Donna Anna and the aggrandizing freedom of Don Giovanni.

Ottavio and Masetto are types often encountered in Mozart's operas. Ottavio has no ideas or direction of his own; he exists only to fulfill Donna Anna's hypocritical wish for an acceptable husband. He is a throwback to Belmonte in *The Abduction from the Seraglio* and a precursor of Tamino in *The Magic Flute*. Masetto is a conventional country bumpkin, who nevertheless displays an ineffective bravery in attempting to defy Don Giovanni.

The three women are clearly differentiated. Donna Anna's furious vengeance conceals an equally furious passion, for we know that she is obsessed by Don Giovanni throughout the opera. We are not surprised at her reluctance to marry Don Ottavio, even when the libertine has finally met his end. Donna Elvira seeks to hold Don Giovanni by the weak social chain of matrimony; when he breaks his vows, she refuses to give him up, not realizing that no woman can intimidate or bind him with any conventional tie. Nor does she completely recognize that it is precisely his fiery iconoclasm to which she so fully responds. She, like Donna Anna, may lack a sense of humor, but neither is backward in demanding her rights. Their best feminine weapons are given to them by society, and so they necessarily fail with Don Giovanni. He neither accepts marriage to Donna Elvira nor repents when Donna Anna's father completes her revenge. Zerlina is a typical Mozart soubrette, more complex than Blonde in *The Abduction from the Seraglio,* but less so than Susanna in *The Marriage of Figaro.* Zerlina is tempted by Don Giovanni's proposals, but they frighten her; actually, she is more eager for security than for adventure. And so we have a clear sense of the limitation of her love for Masetto. She cajoles him; she is tender with him; but she never will passionately love him.

The story of *Don Giovanni* is both amusing and terrifying. Because it embodies the awareness that deep within us all there is something opposed to morality and self-restraint, it never dogmatizes the need for moral reform; in a sense, the opera satirizes all moral complacency. We can note the same strain of rhetoric in certain of Donna Anna's and Donna Elvira's indignant outbursts as in Fiordiligi's arias in *Così fan tutte,* which Mozart and Da Ponte patently intended to be satirical.

Don Giovanni is comic in its parody of moral pretentiousness, but it is tragic in portraying the consequences of freedom from morality, and it is even more ultimately tragic in recognizing that there can be no end, no resolution to the war between social morality and individual desire.

R. P.

SYNOPSIS

ACT ONE

Don Giovanni's attempted seduction of Donna Anna results in a duel in which he kills the Commendatore, her father. Don Giovanni escapes unrecognized with Leporello, his servant, as Donna Anna and her fiancé, Don Ottavio, vow vengeance upon her father's murderer.

Don Giovanni next encounters an old acquaintance, Donna Elvira, whom he had seduced by a promise of marriage. He escapes while Leporello enumerates to the outraged Elvira the varied and extensive conquests of his master.

On the way to her wedding, a peasant girl, Zerlina, is accosted by Don Giovanni. Their flirtation is interrupted by Donna Elvira, who warns the girl to distrust him. Elvira also tries, with some success, to arouse the suspicions of Donna Anna and Don Ottavio. But it is not until Don Giovanni takes leave of Donna Anna that she recognizes his voice as that of the man who killed her father.

A great ball is in progress in Don Giovanni's castle, as Zerlina reassures her bridegroom, Masetto, of her affection for him. Elvira, Anna, and Ottavio, who have now joined forces, appear at the ball as masqueraders, seeking vengeance upon Don Giovanni. They prevent him from seducing Zerlina, but, sword in hand, he escapes from his accusers.

ACT TWO

Exchanging his cloak for Leporello's in order to serenade Donna Elvira's maid, Don Giovanni first entices Donna Elvira down from her balcony and then sends her off with Leporello, whom she believes to be Don Giovanni. Masetto enters. Mistaking Don Giovanni for Leporello, he is beaten after confiding his plans to murder the reprobate.

Meanwhile, Leporello cannot elude Elvira. Anna, Ottavio, Zerlina, and Masetto come upon the pair, and Elvira pleads that they spare Leporello's life, until Leporello reveals his identity. In the general confusion, Leporello escapes.

Leporello rejoins Don Giovanni in a cemetery dominated by a statue of Donna Anna's father. Their laughter at the evening's events is interrupted by the foreboding voice of the Statue, which bids them leave the dead in peace. Don Giovanni, accepting the challenge, invites the Statue to dine, and this invitation is promptly accepted.

The Commendatore, as a marble statue, arrives at Don Giovanni's castle and finds Don Giovanni and Leporello carousing at dinner. Don Giovanni, refusing the Commendatore's offer of a last chance to repent, accepts his return invitation to dine. As the Commendatore exits, flames appear from all directions. Don Giovanni is engulfed by the fire. Informed by Leporello of Don Giovanni's fate, the remaining characters announce their plans: Donna Anna and Don Ottavio will postpone their wedding for a year; Donna Elvira will enter a convent; Zerlina and Masetto will go home to dinner. Leporello announces that he will seek a better master. And all rejoice at "the end of evildoers"!

CHARACTERS

DON GIOVANNI, *a nobleman*	*Bass-baritone or Baritone*
LEPORELLO, *his servant*	*Bass-baritone or Bass*
DONNA ANNA, *a lady of Seville*	*Soprano*
THE COMMENDATORE, *her father*	*Bass*
DON OTTAVIO, *betrothed to* DONNA ANNA	*Tenor*
DONNA ELVIRA, *a lady of Burgos;*	
abandoned by DON GIOVANNI	*Soprano*
ZERLINA, *a peasant girl*	*Soprano*
MASETTO, *her betrothed*	*Bass or Baritone*
CHORUS *of peasants*	
Servants, musicians, guests	

The action takes place in Seville, during the course of one day, in the middle of the seventeenth century.

ATTO PRIMO

Scena I

LEPORELLO *aspetta fuori dalla casa del* COMMENDATORE.

1. Introduzione

LEPORELLO: Notte e giorno faticar,
Per chi nulla sà gradir;
Piova e vento sopportar,
Mangiar male e mal dormir.
Voglio far il gentiluomo,
E non voglio più servir;
No, no, no, non voglio più servir.
Oh che caro galantuomo:
Vuol star dentro colla bella,
Ed io far la sentinella!
Ma mi par, che venga gente,
Non mi voglio far sentir, Ah!
(*Si nasconde. Entrano* DON GIOVANNI, *mascherato, e* DONNA ANNA.)

DONNA ANNA: Non sperar, se non m'uccidi,
Ch'io ti lascio fuggir mai.

DON GIOVANNI: Donna folle, indarno gridi!
Chi son io tu non saprai.

LEPORELLO: Che tumulto! oh ciel, che gridi!
Il padron in nuovi guai.

DONNA ANNA: Gente! Servi! al traditore!

DON GIOVANNI: Taci, e trema al mio furore!

DONNA ANNA: Scelerato!

DON GIOVANNI: Sconsigliata!

DONNA ANNA: Come furia disperata
Ti saprò perseguitar.

DON GIOVANNI: Questa furia disperata
Mi vuol far precipitar.

LEPORELLO: Stà a veder ch'il malandrino
Mi farà precipitar.
(*Esce* DONNA ANNA. *Entra* IL COMMENDATORE, *spada in mano.*)

IL COMMENDATORE: Lasciala, indegno;
Battiti meco.

DON GIOVANNI: Va, non mi degno
Di pugnar teco.

ACT ONE

Scene I

LEPORELLO *is waiting outside the* COMMENDATORE'S *house.*

1. Introduction

LEPORELLO: I must work night and day for someone who doesn't appreciate me; I must bear the wind and rain, scarcely eating or sleeping! I, too, would like to be a gentleman, and no longer a servant, no, no, no, no! Oh, what a worthy nobleman! You revel in there with a beautiful lady, while I have to keep watch. But I hear somebody coming, and I don't want to be seen, no, no, no, no! (*He hides. Enter* DON GIOVANNI, *who is masked, and* DONNA ANNA.)

DONNA ANNA: Unless you kill me, don't think that you'll escape!

DON GIOVANNI: Madwoman! Your shouting is in vain! You'll never discover who I am!

LEPORELLO: What a noise—O God, what shouting! My master's in trouble again!

DONNA ANNA: Servants, come and kill the traitor!

DON GIOVANNI: Be quiet, and tremble at my fury!

DONNA ANNA: Traitor!

DON GIOVANNI: Stupid woman!

DONNA ANNA: I'll pursue you forever like a desperate Fury!

DON GIOVANNI: This raging woman will force me to do something desperate!

LEPORELLO: I'll wait here and see what this libertine expects me to do.

(DONNA ANNA *exits. The* COMMENDATORE *enters, with drawn sword.*)

COMMENDATORE: Let her go, you wretch, and fight with me!

DON GIOVANNI: Go away; it's not my custom to fight with old men.

IL COMMENDATORE: Così pretendi
Da me fuggir?
LEPORELLO (*a parte*): Potessi almeno
Di quà partir.
DON GIOVANNI: Misero! attendi,
Se vuoi morir.
(*Si battono.* IL COMMENDATORE *cade.*)
IL COMMENDATORE: Ah soccorso! son tradito.
L'assassino m'ha ferito,
E dal seno palpitante
Sento l'anima partir.
DON GIOVANNI: Ah! già cade il sciagurato,
Affannoso e agonizzante;
Già dal seno palpitante
Veggo l'anima partir.
LEPORELLO: Qual misfatto! qual eccesso!
Entro il sen dallo spavento
Palpitar il cor mi sento—
Io non so che far, che dir!
(IL COMMENDATORE *muore.*)

Recitativo

DON GIOVANNI (*sotto voce*): Leporello, ove sei?
LEPORELLO: Son quì per mia disgrazia; e voi?
DON GIOVANNI: Son quì.
LEPORELLO: Chi è morto—voi, o il vecchio?
DON GIOVANNI: Che domanda da bestia! il vecchio!

LEPORELLO: Bravo! due imprese leggiadre: sforzar la figlia,
ed ammazzar il padre!
DON GIOVANNI: L'ha voluto suo danno.
LEPORELLO: Ma Donn'Anna cos'ha voluto?

DON GIOVANNI: Taci! Non mi seccar, vien meco, se non
vuoi qualche cosa ancor tu—
LEPORELLO: Non vo' nulla, Signor! non parlo più.
(*Escono* DON GIOVANNI *e* LEPORELLO. *Entrano* DONNA
ANNA, DON OTTAVIO *e servi portando fiaccole.*)

DONNA ANNA: Ah, del padre in periglio in soccorso voliam.

COMMENDATORE: Is that your excuse to avoid me?

LEPORELLO (aside): If only I could get away from here!

DON GIOVANNI: Miserable old man! on guard, then, since you're anxious to die!
(They fight. The COMMENDATORE falls.)
COMMENDATORE: Heaven, aid me! I'm betrayed! This assassin has struck me, and I feel that I am dying.

DON GIOVANNI: Ah, the poor old man is already dying; he's suffering and in agony. I can almost see the spirit departing from his body.

LEPORELLO: What brutality! I feel my heart shuddering within me! I don't know what to do or say.
(The COMMENDATORE dies.)

Recitative

DON GIOVANNI (sotto voce): Leporello, where are you?

LEPORELLO: Here I am, to my shame—and you?

DON GIOVANNI: I'm here.

LEPORELLO: Who's dead—you or the old man?

DON GIOVANNI: What a stupid question! The old man, of course.

LEPORELLO: Wonderful! Two charming projects. Seduce the daughter, and then murder the father!

DON GIOVANNI: He got what he asked for!

LEPORELLO: But Donna Anna—did she ask for what she got?

DON GIOVANNI: Be quiet! You're boring me. Come along, unless you, too, are asking for something—

LEPORELLO: I'm quite satisfied, my Lord. I won't speak another word.
(DON GIOVANNI and LEPORELLO exit. DONNA ANNA and DON OTTAVIO enter, with servants carrying torches.)

DONNA ANNA: My father is in terrible danger; we must help him.

DON OTTAVIO: Tutto il mio sangue verserò, se bisogna. Ma dov'è il scellerato?

DONNA ANNA: In questo loco—(*vedendo il corpo del suo padre*) Ma qual mai s'offre, oh Dei! spettacolo funesto agli occhi miei! Padre mio! mio caro padre!

DON OTTAVIO: Signore!

DONNA ANNA: Ah, l'assassino mel trucidò! Quel sangue, quella piaga—quel volto tinto e coperto del color di morte! Ei non respira più—fredde ha le membra! Padre mio! caro padre! padre amato! Io manco—io moro!
(*Si getta sal corpo del* COMMENDATORE.)

DON OTTAVIO: Ah soccorrete, amici, il mio tesoro! (*ai servi*) Cercatemi, recatemi qualche odor, qualche spirto. Ah non tardate! Donn'Anna, sposa, amica! Il duolo estremo la meschinella uccide.

DONNA ANNA: Ahi!

DON OTTAVIO: Già rinviene! Datele nuovi ajuti.

DONNA ANNA: Padre mio!

DON OTTAVIO: Celate, allontanate agli occhi suoi quell'oggetto d'orrore. Anima mia! consolati, fa core!

2. Duetto

DONNA ANNA: Fuggi, crudele, fuggi!
Lascia che mora anch'io!
Ora ch'è morto, oh Dio!
Chi a me la vita diè!

DON OTTAVIO: Senti cor mio, deh senti!
Guardami un solo istante!
Ti parla il caro amante.
Che vive sol per te!

DONNA ANNA: Tu sei, perdon! mio bene!
L'affanno mio, le pene!
Ah, il padre mio dov'è?

DON OTTAVIO: Il padre? Lascia o cara!
La rimembranza amara:
Hai sposo e padre in me!

DONNA ANNA: Ah! vendicar, s'il puoi,
Giura quel sangue ognor!

DON OTTAVIO: Lo giuro agli occhi tuoi.
Lo giuro al nostro amor!

DON OTTAVIO: I'll gladly pour out all my blood in his defense! Where is the vile wretch?

DONNA ANNA: He was here a moment ago—(*seeing her father's body*) O God! What a horrible sight offends my eyes! Father, my dearest father!

DON OTTAVIO: Your Lordship!

DONNA ANNA: Oh, the assassin has killed him! This blood, this wound, that deadly pallor! He's steeped in the color of death! And he no longer breathes! His limbs are cold! Father! Beloved father! I'm fainting, I'm dying!
(*She throws herself upon the* COMMENDATORE'S *body.*)

DON OTTAVIO: Ah, sustain yourself, my darling! (*to the servants*) Look about—bring me some smelling salts; don't delay! Donna Anna! My bride! My beloved! Poor girl; the sudden shock has almost killed her!

DONNA ANNA: Ah!

DON OTTAVIO: She's reviving now; we must help her.

DONNA ANNA: My father!

DON OTTAVIO: Hide the corpse; take the object of such horror from her eyes. My darling, console yourself—be courageous!

2. Duet

DONNA ANNA: Leave me, cruel one! Leave me here so that I too can die, now that the one who gave me life is dead!

DON OTTAVIO: Listen, my darling, please listen. Look at me for only one moment. Your dear lover is speaking to you—he who lives only for you.

DONNA ANNA: It's you—pardon me, dear—my grief, the pain—oh, where is my dear father?

DON OTTAVIO: Your father? Forget the bitter sight, my dear; in me you will have a father and a husband as well.

DONNA ANNA: Swear to avenge his blood, however you can!

DON OTTAVIO: I swear it by your eyes—and by our love!

DONNA ANNA e DON OTTAVIO: Che giuramenti oh Dei!
Che barbaro momento!
Fra cento affanni e cento
Vammi ondeggiando il cor! (*Partono.*)

Scena II

Strada. Entrano DON GIOVANNI *e* LEPORELLO.

Recitativo

DON GIOVANNI: Orsù spicciati presto—cosa vuoi?

LEPORELLO: L'affar di cui si tratta è importante.

DON GIOVANNI: Lo credo.

LEPORELLO: Importantissimo.

DON GIOVANNI: Meglio ancora. Finiscila.

LEPORELLO: Ma giurate di non andar in collera.

DON GIOVANNI: Lo giuro sul mio onore, purchè non parli
del Commendatore.

LEPORELLO: Siamo soli?

DON GIOVANNI: Lo vedo.

LEPORELLO: Nessun ci sente?

DON GIOVANNI: Via!

LEPORELLO: Vi posso dire tutto liberamente?

DON GIOVANNI: Tutto sì.

LEPORELLO: Dunque quand'è così, caro signor padrone, la
vita che menate è da briccone.

DON GIOVANNI: Temerario! in tal guisa!

LEPORELLO: E il giuramento.

DON GIOVANNI: Zitto! Non so di giuramento, taci, o ch'io—

LEPORELLO: Non parlo più! non fiato, padron mio.

DON GIOVANNI: Così saremo amici. Or odi un poco sai tu
perchè son qui?

LEPORELLO: Non ne so nulla. Ma essendo l'alba chiara,
non sarebbe qualche nuova conquista: io lo devo saper per
porla in lista.

DON GIOVANNI: Va là che sei 'l grand'uom! Sappi ch'io
sono innamorato d'una bella dama, e son certo che m'ama.
La vidi, le parlai: meco al Casino questa notte verrà; zitto
mi pare sentir odor di femmina.

DONNA ANNA *and* DON OTTAVIO: O God, what an oath I have sworn! What a dreadful moment! A hundred afflictions tear my heart! (*Exit.*)

Scene II

A street. Enter DON GIOVANNI *and* LEPORELLO.

Recitative

DON GIOVANNI: All right, hurry up, now— What do you want to say?

LEPORELLO: It's an important matter!

DON GIOVANNI: I believe you.

LEPORELLO: It's very important!

DON GIOVANNI: Better still. Tell me and get it over with.

LEPORELLO: Promise me not to be angry.

DON GIOVANNI: I swear it on my honor—as long as you don't mention the Commendatore.

LEPORELLO: We're alone?

DON GIOVANNI: As you see.

LEPORELLO: Nobody's listening?

DON GIOVANNI: Speak!

LEPORELLO: I can tell you all freely?

DON GIOVANNI: Yes.

LEPORELLO: Well, then, it's this way; my dear lord and master, you are leading the life of a scoundrel!

DON GIOVANNI: Idiot! How dare you?

LEPORELLO: Remember your promise!

DON GIOVANNI: I don't remember any promises. Be quiet now, or I'll—

LEPORELLO: Not a word, not a breath, dear master.

DON GIOVANNI: That's fine; then we'll be friends. Now, listen to me. Do you know why we're here?

LEPORELLO: I don't know anything about it. But since a new day is dawning, it must be some new conquest. Tell me all about it, so that I can add it to my list.

DON GIOVANNI: What a great man you are! You must know that I'm in love with a beautiful lady, and I'm certain that she loves me in return. I spoke to her; I saw her; she'll come to meet me in the summerhouse tonight. Hush! I can smell the approach of a woman!

LEPORELLO (*a parte*): Cospetto! che odorato perfetto!

DON GIOVANNI: All'aria mi par bella.

LEPORELLO (*a parte*): E che occhio, dico!

DON GIOVANNI: Ritiriamoci un poco, e scopriamo terren.

LEPORELLO (*a parte*): Già prese foco.

(DON GIOVANNI e LEPORELLO *in disparte*. *Entra* DONNA ELVIRA.)

3. Aria

DONNA ELVIRA: Ah chi mi dice mai,
Quel barbaro dov'è?
Che per mio scorno amai,
Che mi mancò di fè.
Ah se ritrovo l'empio,
E a me non torna ancor,
Vo' farne orrendo scempio,
Gli vo' cavar il cor!

DON GIOVANNI (*a* LEPORELLO): Udisti? Qualche bella del vago abbandonata. Poverina! Poverina! Cerchiam di consolare il suo tormento.

LEPORELLO: Così ne consolò mille e ottocento.

DON GIOVANNI: Signorina!

Recitativo

DONNA ELVIRA: Chi è là?

DON GIOVANNI: Stelle! che vedo!

LEPORELLO (*a parte*): Oh bella! Donna Elvira!

DONNA ELVIRA: Don Giovanni! Sei quì? Mostro, fellon, nido d'inganni!

LEPORELLO (*a parte*): Che titoli cruscanti! Manco male che lo conosce bene.

DON GIOVANNI: Via, cara Donna Elvira, calmate quella collera—sentite—lasciatemi parlar!

DONNA ELVIRA: Cosa puoi dire dopo azion sì nera? In casa mia entra furtivamente, a forza d'arte, di giuramenti e di lusinghe arrivi a sedurre il cor mio! m'innamori, o crudele! Mi dichiari tua sposa, e poi—mancando della terra e del ciel al santo dritto—con enorme delitto, dopo tre dì da Burgos t'allontani. M'abbandoni, mi fuggi—e lasci in preda al rimorso ed al pianto per pena forse che t'amai cotanto!

LEPORELLO (*aside*): Good heavens, what a perfect sense of smell!

DON GIOVANNI: From here she seems to be beautiful.

LEPORELLO (*aside*): Good Lord, what eyesight!

DON GIOVANNI: Let's retire for a while, and examine the situation.

LEPORELLO (*aside*): He's on fire already!

(DON GIOVANNI *and* LEPORELLO *hide in the background.* DONNA ELVIRA *enters.*)

3. Aria

DONNA ELVIRA: Ah, who can tell me where that wretch has gone? I loved him, to my shame, and he broke his faith to me. If I find him again, and he tries to escape, I'll make a horrible scandal; I'll tear his heart from his breast!

DON GIOVANNI (*to* LEPORELLO): You hear? This beauty's been abandoned by her lover. Poor girl! Poor girl! We'll try to console her.

LEPORELLO: Just as you've consoled all the others.

DON GIOVANNI: Signorina!

Recitative

DONNA ELVIRA: Who is it?

DON GIOVANNI: Good Lord! It's she!

LEPORELLO (*aside*): Oh, lovely! Donna Elvira!

DONNA ELVIRA: Don Giovanni! You're here? Monster! Seducer! Liar!

LEPORELLO (*aside*): What pleasant titles! One can see that she knows him well.

DON GIOVANNI: Come, dearest Elvira, calm your anger! Listen for a moment—let me speak!

DONNA ELVIRA: What can you say after such evil actions? You entered my house furtively, and with oaths and flattery, you seduced my heart and made me fall in love with you! You called me your wife, and then, disregarding all the sacred ties of heaven and earth—oh, horrible crime—you left Burgos after three days! You abandoned me and left me prey to remorse and tears, a fitting punishment for having loved you so much!

LEPORELLO (*a parte*): Pare un libro stampato!

DON GIOVANNI: Oh, in quanto a questo ebbi le mie ragioni. (*a* LEPORELLO) È vero?

LEPORELLO: È vero. (*ironicamente*) E che ragioni forti!

DONNA ELVIRA: E quali sono, se non la tua perfidia, la leggerezza tua? Ma il giusto cielo vuole, ch'io ti trovassi per far le sue, le mie vendette.

DON GIOVANNI: Eh via, cara Donna Elvira, siate più ragionevole! (*a parte*) Mi pone a cimento costei. (*forte*) Se non credete al labbro mio, credete a questo galantuomo.

LEPORELLO: Salvo il vero.

DON GIOVANNI: Via dille un poco.

LEPORELLO (*piano*): E cosa devo dirle?

DON GIOVANNI (*forte*): Si, si, dille pur tutto.

DONNA ELVIRA (*a* LEPORELLO): Ebben, fa presto.

LEPORELLO: Madama—veramente—in questo mondo conciòsia cosa quando fosse che il quadro non è tondo— (DON GIOVANNI *parte*.)

DONNA ELVIRA: Sciagurato! Così del mio dolor gioco ti prendi? Ah voi— Stelle! l'iniquo fuggì! Misera me! dove? In qual parte?

LEPORELLO: Eh, lasciate che vada! Egli non merita ch'a lui voi più pensiate.

DONNA ELVIRA: Il scelerato m'ingannò, mi tradì!

LEPORELLO: Eh consolatevi! Non siete voi, non foste, e non sarete nè la prima, nè l'ultima. Guardate questo non piccolo libro: è tutto pieno dei nomi di sue belle. Ogni villa, ogni borgo, ogni paese è testimone di sue donnesche imprese.

4. Aria

Madamina!
Il catalogo è questo,
Delle belle, che amò il padron mio!
Un catalogo egli è ch'ho fatto io:
Osservate, leggete con me!
In Italia sei cento e quaranta,
In Alemagna due cento trent'una;
Cento in Francia, in Turchia novant'una,

LEPORELLO (*aside*): As if she read it from a book!

DON GIOVANNI: Oh, as to that, I had my reasons! (*to* LEPORELLO) Isn't that true?

LEPORELLO: Yes, it's true. (*ironically*) And what important reasons!

DONNA ELVIRA: And what were they if not your own perfidy and shallowness? But God willed that I should find you, to take his revenge, and my own as well!

DON GIOVANNI: Come now; be more reasonable. (*aside*) This woman will drive me insane! (*aloud*) If you won't believe it from my lips, perhaps you'll believe this gentleman.

LEPORELLO: It's the truth.

DON GIOVANNI: Go ahead, tell her the story.

LEPORELLO (*softly*): And what shall I tell her?

DON GIOVANNI (*aloud*): Yes, yes. Tell her everything.

DONNA ELVIRA (*to* LEPORELLO): Well, hurry up then!

LEPORELLO: Madame—really—in this world you must know that sometimes a square is not a circle—
(DON GIOVANNI *escapes.*)

DONNA ELVIRA: Monster! Are you laughing at my grief? And as for you—heavens! The wretch has gone! I'm miserable! Where? In what direction?

LEPORELLO: Let him go! He doesn't merit a single one of your thoughts.

DONNA ELVIRA: The scoundrel has deceived and betrayed me!

LEPORELLO: Well, console yourself. You're not the first, nor will you be the last. Look here—this good-sized book is filled with the names of his conquests: every village, every town, every country, bears witness to his triumphs of love!

4. Aria

My dear lady! This is the catalogue of the women my master has loved. It's a list that I've compiled—look at it; read it over with me! In Italy, six hundred and forty; in Germany, two hundred and thirty-one; a hundred in France; ninety-one in Turkey—but in Spain there are already a thousand and three. Among them are country girls, ladies from the city, chambermaids, countesses, baronesses, marchionesses, princesses, and women of every

Ma, ma in Ispagna, son già mille e tre!
V'han fra queste contadine.
Cameriere cittadine;
V'han Contesse, Baronesse,
Marchesane, Principesse,
E v'han donne d'ogni grado,
D'ogni forma d'ogni età.
Nella bionda, egli ha l'usanza
Di lodar la gentilezza—
Nella bruna la costanza,
Nella bianca la dolcezza!
Vuol d'inverno la grassotta
Vuol d'estate la magrotta;
E la grande, maestosa;
La piccina, ognor vezzosa.
Delle vecchie fa conquista
Per piacer di porle in lista:
Sua passion predominante
E la giovin principiante
Non si picca, se sia ricca—
Se sia brutta, se sia bella!
Purchè porti la gonnella,
Voi sapete quel che fa!
(DONNA ELVIRA *e* LEPORELLO *partono. Entrano* ZERLINA *e*
MASETTO *e* CORO *di contadini.*)

5. Duetto e Coro

ZERLINA: Giovinette, che fate all'amore,
Non lasciate, che passi l'età;
Se nel seno vi bulica il core,
Il rimedio vedetelo quà!
La la la, la la la!
Che piacer, che sarà.

MASETTO: Giovinetti leggieri di testa,
Non andate girando quà e là
Poco dura dei matti la festa,
Ma per me cominciata non ha!
Lera, lera la!
Che piacer, che piacer, che sarà!
Lera la, lera la!

ZERLINA, MASETTO, CORO: Vieni, vieni, carina godiamo,
E cantiamo, e balliamo, e suoniamo!
Che piacer, che piacer, che sarà!
(*Entrano* DON GIOVANNI *e* LEPORELLO.)

class, every figure, every age! With blondes, it's his habit
to praise their sweetness; with brunettes, their constancy;
with old women, their tenderness. In winter he likes them
plump; and in the summer, slender, tall, and majestic. But
still he finds the little ones charming. He even seduces the
old women, simply for the pleasure of adding them to his
list. But his preference is really for the young beginners.
He never thinks of whether she's rich, ugly or beautiful—
as long as she wears a skirt, you know very well what he
does!

(DONNA ELVIRA and LEPORELLO exit. Enter ZERLINA and
MASETTO, with a CHORUS of peasants.)

5. Duet and Chorus

ZERLINA: You young girls who play at falling in love, don't
wait for your summer to pass! If your heart is bubbling
over, here you see the remedy for it! How happy we will
be!

MASETTO: Lightheaded young men, don't wander from one
girl to another. Your happiness will soon be over, but
mine hasn't even begun! How happy we will be!

ZERLINA, MASETTO, CHORUS: Come, my darling, let's enjoy ourselves, and sing and dance and play. How happy
we will be!

(DON GIOVANNI and LEPORELLO enter.)

Recitativo

DON GIOVANNI: Manco male è partita! Oh guarda, guarda, che bella gioventù! Che belle donne!

LEPORELLO (*a parte*): Tra tante per mia fè, vi sarà qualche cosa anche per me.

DON GIOVANNI: Cari amici, buon giorno! Seguitate a stare allegramente; seguitate a suonar o buona gente. C'è qualche sposalizio?

ZERLINA: Si, signore; e la sposa son io.

DON GIOVANNI: Me ne consolo. Lo sposo?

MASETTO: Io per servirla.

DON GIOVANNI: Oh bravo! per servirmi! Questo è vero parlar da galantuomo.

LEPORELLO (*a parte*): Basta che sia marito.

ZERLINA: Oh, il mio Masetto è un uom d'ottimo core!

DON GIOVANNI: Oh anch'io, vedete: voglio che siamo amici. Il vostro nome?

ZERLINA: Zerlina.

DON GIOVANNI: E il tuo?

MASETTO: Masetto.

DON GIOVANNI: Oh, caro il mio Masetto! cara la mia Zerlina, v'esibisco la mia protezione. Leporello—cosa fai là, birbone?

LEPORELLO: Anch'io caro padrone, esibisco la mia protezione.

DON GIOVANNI: Presto va con costor, nel mio palazzo conducili sul fatto: ordina ch'abbiano cioccolatte, caffè, vini, prosciutti—cerca divertir tutti. Mostra loro il giardin, la galleria, le camere; in effetto fa che resti contento il mio Masetto. Hai capito?

LEPORELLO: Ho capito. Andiam.

MASETTO: Signore!

DON GIOVANNI: Cosa c'è?

MASETTO: La Zerlina senza me non può star.

LEPORELLO: In vostro loco ci starà sua Eccellenza—e saprà bene fare le vostre parti.

DON GIOVANNI: Oh la Zerlina è in man d'un cavalier. Va pur; fra poco ella meco verrà.

ZERLINA: Va; non temere! nelle mani son io d'un cavaliere.

Recitative

DON GIOVANNI: Thank heaven I got rid of Elvira! Oh, look here, what charming young people. What pretty girls!

LEPORELLO (*aside*): Among so many, perhaps there may be something here for me as well!

DON GIOVANNI: My friends, good morning! Continue your amusements; go on with the music, good people. Is this a betrothal?

ZERLINA: Yes, my Lord, and I am the bride.

DON GIOVANNI: Well, well—the groom?

MASETTO: Here, at your service.

DON GIOVANNI: Oh, charming! At my service—that's really the remark of a gallant man.

LEPORELLO (*aside*): It's enough that he'll be a husband.

ZERLINA: Oh, my Masetto is very good-natured!

DON GIOVANNI: So am I; I'll show you. I think we shall all be friends. What is your name?

ZERLINA: Zerlina.

DON GIOVANNI: And yours?

MASETTO: Masetto.

DON GIOVANNI: Oh, my dear Masetto! my dearest Zerlina, I offer my protection to you. Leporello—what are you doing over there, you rascal?

LEPORELLO: I, too, dear master, was offering my protection.

DON GIOVANNI: That's enough of that; invite them all to my castle, at once. Order chocolate, coffee, wines, meat—try to amuse everybody. Show them the garden, the gallery, the rooms; in other words, be sure that you keep my dear Masetto occupied— You understand me?

LEPORELLO: I understand you. Let's go.

MASETTO: My Lord!

DON GIOVANNI: What's the matter?

MASETTO: Zerlina won't stay here without me.

LEPORELLO: His lordship will be here in your place—and he knows well how to take your part.

DON GIOVANNI: Oh, Zerlina is in a nobleman's hands. Go ahead; she'll come along soon with me.

ZERLINA: Go! Don't worry; I'm with a nobleman.

MASETTO: E per questo?

ZERLINA: E per questo non c'è da dubitar.

MASETTO: Ed io, cospetto!

DON GIOVANNI: Olà! Finiam le dispute; se subito senz'altro replicar, non te ne vai, Masetto, guarda ben, ti pentirai.

6. *Aria*

MASETTO: Hò capito, signor sì!
Chino il capo, e me ne vo'
Giacchè piace a voi così
Altre repliche non fo'.
Cavalier voi siete già,
Dubitar non posso affè,
Me lo dice la bontà,
Che volete aver per me. (*a* ZERLINA)
Bricconaccia! malandrina!
Fosti, ognor, la mia ruina! (*a* LEPORELLO)
Vengo, vengo. (*a* ZERLINA)
Resta! resta!
È una cosa molto onesta;
Faccia il nostro cavaliere,
Cavaliera ancora te.
(MASETTO *parte con* LEPORELLO *e il* CORO.)

Recitativo

DON GIOVANNI: Alfin siam liberati, Zerlinetta gentile da quel scioccone. Che ne dite, mio ben, so far pulito?

ZERLINA: Signore, è mio marito.

DON GIOVANNI: Chi! colui? Vi par ch'un'onest'uomo, un nobil cavalier, qual io mi vanto, possa soffrir che quel visetto d'oro, quel viso inzuccherato da un bifolcaccio vil sia strapazzato.

ZERLINA: Ma, signore, io gli diedi parola di sposarlo.

DON GIOVANNI: Tal parola non vale un zero, voi non siete fatta per esser paesana. Un'altra sorte vi procuran quegli occhi bricconcelli, quei labretti sì belli, quelle dituccie candide, e odorose, parmi toccar giuncata, e fiutar rose.

ZERLINA: Ah, non vorrei—

DON GIOVANNI: Che non vorreste?

MASETTO: And so?

ZERLINA: And so there's no cause for concern.

MASETTO: And I, damn it!

DON GIOVANNI: Very well, stop arguing. Masetto, listen to me—if you don't leave us without any more chatter, I can assure you that you'll repent it!

6. Aria

MASETTO: Yes, my Lord, I understand. I must bow to you and go away, because that pleases you, and I mustn't argue any more, no, no, no! You're a gentleman, after all, and I can't doubt your honor—you speak of the esteem that you have for me. (*to* ZERLINA) You flirt! You witch! You were always my ruin! (*to* LEPORELLO) Yes, I'm going. (*to* ZERLINA) You'll stay here! It's a very honest bargain. This nobleman will make a noblewoman out of you!

(MASETTO *exits with* LEPORELLO *and* CHORUS.)

Recitative

DON GIOVANNI: At last we're free, sweet Zerlina; that stupid idiot is gone. What do you think, my dear, didn't I manage it neatly?

ZERLINA: My Lord, he's my fiancé!

DON GIOVANNI: Who, that creature? Do you think that an honest man, a nobleman such as myself, could allow that lovely face, that sweet appearance to be wasted on such a vile scarecrow?

ZERLINA: But, my Lord, I have promised to marry him.

DON GIOVANNI: Such a promise means nothing; you weren't made to be a peasant; you're assured of a higher lot by your sparkling eyes, your beautiful lips, your white and fragrant fingers, which smell like roses and are as smooth as cream.

ZERLINA: Ah, I wouldn't like—

DON GIOVANNI: What wouldn't you like?

ZERLINA: Alfine ingannata restar. Io so che raro colle donne voi altri cavalieri siete onesti e sinceri.

DON GIOVANNI: È un'impostura della gente plebea: la nobiltà ha dipinta negli occhi l'onestà. Orsù non perdiamo tempo in quest'istante io vi voglio sposar.

ZERLINA: Voi?

DON GIOVANNI: Certo io. Quel casinetto è mio: soli saremo: e là giojello mio, ci sposeremo.

7. Duettino

Là ci darem la mano,
Là mi dirai di sì!
Vedi, non è lontano
Partiam, ben mio, da quì!

ZERLINA: Vorrei, e non vorrei;
Mi trema un poco il cor:
Felice, è ver sarei,
Ma può burlarmi ancor.

DON GIOVANNI: Vieni mio bel diletto!

ZERLINA: Mi fa pietà Masetto.

DON GIOVANNI: Io cangierò tua sorte.

ZERLINA: Presto, non son più forte.

DON GIOVANNI: Vieni! Vieni! Là ci darem la mano,
Là mi dirai di sì!

ZERLINA: Vorrei e non vorrei;
Mi trema un poco il cor.

ZERLINA e DON GIOVANNI: Andiam, andiam mio bene,
A ristorar le pene
D'un innocente amor!
(*Entra* DONNA ELVIRA.)

Recitativo

DONNA ELVIRA: Fermati, scelerato! Il ciel mi fece udir le tue perfidie; io sono a tempo di salvar questa misera innocente dal tuo barbaro artiglio.

ZERLINA: Meschina! cosa sento!

DON GIOVANNI (*a parte*): Amor, consiglio! (*a* DONNA ELVIRA) Idol mio, non vedete ch'io voglio divertirmi?

DONNA ELVIRA: Divertirti, è vero, divertirti? Io so, crudele, come tu ti diverti.

ZERLINA: To be deceived after a while. I've heard that you noblemen are seldom honest and sincere with women.

DON GIOVANNI: That's a lie invented by peasants! A nobleman's honesty is written in his eyes. Come on, let's not waste time. I'll marry you this very day.

ZERLINA: You?

DON GIOVANNI: Certainly, I. That little castle is mine. We'll be alone there, and there, my dearest jewel, we'll be married!

7. Duet

There we'll take each other's hands, and then you'll tell me "yes." See; it isn't far; let's go there together, my darling!

ZERLINA: I'd like to, and yet I'm afraid—something within me holds me back. Perhaps I would be happy—but still he may be deceiving me!

DON GIOVANNI: Come, my beautiful delight!

ZERLINA: And yet I pity Masetto.

DON GIOVANNI: Your rank will equal mine!

ZERLINA: Suddenly I'm not strong enough to resist him!

DON GIOVANNI: Come with me! Come with me!

ZERLINA: I will! My heart trembles.

ZERLINA *and* DON GIOVANNI: Together, my dearest, we'll soothe the pangs of innocent love!
(DONNA ELVIRA *enters.*)

Recitative

DONNA ELVIRA: Stop, you wretch! Heaven has sent me to refute your lies; I'm just in time to save this innocent girl from your horrible designs!

ZERLINA: What is she saying? Poor me!

DON GIOVANNI (*aside*): God of Love, inspire me now! (*to* DONNA ELVIRA) My dearest, don't you see that I'm merely amusing myself?

DONNA ELVIRA: Amusing yourself? How interesting! I know well, cruel man, what your amusements are!

ZERLINA: Ma, signor cavaliere, è ver quel ch'ella dice?

DON GIOVANNI: La povera infelice è di me innamorata, e per pietà deggio fingere amore, ch'io son per mia disgrazia uom di buon core.

8. Aria

DONNA ELVIRA: Ah fuggi il traditor,
Non lo lasciar più dir!
Il labbro è mentitor,
Fallace il ciglio.
Da miei tormenti impara
A creder a quel cor,
E nasca il tuo timor
Dal mio periglio!
(*Partono* DONNA ELVIRA *e* ZERLINA.)

Recitativo

DON GIOVANNI: Mi par ch'oggi il demonio si diverta d'opporsi ai miei piacevoli progressi, vanno mal tutti quanti.
(*Entrano* DONNA ANNA *e* DON OTTAVIO.)

DON OTTAVIO: Ah! ch'ora, idolo mio, son vani i pianti! Di vendetta si parli. Oh, Don Giovanni!

DON GIOVANNI (*a parte*): Mancava questo in ver!

DONNA ANNA: Amico! a tempo vi ritroviam! Avete core, avete anima generosa?

DON GIOVANNI (*a parte*): Sta a vedere ch'il diavolo gli ha detto qualche cosa? (*forte*) Che domanda! perchè?

DONNA ANNA: Bisogno abbiamo della vostra amicizia.

DON GIOVANNI (*a parte*): Respiro. (*forte*) Comandate: i congiunti, i parenti; questa man, questo ferro, i beni, il sangue spenderò per servirvi. Ma voi, bella Donn'Anna, perchè così piangete? Sì crudele chi fù, ch'osò la calma turbar del viver vostro?
(*Entra* DONNA ELVIRA.)

DONNA ELVIRA: Ah ti ritrovo ancor, perfido mostro. (*a* DONNA ANNA)

9. Quartetto

Non ti fidar, o misera!
Di quel ribaldo cor!
Me già tradì quel barbaro—
Ti vuol tradir ancor.

ZERLINA: But, my Lord, is she telling the truth?

DON GIOVANNI: This poor unhappy lady is madly in love with me, and from pity I pretend to love her in return. I'm far too sympathetic for my own good!

8. Aria

DONNA ELVIRA: Ah, flee from this traitor! Don't let him say another word! His lips are lying; his glances are deceitful! Learn from my suffering to distrust his heart, and let your fear be born of my danger!

(DONNA ELVIRA and ZERLINA exit.)

Recitative

DON GIOVANNI: It seems that the devil amuses himself today by impeding the progress of my pleasures; everything has gone badly.

(DONNA ANNA and DON OTTAVIO enter.)

DON OTTAVIO: Since tears are in vain, my darling, let's think of vengeance. Oh, Don Giovanni!

DON GIOVANNI (aside): This is all I need!

DONNA ANNA: My Lord! We meet most opportunely! Have you a noble heart, and a generous soul?

DON GIOVANNI (aside): Let's see if the devil has told her anything. (aloud) What a question! Why do you ask me?

DONNA ANNA: We have need of your friendship.

DON GIOVANNI (aside): What a relief! (aloud) Command me! My vassals, relatives, this hand, this sword, my possessions, my blood, will flow to serve you. But you, beautiful Donna Anna, why are you weeping? Who is the villain who has dared to disturb your life's serenity?

(DONNA ELVIRA enters.)

DONNA ELVIRA: Ah, here you are again, perfidious monster! (to DONNA ANNA)

9. Quartet

Unhappy girl, don't trust in this barbarous man's ribald heart! He has betrayed me already—and he'll betray you as well.

DONNA ANNA e DON OTTAVIO: Cieli! che aspetto nobile!
Che dolce maestà!
Il suo dolor, le lagrime
M'empiono di pietà.
DON GIOVANNI: La povera ragazza
E pazza, amici miei:
Lasciatemi con lei!
Forse si calmerà.
DONNA ELVIRA (*a* DONNA ANNA): Ah non credete al perfido!
DON GIOVANNI (*a* DONNA ANNA e DON OTTAVIO): È pazza;
non badate.
DONNA ELVIRA (*a* DONNA ANNA e DON OTTAVIO): Restate,
oh Dei! restate.
DONNA ANNA e DON OTTAVIO: A chi si crederà?
DONNA ANNA, DON OTTAVIO, DON GIOVANNI: Certo moto
d'ignoto tormento
Dentro l'alma girare mi sento,
Che mi dice per quella infelice
Cento cose che intender non sa.
DONNA ELVIRA: Sdegno, rabbia, dispetto, spavento
Dentro l'alma girare mi sento,
Che mi dice di quel traditore
Cento cose che intender non sa.
DON OTTAVIO: Io di quà non vado via,
Se non so com'è l'affar.
DONNA ANNA: Non ha l'aria di pazzia
Il suo tratto, il suo parlar.
DON GIOVANNI (*a parte*): Se men vada, si potria
Qualche cosa sospettar.
DONNA ELVIRA: Da quel ceffo si dovria
La ner'alma giudicar.
DON OTTAVIO (*a* DON GIOVANNI): Dunque quella?
DON GIOVANNI: È pazzarella.
DONNA ANNA (*a* DONNA ELVIRA): Dunque quegli?
DONNA ELVIRA: È un traditore.
DON GIOVANNI: Infelice!
DONNA ELVIRA: Mentitore! Mentitore!
DONNA ANNA e DON OTTAVIO: Incomincio a dubitar.

DONNA ANNA *and* DON OTTAVIO: Heavens! What a noble manner! What sweet majesty! Her grief and tears move me to pity.

DON GIOVANNI: This poor girl is crazy, my friends! Leave me alone with her, and perhaps I can persuade her to calm herself.

DONNA ELVIRA (*to* DONNA ANNA): Ah, don't believe this traitor!

DON GIOVANNI (*to* DONNA ANNA *and* DON OTTAVIO): She's crazy; don't listen to her!

DONNA ELVIRA (*to* DONNA ANNA *and* DON OTTAVIO): Stay with me—O God! Stay with me!

DONNA ANNA *and* DON OTTAVIO: Whom can we believe?

DONNA ANNA, DON OTTAVIO, DON GIOVANNI: I feel a torment in my soul that secretly reveals to me a hundred things about this poor unhappy girl that I don't yet understand.

DONNA ELVIRA: I feel scorn, rage, spite, and fear turning within my soul, telling me a hundred things about this libertine that I don't yet understand!

DON OTTAVIO: I won't leave this place until I know the true state of affairs!

DONNA ANNA: Her bearing and speech are not those of a madwoman.

DON GIOVANNI (*aside*): If I leave them now, they may begin to suspect something.

DONNA ELVIRA: You may judge his black soul from his expression!

DON OTTAVIO (*to* DON GIOVANNI): Then, this lady—

DON GIOVANNI: Is insane.

DONNA ANNA (*to* DONNA ELVIRA): Then, this man—

DONNA ELVIRA: Is a traitor!

DON GIOVANNI: Poor girl!

DONNA ELVIRA: Liar, liar!

DONNA ANNA *and* DON OTTAVIO: I'm beginning to doubt his word.

DON GIOVANNI (*a* DONNA ELVIRA): Zitto, zitto, che la gente
Si raduna a noi d'intorno:
Siate un poco più prudente—
Vi farete criticar.

DONNA ELVIRA: Non sperarlo, o scellerato!
Ho perduta la prudenza—
Le tue colpe ed il mio stato
Voglio a tutti palesar.

DONNA ANNA *e* DON OTTAVIO: Quegli accenti sì sommessi!
Quel cangiarsi di colore
Sono indizi troppo espressi
Che mi fan determinar.
(DONNA ELVIRA *parte.*)

Recitativo

DON GIOVANNI: Povera sventurata! i passi suoi voglio seguir,
non voglio che faccia un precipizio. Perdonate, bellissima
Donn'Anna; se servirvi poss'io, in mia casa v'aspetto.
Amici, addio! (*Parte.*)

DONNA ANNA: Don Ottavio, son morta.

DON OTTAVIO: Cos'è stato?

DONNA ANNA: Per pietà soccorretemi!

DON OTTAVIO: Mio ben, fate coraggio!

DONNA ANNA: Oh Dei! Quegli è il carnefice del padre mio!

DON OTTAVIO: Che dite?

DONNA ANNA: Non dubitate più. Gli ultimi accenti che
l'empio proferì, tutta la voce richiama nel cor mio di quell-
l'indegno, che nel mio appartamento—

DON OTTAVIO: Oh ciel! possibile, che sotto il sacro manto
d'amicizia—ma come fu? Narratemi lo strano avvenimento.

DONNA ANNA: Era già alquanto avanzata la notte, quando
nelle mie stanze, ove, soletta mi trovai per sventura, entrar
io vidi in un mantello avvolto un uom, ch'al primo istante
avea preso per voi; ma riconobbi poi ch'un inganno era il
mio.

DON OTTAVIO: Stelle! Seguite.

DONNA ANNA: Tacito a me s'appressa, e mi vuol abbracciar;
sciogliermi cerco, ei più mi stringe, io grido; non viene
alcun; con una mano cerca d'impedire la voce, e coll'altra
m'afferra stretta così, che già mi credo vinta.

DON GIOVANNI (*to* DONNA ELVIRA): Be quiet, or a crowd will gather. Be a little more prudent—you're making a spectacle of yourself!

DONNA ELVIRA: Don't hope to escape me, you scoundrel! I've lost all my prudence— I'll publish my wrongs and your misdeeds to all the world!

DONNA ANNA *and* DON OTTAVIO: His whispers and expressions incline me to decide in her favor!
(DONNA ELVIRA *exits.*)

Recitative

DON GIOVANNI: Poor unhappy woman! I'll follow her so that she won't do anything desperate. Forgive me, most beautiful Donna Anna; I'll await your commands at my castle. My friends, good morning! (*Exits.*)

DONNA ANNA: Don Ottavio, I'm dying!

DON OTTAVIO: What has happened?

DONNA ANNA: For heaven's sake, help me!

DON OTTAVIO: My darling, take courage!

DONNA ANNA: O God! That was the man who murdered my father!

DON OTTAVIO: What are you saying?

DONNA ANNA: I can't doubt it any longer. The last words that the villain spoke, his very voice recalled to my heart that wretch who came to my apartments—

DON OTTAVIO: O heavens! is it possible that under the sacred cloak of friendship— But what did he do then? Tell me the whole story!

DONNA ANNA: It was already late at night when unfortunately I found myself alone in my rooms. I saw a man come in, wrapped in a cloak; at first I mistook him for you, but I soon realized that I was deceived!

DON OTTAVIO: Good Lord! Go on.

DONNA ANNA: He quietly approached me and attempted to embrace me. I tried to escape him; he held me closer. I screamed, but nobody came. He put a hand on my mouth and held me so tightly that I believed myself conquered.

DON OTTAVIO: Perfido! e alfin?

DONNA ANNA: Alfine il duol, l'orrore dell'infame attentato accrebbe sì la lena mia; che a forza di svincolarmi, torcermi, e piegarmi, da lui mi sciolsi.

DON OTTAVIO: Ohimè! respiro!

DONNA ANNA: Allora rinforzo i stridi miei, chiamo soccorso —fugge il fellon, arditamente il seguo fin nella strada per fermarlo; e sono assalitrice d'assalita. Il padre v'accorre, vuol conoscerlo, e l'indegno; che del povero vecchio era più forte. Compiè il misfatto suo col dargli morte.

10. Aria
Or sai chi l'onore rapir a me volse,
Chi fu il traditore, ch'il padre mi tolse.
Vendetta ti chieggo—la chiede il tuo cor.
Rammenta la piaga del misero seno—
Rimira di sangue coperto il terreno,
Se 'l cor in te langue d'un giusto furor. (*Parte*.)

Recitativo
DON OTTAVIO: Come mai creder deggio di sì nero delitto capace un cavaliere! Ah di scoprire il vero ogni mezzo si cerchi, io sento in petto e di sposo, e d'amico il dover che mi parla: Disingannarla voglio, o vendicarla.

11. Aria
Dalla sua pace la mia dipende—
Quel ch'a lei piace vita mi rende;
Quel che le incresce morte mi da;
S'ella sospira, sospiro anch'io;
E mia quell'ira, quel pianto è mio—
E non ho bene se non l'ha.
(DON OTTAVIO *parte. Entrano* DON GIOVANNI *e* LEPORELLO.)

Recitativo
LEPORELLO: Io deggio ad ogni patto per sempre abbandonar questo bel matto. Eccolo qui: guardate con quell'indifferenza se ne viene.

DON GIOVANNI: Leporellino mio, va tutto bene?

LEPORELLO: Don Giovannino mio, va tutto male.

DON GIOVANNI: Come va tutto male?

DON OTTAVIO: Wretch! And then?

DONNA ANNA: Finally the dread and horror of the infamous attack increased my strength, and by twisting and struggling I tore myself away.

DON OTTAVIO: Thank heaven!

DONNA ANNA: Then I screamed more loudly, calling for help. The criminal tried to escape, and I followed him into the street, becoming the pursuer of my assailant. My father ran to me, and tried to unmask the wretch, who was stronger than the poor old man. Then he completed his crime by killing my father!

10. Aria

Now you know who tried to steal my honor, and who was the traitor that tore my beloved father from me. I ask for vengeance; your heart must also demand it. Remember the wound gaping in my father's breast! Recall his blood that covered the ground if ever you are tempted to forget your just anger at his murder! (*Exits.*)

Recitative

DON OTTAVIO: How can I believe that a nobleman could be guilty of such a black crime? I will not rest until I discover the truth. I feel a friend's and a lover's duty within my breast which says to me: "You must undeceive her or avenge her!"

11. Aria

My peace depends on her peace. Everything that pleases her gives new life to me. When she is injured, it brings me pain. If she sighs, then I sigh as well. I share her wrath and tears, and while she is sad, I can have no happiness! (DON OTTAVIO *exits.* DON GIOVANNI *and* LEPORELLO *enter.*)

Recitative

LEPORELLO: In any case, I must leave this madman's service. Here he is now—look at him, with what indifference he behaves!

DON GIOVANNI: Well, my dear Leporello, does all go well?

LEPORELLO: My very dear Don Giovanni, everything is going badly.

DON GIOVANNI: What do you mean?

LEPORELLO: Vado a casa, come voi m'ordinaste, con tutta quella gente.

DON GIOVANNI: Bravo!

LEPORELLO: A forza di chiacchere, di vezzi, e di bugie, ch'ho imparato sì bene a star con voi, cerco d'intrattenerli.

DON GIOVANNI: Bravo!

LEPORELLO: Dico mille cose a Masetto per placarlo, per trargli dal pensier la gelosia.

DON GIOVANNI: Ma bravo, in coscienza mia!

LEPORELLO: Faccio che bevano e gli uomini e le donne; son già mezzo ubbriachi. Altri canta, altri scherza—Altri seguita a ber—in sul più bello chi credete che capiti?

DON GIOVANNI: Zerlina!

LEPORELLO: Bravo! e con lei chi viene?

DON GIOVANNI: Donna Elvira.

LEPORELLO: Bravo! e disse di voi.

DON GIOVANNI: Tutto quel mal ch'in bocca le venia!

LEPORELLO: Ma bravo, in coscienza mia!

DON GIOVANNI: E tu cosa facesti?

LEPORELLO: Tacqui.

DON GIOVANNI: Ed ella?

LEPORELLO: Seguì a gridar.

DON GIOVANNI: E tu?

LEPORELLO: Quando mi parve, che già fosse sfogata, dolcemente fuor dell'orto la trassi, e con bell'arte chiusa la porta a chiave io me n'andai, e sulla via soletta io la lasciai.

DON GIOVANNI: Bravo! Bravo! arcibravo! L'affar non può andar meglio; incominciasti, io saprò terminar. Troppo mi premono queste contadinotte: le voglio divertir finchè vien notte.

12. Aria

Finch'han del vino
Calda la testa,
Una gran festa,
Fa preparar:
Se trovi in piazza,
Qualche ragazza,
Teco ancor quella

LEPORELLO: I went home, as you ordered me, with all those people.

DON GIOVANNI: Bravo!

LEPORELLO: By chattering, by flattery and lies, which I have learned to do so well by being near you, I tried to detain them.

DON GIOVANNI: Bravo!

LEPORELLO: I said a thousand things to Masetto to please him, to soothe his jealousy.

DON GIOVANNI: Bravo! By my conscience!

LEPORELLO: I made them drink, and the men and women were half-drunk already. Some sang, some joked—some continued with their drinking. At the height of this confusion, who do you think arrived?

DON GIOVANNI: Zerlina!

LEPORELLO: Bravo! And who do you think came with her?

DON GIOVANNI: Donna Elvira!

LEPORELLO: Bravo! And they spoke of you.

DON GIOVANNI: Everything evil that they could think of!

LEPORELLO: Bravo, by my conscience!

DON GIOVANNI: And you, what were you doing?

LEPORELLO: I was silent.

DON GIOVANNI: And Elvira?

LEPORELLO: She continued to accuse you.

DON GIOVANNI: And you?

LEPORELLO: When she appeared to be calmer, I gently led her outside to the orchard, and I very artfully locked the door with my own key, leaving her all alone on the street.

DON GIOVANNI: Bravo, bravo! More than bravo! It couldn't have been done better. You've begun well; now I'll be able to finish the matter. These country girls tempt me so much that I wish to entertain them all night long!

12. Aria

While they are flushed with wine; prepare everything for a great party! If you find some girls in the village square, bring them along with you. Let the dancing be without special order—let there be minuets; let there be country dances—let the dancers do whatever dances they please. And I, on the other hand, among so many, can make love to whomever I please. Ah,

Cerca menar;
Senz'alcun ordine,
La danza sia,
Ch'il minuetto,
Chi la follia
Chi l'Alemana,
Farai ballar;
Ed io frattanto,
Dall'altro canto,
Con questa e quella,
Vo' amoreggiar.
Ah la mia lista,
Doman mattina,
D'una decina deve aumentar.
(*Partono* DON GIOVANNI *e* LEPORELLO. *Entrano* ZERLINA *e*
MASETTO.)

Recitativo

ZERLINA: Masetto, senti un pò! Masetto, dico!
MASETTO: Non mi toccar.
ZERLINA: Perchè?
MASETTO: Perfida! il tutto sopportar dovrei d'una mano
infedele?
ZERLINA: Ah, no! taci, crudele, io non merto da te tal
trattamento.
MASETTO: Come! ed hai l'ardimento di scusarti? Star sola
con un uom; abbandonarmi il dì delle mie nozze—porre in
fronte a un villano d'onore questa marca d'infamia! Ah, se
non fosse, se non fosse lo scandalo, vorrei—

ZERLINA: Ma se colpa io non ho—ma se da lui ingannata
rimasi? E poi che temi? Tranquillati, mia vita! Non mi
toccò la punta delle dita. Non me lo credi, ingrato? Vien
qui, sfogati, ammazzami—fa pur tutto di me quel che ti
piace! Ma poi, Masetto poi, ma poi fa pace.

13. *Aria*

Batti, batti, o bel Masetto,
La tua povera Zerlina;
Starò qui come agnellina,
Le tue botte ad aspettar.
Lascierò straziarmi il crine;

by tomorrow morning a dozen names must be added to my list!
(DON GIOVANNI *and* LEPORELLO *exit.* ZERLINA *and* MASETTO *enter.*)

Recitative

ZERLINA: Masetto, listen to me! Masetto, I want to explain!

MASETTO: Don't touch me!

ZERLINA: Why not?

MASETTO: Slut! How can you ask me? Who could bear the touch of an unfaithful hand?

ZERLINA: Ah, no, don't say any more; I don't deserve such treatment from you!

MASETTO: What? And you have the audacity to argue with me? You were alone with that man; you abandoned me on our wedding day—and you planted the infamous horns on the forehead of an honest man! Ah, if only there would be no scandal, I would—

ZERLINA: But if it wasn't my fault—if I was deceived by him? Anyway, what are you afraid of? Be calm, my darling! He didn't even touch the tip of my finger. Don't you believe me? Ungrateful! Come here, strike me, kill me— do anything you please to me! But then, my dear Masetto, then let's be friends again.

13. Aria

Beat me, dear Masetto, beat your poor Zerlina! I'll stand here like a little lamb, awaiting your blows. I'll let you pull my hair out; I'll let you tear my eyes out, and even then I'll kiss your dear hands! Ah, I see that you haven't the heart to do it! Peace, peace, my darling—we'll pass our

Lascierò cavarmi gli occhi;
E le care tue manine
Lieta poi saprò baciar.
Ah! lo vedo, non hai core!
Pace, pace, o vita mia!
In contenti, ed allegria,
Notte e dì vogliam passar.

Recitativo

MASETTO: Guarda un pò, come seppe questa strega sedurmi! Siamo pure i deboli di testa!

DON GIOVANNI (*di dentro*): Sia preparato tutto a una gran festa.

ZERLINA: Ah, Masetto, Masetto! odi la voce del monsù cavaliere!

MASETTO: Ebben, che c'è?

ZERLINA: Verrà.

MASETTO: Lascia che venga.

ZERLINA: Ah! se vi fosse un buco da fuggir—

MASETTO: Di cosa temi? Perchè diventi pallida? Ah, capisco! Capisco, bricconcella! Hai timor, ch'io comprenda com'è tra voi passata la faccenda.

14. Finale

Presto, presto! pria ch'ei venga
Por mi vò da qualche lato:
V'è una nicchia, qui celato
Cheto, cheto, mi vo' star

ZERLINA: Senti, senti! dove vai!
Ah, non t'asconder, o Masetto!
Se ti trova, poveretto,
Tu non sai quel che può far.

MASETTO: Faccia, dica quel che vuole.

ZERLINA: Ah! non giovan le parole!

MASETTO: Parla forte e qui t'arresta.

ZERLINA: Che capriccio ha nella testa?

MASETTO (*a parte*): Capirò se m'è fedele,
E in qual modo andò l'affar.
(*Si nasconde.*)

ZERLINA: Quell'ingrato, quel crudele
Oggi vuol precipitar.

DON GIOVANNI (*di dentro*): Su svegliatevi da bravi!

days and nights in happiness! Yes, yes, yes, we'll be happy day and night!

Recitative

MASETTO: Just look at how this little witch can get around me. Men are all weak in the head!

DON GIOVANNI (*off-stage*): Let everything be prepared for a huge celebration!

ZERLINA: Ah, Masetto, Masetto, that's the voice of Don Giovanni!

MASETTO: And what about it?

ZERLINA: He's coming here!

MASETTO: Well, let him.

ZERLINA: Ah, if there were only a hole for us to hide in—

MASETTO: What are you afraid of? Why are you so pale? Ah, I understand, you traitress! You're afraid that I'll discover how things are between you!

14. Finale

Quickly, quickly, before he gets here, I'll place myself to one side. Here's a secluded spot— I'll silently hide myself here.

ZERLINA: Come back! Where are you going? Ah, don't hide yourself here, Masetto! If he finds you, you poor thing, you don't know what he will do!

MASETTO: Let him do and say what he likes!

ZERLINA: Your boasting is all in vain!

MASETTO: Speak louder, and stay right here!

ZERLINA: What nonsense is in your head?

MASETTO (*aside*): I'll learn if she's faithful to me, and exactly what has happened!

(*He hides.*)

ZERLINA: How cruel! How suspicious! Now he's sure to do something rash!

DON GIOVANNI (*off-stage*): Continue your celebration!

Su coraggio, o buona gente.
Vogliam star allegramente!
Vogliam ridere e scherzar.
Alla stanza della danza. (*ai servi*)
Conducete tutti quante;
Ed a tutti in abbondanza
Gran rinfreschi fate dar—
CORO (*di dentro*): Su, svegliatevi da bravi!
Su coraggio, o buona gente.
Vogliam star allegramente!
Vogliam ridere e scherzar—
ZERLINA: Tra questi arbori celata,
Si può dar che non mi veda.
(*Entra* DON GIOVANNI.)
DON GIOVANNI: Zerlinetta mia garbata!
Ti ho già vista—non scappar!
ZERLINA: Ah! lasciatemi andar via!
DON GIOVANNI: No, no, resta, gioja mia!
ZERLINA: Se pietade avete in core—
DON GIOVANNI: Sì, ben mio, son tutto amore.
Vieni un poco, in questo loco,
Fortunata io ti vo' far.
ZERLINA (*a parte*): Ah! s'ei vede il sposo mio,
So ben io quel che può far.
DON GIOVANNI (*vede* MASETTO, *che emerge dal suo nascondiglio*): Masetto!
MASETTO: Sì, Masetto!
DON GIOVANNI: E chiuso là perchè?
La bella tua Zerlina—
Non può la poverina
Più star senza di te.
MASETTO: Capisco, sì signore.
DON GIOVANNI: Adesso fate core!
I suonatori udite,
Venite omai con me!
ZERLINA e MASETTO: Si, si facciamo core,
Ed a ballar cogli altri
Andiamo tutti tre.
(ZERLINA, MASETTO e DON GIOVANNI *partono*. DONNA ANNA,
DONNA ELVIRA *e* DON OTTAVIO *entrano, in maschera.*)

Good people, amuse yourselves! I want you to be happy; I want you to laugh and dance. (*to servants*) Lead everyone into the ballroom and give them all the refreshments that they can eat!

CHORUS (*off-stage*): Continue your celebration! Amuse yourselves, good people! Be happy, laugh—

ZERLINA: Perhaps he won't find me here among these secluded trees.
(DON GIOVANNI *enters.*)
DON GIOVANNI: My sweet Zerlina, I've already seen you! You can't escape from me!
ZERLINA: Ah, let me go away!
DON GIOVANNI: No, no, stay with me, my darling!
ZERLINA: If you have any pity in your heart—
DON GIOVANNI: Yes, my dear, my heart is full of love. Come into this arbor for a moment, and I'll make you very happy.
ZERLINA (*aside*): Ah! If he should ever see Masetto, I know very well what he would do!
DON GIOVANNI (*seeing* MASETTO, *who has emerged from his hiding place*): Masetto!
MASETTO: Yes, Masetto!
DON GIOVANNI: You were hidden there—but why? Your pretty Zerlina, poor girl, won't stay here another moment without you.

MASETTO: I understand, my Lord.
DON GIOVANNI: Well, then, let's be cheerful! Listen to the music, and come inside with me!

ZERLINA *and* MASETTO: Yes, yes, let's be cheerful, and go inside to dance with the others!
(ZERLINA, MASETTO, *and* DON GIOVANNI *exit.* DONNA ANNA, DONNA ELVIRA, *and* DON OTTAVIO *enter, masked.*)

DONNA ELVIRA: Bisogna aver coraggio,
O cari amici miei;
E i suoi misfatti rei
Scoprir potremo allor.
DON OTTAVIO: L'amica dice bene—
Coraggio aver conviene. (*a* DONNA ANNA)
Discaccia, o vita mia!
L'affanno ed il timor.
DONNA ANNA: Il passo e periglioso,
Può nascer qualche imbroglio;
Temo pel caro sposo—
E per noi temo ancor.
(LEPORELLO *apre una finestra dal palazzo.*)
LEPORELLO: Signor, guardate un poco!
Che maschere galanti!
DON GIOVANNI (*di dentro*): Falle passar avanti,
Dì che ci fanno onor.
DONNA ANNA, DONNA ELVIRA, DON OTTAVIO: Al volto, ed alla
voce
Si scopre il traditore.
LEPORELLO: Zi! Zi! signore maschere!
DONNA ANNA *e* DONNA ELVIRA (*a* DON OTTAVIO): Via rispondete.
DON OTTAVIO: Cosa chiedete?
LEPORELLO: Al ballo, se vi piace
V'invita il mio signor.
DON OTTAVIO: Grazie di tanto onore.
Andiam, compagne belle.
LEPORELLO (*a parte*): L'amico anche su quelle
Prova farà d'amor.
(*Chiude la finestra.*)
 Trio
DONNA ANNA *e* DON OTTAVIO: Protegga il giusto cielo
Il zelo del mio cor!
DONNA ELVIRA: Vendichi il giusto cielo
Il mio tradito amor!
(*Partono* DONNA ANNA, DONNA ELVIRA *e* DON OTTAVIO.)
 Scena III
Sala da ballo nel palazzo di DON GIOVANNI. DON GIOVANNI,
LEPORELLO, ZERLINA, MASETTO, *suonatori, servi, contadini
e contadine.*

DONNA ELVIRA: We must be courageous now, my dear friends; only then can we uncover all his black crimes!

DON OTTAVIO: Our friend is right—we must have courage. (*to* DONNA ANNA) Try to dispel your grief and fear!

DONNA ANNA: Our situation is dangerous, and the danger increases. I'm afraid for both of you, and for myself as well.
(LEPORELLO *opens a window of the palace.*)

LEPORELLO: My Lord, look out there— I see three gallant maskers!

DON GIOVANNI (*off-stage*): Call to them and invite them to the ball.

DONNA ANNA, DONNA ELVIRA, DON OTTAVIO: I recognize the traitor's voice!

LEPORELLO: Pst! My Lord maskers!

DONNA ANNA *and* DONNA ELVIRA (*to* DON OTTAVIO): Go and speak to him.

DON OTTAVIO: What did you ask me?

LEPORELLO: If it pleases you, my master invites you to his ball.

DON OTTAVIO: Thank you; we would be honored. Shall we go, my fair companions?

LEPORELLO (*aside*): My master can also give these ladies a proof of his love.
(*He closes the window.*)

   Trio

DONNA ANNA *and* DON OTTAVIO: My heaven protect my heart's resolution!

DONNA ELVIRA: May heaven avenge my betrayed love!
(DONNA ANNA, DONNA ELVIRA, *and* DON OTTAVIO *exit.*)

   Scene III

The ballroom of DON GIOVANNI'S *palace.* DON GIOVANNI, LEPORELLO, ZERLINA, MASETTO, *musicians, servants, and guests.*

DON GIOVANNI: Riposate, vezzose ragazze!

LEPORELLO: Rinfrescatevi, bei giovinotti.

DON GIOVANNI *e* LEPORELLO: Tornerete a far presto le pazze,
Tornerete a scherzar e ballar!

DON GIOVANNI: Ehi caffè!

LEPORELLO: Cioccolatte!

MASETTO: Ah, Zerlina, giudizio!

DON GIOVANNI: Sorbetti!

LEPORELLO: Confetti!

ZERLINA *e* MASETTO (*a parte*): Troppo dolce comincia la scena,
In amaro potria terminar.

DON GIOVANNI: Sei pur vaga, brillante Zerlina!

ZERLINA: Sua bontà!

MASETTO (*a parte*): La briccona fa festa!

LEPORELLO (*fra le ragazze*): Sei pur cara, Giannotta, Sandrina!

MASETTO (*a parte*): Tocca pur, che ti cada la testa!

ZERLINA (*a parte*): Quel Masetto mi par stralunato.
Brutto, brutto si fa quest'affar.

DON GIOVANNI *e* LEPORELLO (*a parte*): Quel Masetto mi par stralunato.
Qui bisogna cervello adoprar.

MASETTO (*a parte*): La briccona mi fa disperar!

(*Entrano* DONNA ANNA, DONNA ELVIRA *e* DON OTTAVIO.)

LEPORELLO: Venite pur avanti,
Vezzose mascherette.

DON GIOVANNI: È aperto a tutti quanti,
Viva la libertà.

DONNA ANNA, DONNA ELVIRA, DON OTTAVIO: Siam grati a tanti segni
Di generosità.

DON GIOVANNI (*ai musicisti*): Ricominciate il suono!
Tu accoppia i ballerini. (*a* LEPORELLO)
Meco tu dei ballare. (*a* ZERLINA)
Zerlina, vien pur quà.

LEPORELLO: Da bravi via! ballate.

DON GIOVANNI: You must rest now, you charming girls!

LEPORELLO: Have something to eat, you handsome young men!

DON GIOVANNI and LEPORELLO: Soon you'll resume your dancing and amusements!

DON GIOVANNI: Here, some coffee!

LEPORELLO: Chocolate, here!

MASETTO: Ah, Zerlina, be careful!

DON GIOVANNI: Sherbets!

LEPORELLO: Candy!

ZERLINA and MASETTO (*aside*): This evening is beginning so sweetly, but it may end in bitterness!

DON GIOVANNI: You're so charming, my dazzling Zerlina!

ZERLINA: You're so kind!

MASETTO (*aside*): The flirt is enjoying herself!

LEPORELLO (*among the girls*): You're so sweet, Gianotta, Sandrina!

MASETTO (*aside*): Take care; I may cut off his head!

ZERLINA: Masetto is quite insane. (*aside*) This affair is becoming very ugly!

DON GIOVANNI and LEPORELLO (*aside*): Masetto is quite insane. Now we must use our brains!

MASETTO (*aside*): The girl is driving me to distraction! (*Enter* DONNA ANNA, DONNA ELVIRA, *and* DON OTTAVIO.)

LEPORELLO: Come forward, noble maskers!

DON GIOVANNI: This ballroom is open to all; you're at liberty to enter.

DONNA ANNA, DONNA ELVIRA, DON OTTAVIO: We thank you for such generosity.

DON GIOVANNI (*to the musicians*): Continue to play! (*to* LEPORELLO) You organize the dances. (*to* ZERLINA) You must dance with me, Zerlina; come over here.

LEPORELLO: That's fine, now go on dancing.

DONNA ELVIRA (*a* DONNA ANNA): Quell'è la contadina.

DONNA ANNA: Io moro!

DON OTTAVIO: Simulate!

DON GIOVANNI *e* LEPORELLO (*a parte*): Va bene in verità!

MASETTO (*ironicamente*): Va bene in verità?

DON GIOVANNI (*a* LEPORELLO): A bada tien Masetto!

LEPORELLO (*a* MASETTO): Non balli, poveretto.

DON GIOVANNI: Il tuo compagno io sono,
Zerlina, vien pur quà.

LEPORELLO (*a* MASETTO): Vien quà, Masetto caro!
Facciam quel ch'altri fa.

MASETTO: No, no, ballar non voglio.

LEPORELLO: Eh balla, amico mio.

MASETTO: No!

LEPORELLO: Sì, caro Masetto!

DONNA ANNA (*a parte*): Resister non poss'io.

DON OTTAVIO *e* DONNA ELVIRA: Fingete per pietà!

MASETTO: Ballare no, non voglio!

LEPORELLO: Balla, amico mio,
Facciam quel ch'altri fa.

DON GIOVANNI (*a* ZERLINA): Vieni con me, mia vita?

MASETTO (*a* LEPORELLO): Lasciami! Ah, no! Zerlina!

DON GIOVANNI: Vieni, vieni!

ZERLINA (DON GIOVANNI *la mena nell' altra stanza*): Oh,
Numi! son tradita!

LEPORELLO: Qui nasce una ruina.

DONNA ANNA, DONNA ELVIRA, DON OTTAVIO (*a parte*): L'iniquo da se stesso,
Nel laccio se ne va.

ZERLINA (*di dentro*): Gente! ajuto! Ajuto gente!

MASETTO: Ah, Zerlina!

ZERLINA (*di dentro*): Scelerato!

DONNA ANNA, DONNA ELVIRA, DON OTTAVIO: Ora grida da
quel lato!

ZERLINA (*di dentro*): Scelerato!

DONNA ELVIRA (*to* DONNA ANNA): That's the country girl.

DONNA ANNA: I'm dying!

DON OTTAVIO: Take courage!

DON GIOVANNI *and* LEPORELLO (*aside*): It's really going well!

MASETTO (*ironically*): It's really going well?

DON GIOVANNI (*to* LEPORELLO): Hold Masetto back!

LEPORELLO (*to* MASETTO): You're not dancing, poor boy.

DON GIOVANNI: I'm your partner, Zerlina; come here with me!

LEPORELLO (*to* MASETTO): Come here, dear Masetto! Do as the others are doing.

MASETTO: No, no, I don't want to dance!

LEPORELLO: Dance, my friend!

MASETTO: No!

LEPORELLO: Yes, dear Masetto!

DONNA ANNA (*aside*): I can't stand it any longer!

DONNA ELVIRA *and* DON OTTAVIO: Pretend, for heaven's sake!

MASETTO: I don't want to dance!

LEPORELLO: Dance, my friend. Do as the others are doing.

DON GIOVANNI (*to* ZERLINA): Come with me, my darling! Come, come!

MASETTO (*to* LEPORELLO): Let me go! Ah, no! Zerlina!

DON GIOVANNI: Come with me!

ZERLINA (*as* DON GIOVANNI *forces her into an adjoining room*): O God! I'm betrayed!

LEPORELLO: That's how he ruins them all.

DONNA ANNA, DONNA ELVIRA, DON OTTAVIO (*aside*): The wretch is falling into our trap.

ZERLINA (*off-stage*): Help me, somebody!

MASETTO: Ah, Zerlina!

ZERLINA (*off-stage*): Let me go!

DONNA ANNA, DONNA ELVIRA, DON OTTAVIO: Her voice is coming from that room!

ZERLINA (*off-stage*): You villain!

DONNA ANNA, DONNA ELVIRA, DON OTTAVIO: Ah gittiamo giù la porta!

ZERLINA (*di dentro*): Soccorretemi! Son morta!

DONNA ANNA, DONNA ELVIRA, DON OTTAVIO, MASETTO: Siam qui per tua difesa!

(MASETTO *rompe la porta dell' altra stanza;* DON GIOVANNI *ritorna, spada in mano, traendo* LEPORELLO. ZERLINA *corre a* MASETTO.)

DON GIOVANNI (*indicando* LEPORELLO): Ecco il birbo che t'ha offesa.
Ma da me la pena avrà! Mori iniquo!

LEPORELLO: Ah cosa fate?

DON GIOVANNI: Mori, dico!

DON OTTAVIO (*spada in mano*): Nol sperate, nol sperate!

DONNA ANNA, DONNA ELVIRA, DON OTTAVIO: L'empio crede con tal frode nasconder l'empietà.
(*Cavonsi le maschere.*)

DON GIOVANNI: Donna Elvira!

DONNA ELVIRA: Sì, malvagio!

DON GIOVANNI: Don Ottavio!

DON OTTAVIO: Sì, signore!

DON GIOVANNI (*a* DONNA ANNA): Ah, credete—

DONNA ANNA, DONNA ELVIRA, ZERLINA, DON OTTAVIO, MASETTO: Traditore, traditore!

ZERLINA: Tutto, tutto già si sa!

DONNA ANNA, DONNA ELVIRA, ZERLINA, DON OTTAVIO, MASETTO: Tutto tutto già si sa! Tutto! (*a* DON GIOVANNI)
Trema, trema, scellerato!
Saprà tosto il mondo intero
Il misfatto orrendo e nero
La tua fiera crudeltà!

DON GIOVANNI *e* LEPORELLO: È confusa la mia testa,
Non so più quel ch'io mi faccia,
E un orribile tempesta,
Minacciando, oh Dio, mi va!
Non mi perdo (si perde) o mi confondo (si confonde),
Se cadesse ancora il mondo,
Nulla mai temer mi fa!

DONNA ANNA, DONNA ELVIRA, DON OTTAVIO: Let's break the door down!

ZERLINA (*off-stage*): Save me! Help me! I'm dying!

DONNA ANNA, DONNA ELVIRA, DON OTTAVIO, MASETTO: We'll save you!

(MASETTO *breaks down the door to the inner room.* DON GIOVANNI *emerges, sword in hand, dragging* LEPORELLO. ZERLINA *runs out to* MASETTO.)

DON GIOVANNI (*pointing to* LEPORELLO): Here's the rascal who attacked her, but I'll see that he gets his just punishment! Die, you wretch!

LEPORELLO: Ah, what are you doing?

DON GIOVANNI: Die, I say!

DON OTTAVIO (*drawing his sword*): You'll never escape!

DONNA ANNA, DONNA ELVIRA, DON OTTAVIO: This scoundrel believes that he can conceal his crimes by such a transparent scheme!

(*They unmask.*)

DON GIOVANNI: Donna Elvira!

DONNA ELVIRA: Yes, you monster!

DON GIOVANNI: Don Ottavio!

DON OTTAVIO: Yes, it's I!

DON GIOVANNI (*to* DONNA ANNA): Ah, believe me—

DONNA ANNA, DONNA ELVIRA, ZERLINA, DON OTTAVIO, MASETTO: Traitor! Traitor!

ZERLINA: Everything is known to us!

DONNA ANNA, DONNA ELVIRA, ZERLINA, DON OTTAVIO, MASETTO: Everything is known! Everything! (*to* DON GIOVANNI) Now, vile wretch, it is your turn to tremble! Soon the whole world will know of your horrid and black crimes and your harsh cruelty!

DON GIOVANNI *and* LEPORELLO: My thoughts are whirling! The situation is out of control. O God, what a horrible tempest threatens! But I do not (he does not) lack courage. Let the heavens fall; I (he) will defy them.

DONNA ANNA, DONNA ELVIRA, ZERLINA, DON OTTAVIO, MA-
SETTO: Odi il tuon della vendetta,
Che ti fischia intorno intorno,
Sul tuo capo in questo giorno
Il suo fulmine cadrà!
(DON GIOVANNI *si scappa.*)

DONNA ANNA, DONNA ELVIRA, ZERLINA, DON OTTAVIO, MASETTO: Hear the thunder of vengeance that approaches, threatening you; soon its lightning will fall upon your head!

(DON GIOVANNI *escapes.*)

ATTO SECONDO

Scena I

Strada. A lato la casa di DONNA ELVIRA. *Entrano* DON GIO-
VANNI *e* LEPORELLO.

15. Duetto

DON GIOVANNI: Eh via, buffone,
Non mi seccar.

LEPORELLO: No no, padrone,
Non vo'restar.

DON GIOVANNI: Sentimi, amico—

LEPORELLO: Vò andar, vi dico.

DON GIOVANNI: Ma che ti ho fatto,
Che vuoi lasciarmi?

LEPORELLO: Oh niente affatto!
Quasi ammazzarmi,
Ed io non burlo,
Ma voglio andar.

DON GIOVANNI: Va, che sei matto.

LEPORELLO: Non vò restar.

Recitativo

DON GIOVANNI: Leporello!

LEPORELLO: Signore?

DON GIOVANNI: Vien quì, facciamo pace. (*da una borsa*)
Prendi!

LEPORELLO: Cosa?

DON GIOVANNI: Quattro doppie.

LEPORELLO: Oh sentite, per questa volta la cerimonia
accetto; ma non vi ci avvezzate—non credeste di sedurre i
miei pari come le donne, a forza di denari.

DON GIOVANNI: Non parliam più di ciò. Ti basta l'animo
di far quel ch'io ti dico?

LEPORELLO: Purchè lasciam le donne.

DON GIOVANNI: Lasciar le donne! Pazzo! Lasciar le donne!

ACT TWO

Scene I

A street. At one side, the house of DONNA ELVIRA. *Enter* DON GIOVANNI *and* LEPORELLO.

15. *Duet*

DON GIOVANNI: Be quiet, you idiot; stop annoying me!

LEPORELLO: No, no, my master, I won't stay with you any longer!

DON GIOVANNI: Listen to me, my friend—

LEPORELLO: I want to go, I tell you!

DON GIOVANNI: What have I done to make you wish to leave?

LEPORELLO: Oh, nothing important—you've almost murdered me, that's all!

DON GIOVANNI: Don't be stupid—it was all only a joke.

LEPORELLO: I won't stay with you any longer!

Recitative

DON GIOVANNI: Leporello!

LEPORELLO: My Lord?

DON GIOVANNI: Come, let's make peace. (*giving him money*) Take this!

LEPORELLO: What is it?

DON GIOVANNI: Four gold pieces.

LEPORELLO: Well, for this time, I'll accept your bribe— but don't flatter yourself that you can cajole a man like me, as you do the women, with money!

DON GIOVANNI: Let's not discuss it any more. Have you the courage now to do whatever I ask?

LEPORELLO: As long as you give up the women.

DON GIOVANNI: Give up the women? Are you insane? Give

Sai ch'esse per me son necessarie più del pan che mangio,
Più dell'aria che spiro!
LEPORELLO: E avete core d'ingannarle poi tutte?

DON GIOVANNI: È tutto amore. Chi a una sola è fedele verso
l'altra è crudele. Io, ch'in me sento si esteso sentimento, vo
bene a tutte quante. Le donne poi, che calcolar non sanno,
il mio buon natural chiamano inganno.

LEPORELLO: Non ho veduto mai naturale più benigno! Orsù
cosa vorreste?

DON GIOVANNI: Odi! Vedesti tu la cameriera di Donna
Elvira?

LEPORELLO: Io no.

DON GIOVANNI: Non hai veduto qualche cosa di bello caro
il mio Leporello! Ora io con lei vo tentar la mia sorte, ed
ho pensato, giacchè siam verso sera, per aguzzarle meglio
l'appetito, di presentarmi a lei col tuo vestito.

LEPORELLO: E perchè non poteste presentarvi col vostro?

DON GIOVANNI: Han poco credito con gente di tal rango gli
abiti signorili Sbrigati via!

LEPORELLO: Signor, per più ragioni—

DON GIOVANNI: Finiscila, non soffro opposizioni.

(*Si cambiano vestiti.* DONNA ELVIRA *viene alla finestra, e
guarda fuori; si diventa buio.*)

16. Terzetto

DONNA ELVIRA: Ah taci, ingiusto core!
Non palpitarmi in seno!
È un empio, è un traditore
È colpa aver pietà.

LEPORELLO (*a* DON GIOVANNI): Zitto! di Donna Elvira.
Signor, la voce io sento.

DON GIOVANNI (*a* LEPORELLO): Cogliere io vo'il momento!
Tu fermati un po'là. (*si metto dietro* LEPORELLO)
Elvira idolo mio!

DONNA ELVIRA: Non è costui l'ingrato?

DON GIOVANNI: Si vita mia, son io,
E chiedo carità.

DONNA ELVIRA: Numi! che strano effetto
Mi si risveglia in petto!

up the women! You know that I need them more than the
food I eat, more than the very air I breathe!

LEPORELLO: And even so, you have the heart to deceive
them?

DON GIOVANNI: You don't understand my love for them.
Whoever is faithful to one woman only betrays the rest.
The bounty of my love embraces all womankind. But
women, confused by my good nature, call it deceit!

LEPORELLO: I've never seen such good nature and such
kindness! Now, what do you want of me?

DON GIOVANNI: Listen! Have you seen Donna Elvira's
maid?

LEPORELLO: I? No.

DON GIOVANNI: You've never seen anything so beautiful, my
dear Leporello. Now I'd like to try my luck with her, and
I've been thinking that since it's near evening, I'll present
myself to her in your clothing.

LEPORELLO: And why can't you appear in your own
clothes?

DON GIOVANNI: With people of her rank, to be a gentleman
bears no credit. Come, take your cloak off!

LEPORELLO: My Lord, for many reasons—

DON GIOVANNI: Don't delay me! I want no opposition!
(*They exchange cloaks.* DONNA ELVIRA *comes to the window
and looks out, as it becomes dark.*)

16. Trio

DONNA ELVIRA: Be silent, foolish heart! Do not tremble in
my breast! He's unfaithful and a traitor; it would be sinful
to pity him!

LEPORELLO (*to* DON GIOVANNI): Quiet, my Lord, I hear
Donna Elvira's voice.

DON GIOVANNI (*to* LEPORELLO): I want to seize the moment! You stay there for a while. (*placing himself behind*
LEPORELLO) My darling Elvira!

DONNA ELVIRA: Can it be that ungrateful man?

DON GIOVANNI: Yes, my love, it's I, and I beg for your pity!

DONNA ELVIRA: Heavens, what a strange feeling rises in my
breast!

LEPORELLO (*a parte*): State a veder la pazza!
Ch'ancor gli crederà.
DON GIOVANNI: Discendi, o gioja bella!
Vedrai che tu sei quella,
Che adora l'alma mia,
Pentito io sono già!
DONNA ELVIRA: No! non ti credo, o barbaro!
DON GIOVANNI: Ah, credimi, o m'uccido!
LEPORELLO (*a parte*): Se seguitate, io rido.

DON GIOVANNI: Idolo mio, vien quà!
DONNA ELVIRA: Dei, che cimento è questo!
Non so s'io vado, o resto;
Ah proteggete voi
La mia credulità!
DON GIOVANNI (*a parte*): Spero che cada presto!
Che bel colpetto è questo!
Più fertile talento
Del mio no non si da.
LEPORELLO (*a parte*): Già quel mendace labbro!
Torna a sedur costei;
Deh proteggete, oh dei!
La sua credulità!
(DONNA ELVIRA *chiude la finestra.*)

Recitativo

DON GIOVANNI: Amico, che ti par?
LEPORELLO: Mi par ch'abbiate un'anima di bronzo.
DON GIOVANNI: Va là, che sè il gran gonzo! Ascolta bene;
quando costei qui viene, tu corri ad abbracciarla, falle quattro carezze, fingi la voce mia, poi con bell'arte cerca teco
condurla in altra parte.

LEPORELLO: Ma signor—
DON GIOVANNI: Non più repliche!
LEPORELLO: E se poi mi conosce?
DON GIOVANNI: Non ti conoscerà, se tu non vuoi—Zitto!
ell'apre—ehi giudizio.
(*Si nasconde indietro, e ascolta. Entra* DONNA ELVIRA.)
DONNA ELVIRA (*vede* LEPORELLO): Eccomi a voi!
DON GIOVANNI (*a parte*): Vediamo che farà.

LEPORELLO (*aside*): Just look at that foolish woman; she's ready to trust him again!

DON GIOVANNI: Come down here, my darling! You'll see that my heart adores you; I'm already penitent.

DONNA ELVIRA: No, I don't trust you, cruel one!

DON GIOVANNI: Ah, believe me! Or I shall kill myself!

LEPORELLO (*aside*): If he goes on with this, I'll laugh out loud!

DON GIOVANNI: My darling, come here!

DONNA ELVIRA: What a strange situation! I don't know whether I should go with him or stay here! Ah, heaven protect my trusting heart!

DON GIOVANNI (*aside*): I hope she'll yield quickly! This was a fortunate stroke! My talents are beyond emulation.

LEPORELLO (*aside*): Again his lying lips deceive her! Ah, heaven protect her trusting heart!
(DONNA ELVIRA *closes the window.*)

Recitative

DON GIOVANNI: Well, my friend, how does it look?

LEPORELLO: It looks to me as if you have a heart of stone!

DON GIOVANNI: There now, don't be so prudish! Listen carefully; when she comes down here you must hurry and embrace her, give her three or four kisses, imitate my voice, and with similar deceptions, manage to lead her away from here with you.

LEPORELLO: But, my Lord!

DON GIOVANNI: Don't waste time in arguments!

LEPORELLO: And if she should recognize me?

DON GIOVANNI: She won't if you don't wish her to— Look! She's coming—be quiet!
(*He hides upstage, listening.* DONNA ELVIRA *enters.*)

DONNA ELVIRA (*seeing* LEPORELLO): Here I am, my love!

DON GIOVANNI (*aside*): Let's see what he can do.

LEPORELLO (*a parte*): Che bell'imbroglio!

DONNA ELVIRA: Dunque creder potrò, ch'i pianti miei abbian vinto quel cor? dunque pentito l'amato Don Giovanni al suo dovere, e all'amor mio ritorna?

LEPORELLO (*finge la voce di* DON GIOVANNI): Si, carina!

DONNA ELVIRA: Crudele! se sapeste quante lagrime, e quanti sospiri voi mi costate!

LEPORELLO: Io, vita mia!

DONNA ELVIRA: Voi.

LEPORELLO: Poverina! quanto mi dispiace!

DONNA ELVIRA: Mi fuggirete più?

LEPORELLO: No, muso bello!

DONNA ELVIRA: Sarete sempre mio?

LEPORELLO: Sempre!

DONNA ELVIRA: Carissimo!

LEPORELLO: Carissima! (*a parte*) La burla mi da gusto!

DONNA ELVIRA: Mio tesoro!

LEPORELLO: Mia venere!

DONNA ELVIRA: Son per voi tutta foco!

LEPORELLO: Io tutto cenere!

DON GIOVANNI (*a parte*): Il birbo si riscalda.

DONNA ELVIRA: E non m'ingannerete?

LEPORELLO: No, sicuro.

DONNA ELVIRA: Giuratelo!

LEPORELLO: Lo giuro a questa mano, che bacio con trasporto, e a quei bei lumi!

DON GIOVANNI (*finge d'inseguirli*): Ih, eh, ah, ih—sei morto!

DONNA ELVIRA *e* LEPORELLO: Oh Numi! (*fuggono.*)

DON GIOVANNI: Ih, eh, ah, ih! Par che la sorte mi secondi. Veggiamo; le finestre son queste: ora cantiamo.

17. Canzonetta

Deh vieni alla finestra,
O mio tesoro,
Deh vieni a consolar,

LEPORELLO (*aside*): What a situation!

DONNA ELVIRA: May I then believe that my tears have conquered your heart? Now, repentant, my beloved Don Giovanni is returning to his duty and his love?

LEPORELLO (*imitating* DON GIOVANNI'S *voice*): Yes, my darling!

DONNA ELVIRA: Cruel one! If you only knew how many tears and sighs you've cost me!

LEPORELLO: I, treasure of my life?

DONNA ELVIRA: You!

LEPORELLO: Poor girl! How sorry I am!

DONNA ELVIRA: You won't leave me again?

LEPORELLO: No, my sweetheart!

DONNA ELVIRA: You'll always be mine?

LEPORELLO: Always!

DONNA ELVIRA: My darling!

LEPORELLO: My dearest! (*aside*) This game is to my taste!

DONNA ELVIRA: My treasure!

LEPORELLO: My Venus!

DONNA ELVIRA: My heart is flaming with love!

LEPORELLO: I'm one huge furnace!

DON GIOVANNI (*aside*): The rascal is warming up!

DONNA ELVIRA: And you're not deceiving me?

LEPORELLO: No, of course not.

DONNA ELVIRA: Swear it to me!

LEPORELLO: I swear it by this hand, which I kiss with ecstasy, and by those beautiful eyes!

DON GIOVANNI (*pretending to chase them*): Ih, eh, ah—I'll kill you!

DONNA ELVIRA *and* LEPORELLO: O heavens! (*Exit.*)

DON GIOVANNI: Ih, eh, ah, ha, ha, ha! It seems that fortune is auspicious; soon I shall see. These are her windows; now to my song.

17. Canzonetta

Come here to your window, O my treasure! Come to console my tears! If you deny me, I will die here before your eyes! Your mouth is sweeter than honey; your heart is

Il pianto mio.
Se neghi a me di dar qualche ristoro;
Davanti agli occhi tuoi, morir vogl'io.
Tu ch'hai la bocca dolce,
Più del miele.
Tu che il zucchero porti in mezzo al core;
Non esser gioja mia con me crudele,
Lasciate almen veder mio bell'amore!

Recitativo

V'è gente alla finestra; forse è dessa. Zi! Zi!
(*Entra* MASETTO, *e contadini armati*.)

MASETTO: Non ci stanchiamo; il cor mi dice che trovarlo
dobbiamo.

DON GIOVANNI (*a parte*): Qualcuno parla.

MASETTO: Fermatevi—mi pare ch'alcuno qui si mova.

DON GIOVANNI (*a parte*): Se non fallo, è Masetto.

MASETTO: Chi va là? Non risponde. Animo, schioppo al
muso: Chi va là?

DON GIOVANNI (*a parte*): Non è solo, ci vuol giudizio.
(*forte*) Amici! (*a parte*) Non mi voglio scoprir. (*forte*)
Sei tu, Masetto?

MASETTO: Appunto quello! e tu?

DON GIOVANNI: Non mi conosci? Un servo son io di Don
Giovanni—

MASETTO: Leporello! Servo di quell'indegno cavaliere?

DON GIOVANNI: Certo, di quel briccone.

MASETTO: Di quell'uom senz'onore, ah dimmi un poco,
dove possiam trovarlo; lo cerco con costor per trucidarlo.

DON GIOVANNI (*a parte*): Bagatelle! (*forte*) Bravissimo
Masetto. Anch'io con voi m'unisco per fargliela a quel
birbo di padrone; ma udite un pò qual è la mia intenzione.

18. Aria

Metà di voi quà vadano,
E gli altri vadan là!
E pian pianin lo cerchino,
Lontan non sia di quà, no!
Se un uom e una ragazza passegian per la piazza
Se sotto a una finestra

made of sugar! Don't be cruel to me, my dearest. Let me see your face, my beautiful love!

Recitative

There's somebody at the window; it may be she. Pst! Pst! (MASETTO *enters, with armed villagers.*)

MASETTO: Don't give up; I know that we will find him.

DON GIOVANNI (*aside*): I hear a voice!

MASETTO: Stop! It seemed to me that somebody moved.

DON GIOVANNI (*aside*): If I don't mistake him, it's Masetto.

MASETTO: Who goes there? He doesn't answer. Aim your guns! Who goes there?

DON GIOVANNI (*aside*): He's not alone; I must be careful. (*aloud*) My friends! (*aside*) I don't want to be found out. (*aloud*) Is it you, Masetto?

MASETTO: Me myself! And who are you?

DON GIOVANNI: You don't know me? I'm the servant of Don Giovanni.

MASETTO: Leporello? Servant of that unworthy nobleman?

DON GIOVANNI: Yes, of that rascal!

MASETTO: Of that man without honor? Ah, only tell me where we can find him! I'm looking for him with these friends, in order to kill him.

DON GIOVANNI (*aside*): Nonsense! (*aloud*) That's wonderful, Masetto. I'll join you, and help you kill that rascal, my master. But listen—I have a plan.

18. Aria

Half of you go this way; and the other half, that way! Look for him silently; he can't be far from here, no! If you see a man and a girl walking on the square, if you hear love-making under a window, then strike—it will be my master. He's wearing a hat with white feathers; a heavy cloak covers his back; a sword hangs at his side. Go, hurry up!

Fare all'amor sentite
Ferite, pur ferite, il mio padron sarà.
In testa egli ha un cappello,
Con candidi pennacchi,
Addosso un gran mantello
E spada al fianco egli ha.
Andate, fate presto! (*a* MASETTO) Tu sol verrai con me.
Noi far dobbiam il resto, e già vedrai cos'e.
(*I contadini partono.*)

Recitativo

Zitto! lascia ch'io senta. Ottimamente! Dunque dobbiamo ucciderlo?

MASETTO: Sicuro.

DON GIOVANNI: E non ti basteria rompergli l'ossa—fracassargli le spalle?

MASETTO: No, no! voglio ammazzarlo! Vò farlo in cento brani.

DON GIOVANNI: Hai buone arme?

MASETTO: Cospetto! Ho pria questo moschetto; e poi questa pistola.

DON GIOVANNI: E poi?

MASETTO: Non basta?

DON GIOVANNI: Eh, basta certo. Or prendi questa per la pistola, (*battendolo*) questa per il moschetto.

MASETTO: Ahi! ahi! La testa mia!

DON GIOVANNI: Taci, o t'uccido! Questa per l'ammazzarlo— Questa per farlo in brani. Villano, mascalzon, ceffo da cani! (*Parte.*)

MASETTO: Ahi, ahi! La testa mia! Ahi, ahi, le spalle! E il petto!
(*Entra* ZERLINA, *con una lanterna.*)

ZERLINA: Di sentire mi parve la voce di Masetto.

MASETTO: Oh Dio! Zerlina! Zerlina mia, soccorso!

ZERLINA: Cos'è stato?

MASETTO: L'iniquo, il scellerato mi ruppe l'ossa, e i nervi.

ZERLINA: O poveretta me! chi?

MASETTO: Leporello, o qualche diavol che somiglia a lui.

(*to* MASETTO) Only you will remain here with me. We'll do the rest, and you'll soon learn what that will be. (*The villagers exit.*)

Recitative

Be quiet, let me listen. Good; nobody's coming. Then you want to kill him?

MASETTO: Certainly!

DON GIOVANNI: And it won't be enough if you merely break his bones—wrench his shoulders?

MASETTO: No! I want to kill him and cut him into a hundred pieces!

DON GIOVANNI: Have you good weapons?

MASETTO: Of course! First have this musket; and then, this pistol.

DON GIOVANNI: And then?

MASETTO: Isn't that enough?

DON GIOVANNI: Oh, it's enough. Now take that for the pistol (*beating him*) and that for the musket!

MASETTO: Oh, my poor head!

DON GIOVANNI: Be quiet, or I'll kill you! Take this for killing him—and this for the hundred pieces! You ill-bred dog! (*Exits.*)

MASETTO: Oh, oh! My head! Oh, oh, my shoulders, my chest!

(ZERLINA *enters, with a lantern.*)

ZERLINA: Is that Masetto's voice?

MASETTO: O God! Zerlina! My Zerlina, help me!

ZERLINA: What has happened?

MASETTO: The wretch, the villain, has torn my flesh from my bones!

ZERLINA: Oh, poor dear! But who has done this?

MASETTO: Leporello, or a devil who greatly resembled him!

ZERLINA: Crudel! non tel diss'io, che con questa tua pazza gelosia ti ridurresti a qualche brutto passo. Dove ti duole?

MASETTO: Quì.

ZERLINA: E poi?

MASETTO: Quì e ancora quì.

ZERLINA: E poi non ti duol altro?

MASETTO: Duolmi un poco questo piè, questo braccio, e questa mano.

ZERLINA: Via via, non è gran mal, s'il resto è sano. Vientene meco a casa. Purchè tu mi prometta d'essere men geloso, io, io ti guarirò, caro il mio sposo.

19. Aria

Vedrai carino,
Se sei buonino,
Che bel rimedio,
Ti voglio dar.
È naturale,
Non da disgusto,
E lo speziale,
Non lo so far, nò.
È un certo balsamo,
Che porto addosso,
Dare tel posso,
S'il vuoi provar!
Saper vorresti?
Dove mi stà? (*mettendo la mano sul core*)
Sentilo battere
Toccami quà!
(ZERLINA *e* MASETTO *partono. Entrano* LEPORELLO *e* DONNA ELVIRA).

Recitativo

LEPORELLO: Di molte faci il lume s'avvicina, o mio ben; stiamo qui un poco, finchè da noi si scosta.

DONNA ELVIRA: Ma che temi, adorato il mio sposo?

LEPORELLO: Nulla, nulla. Certi riguardi—Io vò veder, s'il lume è già lontano. (*a parte*) Ah come da costei liberarmi? (*forte*) Rimanti, anima bella!

DONNA ELVIRA: Ah, non lasciarmi!

ZERLINA: Cruel one! Haven't I told you that your insane jealousy would get you into trouble? Where does it hurt you?

MASETTO: Here.

ZERLINA: Where else?

MASETTO: Here, and also here.

ZERLINA: Is that all?

MASETTO: My foot hurts me a little, this arm, and this hand.

ZERLINA: Come, come, it's not so bad if the rest is well. Now come home with me. If you'll promise me to be less jealous, I myself will cure you, my darling!

19. Aria

Come, my dearest; if you're good, I'll give you the best of all remedies. It's a natural cure, and no chemist can make it. It's a certain balsam that I carry with me. I can give it to you if you'd like to try it. Would you like to know where it is? (*putting her hand on her heart*) Listen to it beating; touch me here!

(ZERLINA *and* MASETTO *exit.* LEPORELLO *and* DONNA ELVIRA *enter.*)

Recitative

LEPORELLO: The lights of many torches surround us, my darling. We can hide here, and they will never see us.

DONNA ELVIRA: But why are you afraid, my adored one?

LEPORELLO: It's really nothing—only certain precautions. I'll see how far away they are. (*aside*) How can I get rid of her? (*aloud*) Wait there, my love!

DONNA ELVIRA: Ah, don't leave me!

20. *Sestetto*

Sola, sola, in bujo loco,
Palpitar il cor mi sento!
E m'assale un tal spavento,
Che mi sembra di morir.

LEPORELLO: Più che cerco men ritrovo
Questa porta sciagurata.
Piano, piano—l'ho trovata,
Ecco il tempo di fuggir.

(LEPORELLO *si nasconde.* DON OTTAVIO *e* DONNA ANNA
entrano.)

DON OTTAVIO: Tergi il ciglio, o vita mia!
E dà calma al tuo dolore!
L'ombra omai del genitore
Pena avrà de tuoi martir.

DONNA ANNA: Lascia almen alla mia pena
Questo piccolo ristoro,
Sol la morte, o mio tesoro—
Il mio pianto può finir!

DONNA ELVIRA (*a parte*): Ah, dov'è lo sposo mio?

LEPORELLO (*a parte*): Se mi trova, son perduto.

DONNA ELVIRA *e* LEPORELLO: Una porta là vegg'io,
Cheta, cheta io vò partir!

(*Entrano* ZERLINA *e* MASETTO.)

ZERLINA *e* MASETTO: Ferma briccone! Dove ten vai?

DONNA ANNA *e* DON OTTAVIO: Ecco il fellone! Com'era quà?

DONNA ANNA, ZERLINA, DON OTTAVIO, MASETTO: Ah! mora
il perfido,
Che m'ha tradito!

DONNA ELVIRA: E mio marito!
Pietà! pietà!

DONNA ANNA, ZERLINA, DON OTTAVIO, MASETTO: È Donna
Elvira
Quello ch'io vedo?
Appena il credo?

DONNA ELVIRA: Pietà!

DONNA ANNA, ZERLINA, DON OTTAVIO, MASETTO: No, no!
Morrà!

LEPORELLO: Perdon, perdono!

20. *Sextet*

All alone in this dark place, I feel my heart pounding in my breast, and I tremble so that I fear that I'm going to die.

LEPORELLO: I'm searching for that damned gate, but I still can't find it. At last—here it is! Now it's safe for me to hide!
(LEPORELLO *hides.* DON OTTAVIO *and* DONNA ANNA *enter.*)

DON OTTAVIO: Dry your eyes, my darling, and calm your grief. Even your father's spirit would feel pain at your grief.

DONNA ANNA: Leave me to my sorrow; I can find no consolation. Only death can end my tears.

DONNA ELVIRA (*aside*): Ah, where is my husband?
LEPORELLO (*aside*): If she sees me, I'm lost.
DONNA ELVIRA *and* LEPORELLO: Here is the door; I'll quietly escape from this place!
(*Enter* ZERLINA *and* MASETTO.)
ZERLINA *and* MASETTO: Stop, you rascal! You can't escape us!
DONNA ANNA *and* DON OTTAVIO: Here's the murderer! Why is he here?
DONNA ANNA, ZERLINA, DON OTTAVIO, MASETTO: Let the wretch die! He has betrayed us!

DONNA ELVIRA: He is my husband! Have pity!

DONNA ANNA, ZERLINA, DON OTTAVIO, MASETTO: This woman is Donna Elvira! I can hardly believe it!

DONNA ELVIRA: Have pity!
DONNA ANNA, ZERLINA, DON OTTAVIO, MASETTO: No, no! He must die!
LEPORELLO: Forgive me, ladies and gentlemen! I'm not

Signori miei;
Quell'io non sono,
Sbaglia costei.
Viver lasciatemi
Per carità!

DONNA ANNA, DONNA ELVIRA, ZERLINA, DON OTTAVIO, MA-
SETTO: Dei! Leporello!
Che inganno è questo!
Stupida resto.
Che mai sarà!

TUTTI: Mille torbidi pensieri
Mi s'aggiran per la testa!

LEPORELLO: Se mi salvo in tal tempesta,
È un prodigio in verità!

DONNA ANNA, DONNA ELVIRA, ZERLINA, DON OTTAVIO, MA-
SETTO: Che giornata, o stelle, è questa—
Che impensata novità?

(DONNA ANNA *parte*.)

Recitativo

ZERLINA: Dunque quello sei tu che il mio Masetto poco fà
crudelmente maltrattasti?

DONNA ELVIRA: Dunque tu m'ingannasti, o scellerato, spac-
ciandoti con me da Don Giovanni?

DON OTTAVIO: Dunque tu in questi panni venisti quì per
qualche tradimento!

ZERLINA: A me tocca punirlo!

DONNA ELVIRA: Anzi a me!

DON OTTAVIO: No, no, a me!

MASETTO: Accoppatela meco tutti trè!

21. Aria

LEPORELLO: Ah, pietà, signori miei!
Dò ragione a voi a lei.
Ma il delitto, mio non è,
Il padron con prepotenza l'innocenza mi rubò.
Donna Elvira! Compatite! Già capite come andò.
Di Masetto non sò nulla, (*accennando* DONNA ELVIRA) vel
dirà questa fanciulla.
E un'oretta circumcirca che con lei girando vo. (*a* DON
OTTAVIO)
Ah voi, signore, non dico niente,

Don Giovanni; you've made an error. Please let me live,
for pity's sake!

DONNA ANNA, DONNA ELVIRA, ZERLINA, DON OTTAVIO,
MASETTO: Heavens! Leporello! What trick is this? I'm
amazed! Whatever will happen?

ALL: A thousand dark thoughts are running through my
head.

LEPORELLO: If I'm saved from this tempest it will really
be a miracle!

DONNA ANNA, DONNA ELVIRA, ZERLINA, DON OTTAVIO,
MASETTO: What a day of darkness! O heavens—what new
deceit!

(DONNA ANNA exits.)

Recitative

ZERLINA: Then it was you who cruelly beat my Masetto!

DONNA ELVIRA: Then it was you who deceived me, you
scoundrel, pretending to be Don Giovanni!

DON OTTAVIO: And you came here in his clothing, intending
to deceive us all!

ZERLINA: It's my duty to punish him.

DONNA ELVIRA: No, it's mine!

DON OTTAVIO: No, no, it's mine!

MASETTO: I'll help all of you to kill him!

21. Aria

LEPORELLO: Ah, have pity, good people! You're all very
right to be angry, but the crimes weren't mine. My master
robbed me of my innocence. Donna Elvira, tell them! You
know what happened. I don't know anything about Masetto,
as this young lady (*pointing to* DONNA ELVIRA) can tell
you. It was a peculiar situation; she thought she was going
for a walk with him. (*to* DON OTTAVIO) And you, my
Lord! I can't say a word. Certainly my fear, my ill-fortune
—it was light outside—and dark inside—I couldn't find
—the door—the wall—I took myself off—I hid over there

Certo timore, certo accidente—
Di fuori chiaro—di dentro oscuro—
Non c'è riparo—la porta—il muro—io—me—ne—vo'—
Da quel lato—poi qui celato—l'affar si sa,
Oh, si sa! Ma, s'io sapeva, fuggia per quà! (*Parte.*)

Recitativo

DONNA ELVIRA: Ferma, perfido, ferma!
MASETTO: Il birbo ha l'ali ai piedi!
ZERLINA: Con qual arte si sottrasse l'iniquo!
DON OTTAVIO: Amici miei, dopo eccessi sì enormi, dubitar
non possiam, che Don Giovanni non sia l'empio uccisore
del padre di Donn'Anna. In questa casa per poche ore fermatevi—un ricorso vò far a chi si deve; e in pochi istanti
vendicarvi prometto; così vuole dover, pietade, affetto.
(DONNA ELVIRA, ZERLINA e MASETTO *partono.*)

22. *Aria*

Il mio tesoro intanto
Andate, andate a consolar,
E del bel ciglio il pianto
Cercate di asciugar.
Ditele che i suoi torti
A vendicar io vado.
Che sol di stragi e morti
Nunzio vogl'io tornar.
(DON OTTAVIO *parte. Entra* DONNA ELVIRA.)

Recitativo

DONNA ELVIRA: In quale eccessi, oh, Numi! in quali misfatti
orribili, tremendi, è avvolto il sciagurato! Ah no! non puote
tardar l'ira del cielo. La giustizia tardar! Sentir già parmi
la fatale saetta, che gli piomba sul capo—aperto veggio il
baratro mortal—Misera Elvira! Che contrasto d'affetti in
sen ti nasce! Perchè questi sospiri, e queste ambascie?

23. *Aria*

Mi tradì quell'alma ingrata,
Infelice oh Dio! mi fa!
Ma, tradita e abbandonata,
Provo ancor per lui pietà
Quando sento il mio tormento,
Di vendetta il cor favella;
Ma se guardo il suo cimento,
Palpitando il cor mi va. (*Parte.*)

—you'll understand! But if I had known, I would have run
the other way! (*Exits.*)

Recitative

DONNA ELVIRA: Stop, wretch, stop!

MASETTO: The rascal has wings on his feet!

ZERLINA: How cleverly he escaped us!

DON OTTAVIO: My friends, after such a scene, who can
doubt that Don Giovanni is the evil murderer of Donna
Anna's father? Wait in her house for a few hours. I'll go
to the authorities, and in a short time she'll be avenged.
Duty, pity, and affection demand it.

(DONNA ANNA, ZERLINA, *and* MASETTO *exit.*)

22. Aria

Go to my love, meanwhile, and console her. Try to dry
her beautiful eyes. Tell her that I will avenge her wrongs.
Nothing can stop me from completing her revenge!

(DON OTTAVIO *exits.* DONNA ELVIRA *enters.*)

Recitative

DONNA ELVIRA: O God, to what crimes and excesses has he
descended! Ah, no! heaven will not delay its wrath or its
justice! Already I can feel the fatal lightning that will fall
upon his head. Already I can see the last abyss opening.
Wretched Elvira! What a conflict of emotions contends in
your breast! Why are you sighing? Why are you so unhappy?

23. Aria

That ungrateful man has betrayed me! Oh, God, he has
ruined my happiness! But, although he's betrayed me and
abandoned me, I still feel pity for him. When I suffer my
torments, my heart cries out for vengeance, but when I
hear his voice, my heart murmurs of love. (*Exits.*)

Scena II

Recinto murato, in mezzo al quale si vede la statua del COMMENDATORE. DON GIOVANNI, *salendo il muro; indi* LEPO-RELLO.

Recitativo

DON GIOVANNI: Ah! ah! ah! questa è buona! or lasciala cer-car: Che bella notte! È più chiara del giorno, sembra fatta per gir a zonzo, a caccia di ragazze. Vediam s'è tardi? Ah, no! Ancor non son le due di notte. Avrei voglia un pò di saper com'è finito l'affar tra Leporello e Donna Elvira; s'egli ha avuto giudizio—

LEPORELLO (*dietro il muro*): Alfin vuole ch'io faccia un precipizio!

DON GIOVANNI: È desso! Oh, Leporello!

LEPORELLO: Chi mi chiama?

DON GIOVANNI: Non conosci il padron?

LEPORELLO: Così nol conoscessi!

DON GIOVANNI: Come? birbo!

LEPORELLO: Ah, siete voi? Scusate!

DON GIOVANNI: Cos'è stato?

LEPORELLO: Per cagion vostra io fui quasi accoppato.

DON GIOVANNI: Ebben, non era questo un onore per te?

LEPORELLO: Signor, vel dono!

DON GIOVANNI: Via, via, vien quà! Che belle cose ti deggio dir!

LEPORELLO: Ma cosa fate quì?

DON GIOVANNI: Vien dentro, e lo saprai. Diverse istorielle, che accadute mi son dacchè partisti, ti dirò un'altra volta; or la più bella ti vò solo narrar.

LEPORELLO: Donnesca, al certo.

DON GIOVANNI: C'è dubbio! Una fanciulla, bella, giovin, galante, per la strada incontrai; le vado appresso, la prendo per la man—fuggir mi vuole; dico poche parole, ella mi piglia—sai per chi?

LEPORELLO: Non lo so.

DON GIOVANNI: Per Leporello!

LEPORELLO: Per me?

DON GIOVANNI: Per te!

LEPORELLO: Va bene!

Scene II

A cemetery with a statue of the COMMENDATORE. DON GIOVANNI *leaps over the wall, to meet* LEPORELLO.

Recitative

DON GIOVANNI: Ha, ha! This is amusing! Now let her look for me. What a beautiful night! It's brighter than the day —perfect for making love! I wish I knew what is happening between Leporello and Elvira; if only he is clever—

LEPORELLO (*behind the wall*): I think he wants to get me in trouble!

DON GIOVANNI: He's there! O Leporello!

LEPORELLO: Who's calling me?

DON GIOVANNI: Don't you know your master?

LEPORELLO: No, I don't know him!

DON GIOVANNI: What? You rascal!

LEPORELLO: Ah, is it you, Sir? Excuse me!

DON GIOVANNI: Tell me what has happened.

LEPORELLO: I've been almost killed for your sake.

DON GIOVANNI: I'd say that that was an honor for you.

LEPORELLO: I return that honor to you, Sir!

DON GIOVANNI: Come nearer! I have a delightful tale to tell you!

LEPORELLO: But what are you doing here?

DON GIOVANNI: Come in here and I'll tell you. Things have happened—but I'll discuss it with you another time. Now I only want you to know the funniest story.

LEPORELLO: About a woman, of course.

DON GIOVANNI: Can you doubt it? I met a pretty young girl in the street; I went near her and took her hand—she tried to escape; I said a few words to her; she took me for— Do you know for whom?

LEPORELLO: I don't know.

DON GIOVANNI: For Leporello!

LEPORELLO: For me?

DON GIOVANNI: For you.

LEPORELLO: Good enough!

DON GIOVANNI: Per la mano essa allora mi prende.

LEPORELLO: Ancora meglio.

DON GIOVANNI: M'accarezza, m'abbraccia—"Caro il mio Leporello! Leporello, mio caro!" Allor m'accorse ch'era qualche tua bella.

LEPORELLO (*a parte*): Oh, maledetto!

DON GIOVANNI: Dell'inganno approfitto; non so come mi riconosce, grida, sento gente, a fuggire mi metto, e pronto pronto per quel muretto in questo loco io monto.

LEPORELLO: E mi dite la cosa con tal indifferenza?

DON GIOVANNI: Perchè no?

LEPORELLO: Ma se fosse costei stata mia moglie?

DON GIOVANNI (*ridendo*): Meglio ancora!

LA STATUA DEL COMMENDATORE: Di rider finirai pria dell'aurora!

DON GIOVANNI: Chi ha parlato?

LEPORELLO: Ah! qualch'anima sarà dall'altro mondo vi conosce a fondo.

DON GIOVANNI: Taci, sciocco! Chi va la?

LA STATUA DEL COMMENDATORE: Ribaldo, audace! lascia ai morti la pace!

LEPORELLO: Ve l'hò detto!

DON GIOVANNI: Sarà qualcun di fuori, che si burla di noi. Ehi! del Commendatore non è questa la statua? Leggi un poco quell'iscrizion!

LEPORELLO: Scusate, non hò imparato a leggere a'raggi della luna.

DON GIOVANNI: Leggi, dico!

LEPORELLO (*legge*): "Dell'empio, chi mi trasse al passo estremo, qui attendo la vendetta." Udiste? io tremo!

DON GIOVANNI: O vecchio buffonissimo! Digli che questa sera l'attendo a cena meco.

LEPORELLO: Che pazzia! Ma mi par— Oh, Dei! mirate che terribili occhiate egli ci da! Par vivo—par che senta—e che voglia parlar!

DON GIOVANNI: Orsù va là o qui t'ammazzo! E poi ti seppellisco!

LEPORELLO: Piano, piano, signore—ora ubbidisco.

DON GIOVANNI: Then she took me by the hand.

LEPORELLO: The story is improving.

DON GIOVANNI: She caressed and embraced me. "O my dear Leporello! Leporello, my dear!" Then I thought it must be one of your mistresses.

LEPORELLO (*aside*): Damn you!

DON GIOVANNI: I profited by the deceit! I don't know how she recognized me; she screamed; I heard footsteps, and I fled and quickly leaped over this wall.

LEPORELLO: And can you tell me that with such indifference?

DON GIOVANNI: Why not?

LEPORELLO: But if she had been my wife?

DON GIOVANNI (*laughing*): Better still!

STATUE OF THE COMMENDATORE: By dawn your laughter will be ended.

DON GIOVANNI: Who spoke?

LEPORELLO: It must have been a spirit from the other world, one who knows you well.

DON GIOVANNI: Be quiet, rascal! Who was it?

STATUE OF THE COMMENDATORE: Audacious ribald! Leave the dead in peace!

LEPORELLO: I told you so!

DON GIOVANNI: It's somebody in the street making a joke of us— Isn't that the Commendator's statue? Read me that inscription!

LEPORELLO: Excuse me, but I've never learned to read by moonlight.

DON GIOVANNI: Read, I tell you!

LEPORELLO (*reading*): "Revenge awaits the villain who killed me." Do you hear that? It makes me shiver!

DON GIOVANNI: Oh, stupid old man! Tell him that I will await him at dinner this evening.

LEPORELLO: What madness! It seems— O God! look at his horrible eyes! He seems to be alive—and listening—he's going to speak.

DON GIOVANNI: Hurry; go over there, or I'll kill you and bury you here!

LEPORELLO: Be calm, my Lord—I'll obey you!

24. Duetto

O statua gentilissima
Del gran Commendatore—
Padron, mi trema il core;
Non posso terminar.

DON GIOVANNI: Finiscila, o nel petto
Ti metto questo acciar.

LEPORELLO (*a parte*): Che impiccio! che capriccio!
Io sentomi gelar!

DON GIOVANNI (*a parte*): Che gusto, che spassetto!
Lo voglio far tremar.

LEPORELLO: O, statua gentilissima,
Benchè di marmo siate—
Ah, padron mio! mirate!
Che seguita a guardar.

DON GIOVANNI: Mori, mori!

LEPORELLO: No, no—attendete! (*alla* STATUA)
Signore, il padron mio—
Badate ben, non io—
Ah! ah! che scena è questa!
(LA STATUA *china la testa.*)
Oh, ciel! chinò la testa!

DON GIOVANNI: Va là che sei un buffone!

LEPORELLO: Guardate! Guardate ancor, padrone!

DON GIOVANNI: E che deggio guardar?

LEPORELLO: Colla marmorea testa
Ei fa così così.

DON GIOVANNI (*alla* STATUA): Parlate, se potete,
Verrete a cena?

LA STATUA DEL COMMENDATORE: Si!

LEPORELLO: Mover mi posso appena—
Mi manca, oh Dei, la lena!
Per carità partiamo:
Andiamo via di quà!

DON GIOVANNI: Bizzarra è inver la scena—
Verrà il buon vecchio a cena
A prepararla andiamo,
Partiamo via di quà.

(DON GIOVANNI *e* LEPORELLO *partono. Entrano* DONNA ANNA
e DON OTTAVIO.)

24. Duet

Oh, most honorable statue of the great Commendatore—
Master! My heart is trembling! I cannot finish!

DON GIOVANNI: Go on, or I'll kill you with this sword!

LEPORELLO (*aside*): What a disastrous caprice! I feel my
blood run cold.

DON GIOVANNI (*aside*): What an original amusement! I like
to make him tremble.

LEPORELLO: Oh, most honorable statue, even though you're
made of marble—ah, Master, look at him! He's staring
straight at me!

DON GIOVANNI: Die, then!

LEPORELLO: No, no—wait! (*to the* STATUE) My Lord, my
master—you understand, not I—wishes to dine with you
this evening! Ah, ah, ah! What a scene of madness!
(*The* STATUE *nods its head.*)
O heavens, he's nodding his head!

DON GIOVANNI: You're a stupid buffoon!

LEPORELLO: Look! Look again, my Lord!

DON GIOVANNI: And what must I look at?

LEPORELLO: With his marble head he nods at us just like
this!

DON GIOVANNI (*to the* STATUE): Speak if you can! Will you
dine with me?

STATUE OF COMMENDATORE: Yes!

LEPORELLO: I can hardly move—my strength is gone. For
pity's sake, let's escape from this place!

DON GIOVANNI: This truly is strange—the good old man
accepts my invitation. Let's go and make sure that dinner
is prepared for him.
(DON GIOVANNI *and* LEPORELLO *exit.* DONNA ANNA *and*
DON OTTAVIO *enter.*)

Recitativo

DON OTTAVIO: Calmatevi, idol mio, di quel ribaldo vedrem
puniti in breve i gravi eccessi, vendicati sarem.

DONNA ANNA: Ma il padre, oh Dio!

DON OTTAVIO: Convien chinar il ciglio al volere del ciel.
Respira, o cara. Di tua perdita amara fia domani, se vuoi,
dolce compenso questo cor, questa mano, ch'il mio tenero
amor!

DONNA ANNA: Oh Dei! che dite, in sì tristi momenti?

DON OTTAVIO: E che? Vorresti con indugi novelli accrescer
le mie pene? Crudele!

DONNA ANNA: Crudele! ah no, mio ben. Troppo mi spiace
allontanarti un ben che lungamente la nostr'alma desia—mà
il mondo—oh Dio! Non sedur la costanza del sensibil mio
core! Abbastanza per te mi parla amore.

25. *Aria*

Non mi dir, bell'idol mio,
Che son io crudel con te;
Tu ben sai quant'io t'amai,
Tu conosci la mia fè.
Calma, calma il tuo tormento,
Se di duol non vuoi ch'io mora!
Forse un giorno il cielo ancora
Sentirà pietà di me.

(DONNA ANNA *e* DON OTTAVIO *partono.*)

Scena III

Gran sala del palazzo di DON GIOVANNI. *Una mensa preparata per mangiare. Entrano* DON GIOVANNI *e* LEPORELLO.

26. *Finale*

DON GIOVANNI: Già la mensa è preparata—
Voi suonate, amici cari!
Già che spendo i miei danari,
Io mi voglio divertir!
Leporello, presto in tavola!

LEPORELLO: Son prontissimo a servir.

(*I musicisti suonano;* LEPORELLO *serve.*)
Bravi! *Cosa Rara!*

DON GIOVANNI: Che ti par del bel concerto?

Recitative

DON OTTAVIO: Calm yourself, my darling. We'll soon see the great crimes of that wretch punished and avenged.

DONNA ANNA: But my father, O God!

DON OTTAVIO: We must abide by God's will. Be comforted, my dear. Your loss is bitter, but I will try to recompense it by my hand, my heart, and my tender love.

DONNA ANNA: O God! What are you saying at such a sad time?

DON OTTAVIO: Well then? Will you add to my unhappiness with fresh refusals? Cruel one!

DONNA ANNA: Cruel one? Ah, no, my darling! I don't enjoy denying you something that both of us have long desired. But the world's conventions—O God! Even they can't change the constancy of my faithful heart! Let it be enough that my love is unchanging!

25. *Aria*

Do not tell me, my darling, that I am cruel to you! You know very well how much I love you—you know my unchanging faith. Calm your torments, if you don't wish me to perish of sorrow! Perhaps some day heaven will take pity on me.

(DONNA ANNA *and* DON OTTAVIO *exit.*)

Scene III

A large room in DON GIOVANNI'S *palace. A meal is laid out, ready to be eaten.* DON GIOVANNI *and* LEPORELLO *enter.*

26. *Finale*

DON GIOVANNI: Already the meal is prepared— Play your music, dear friends! If I spend my money, I want to be entertained! Leporello, come to the table!

LEPORELLO: I'm delighted to serve you!
(*The band plays while* LEPORELLO *serves.*)
Bravo! That's from *Cosa Rara!*

DON GIOVANNI: What do you think of the music?

LEPORELLO: È conforme al vostro merto.
DON GIOVANNI: Ah che piatto saporito!
LEPORELLO: Ah che barbaro appetito!
Che bocconi di gigante!
Mi par proprio di svenir.
DON GIOVANNI: Piatto!
LEPORELLO: Servo!
(*La musica continua.*)
Evivano *I Litiganti!*
DON GIOVANNI: Versa il vino.
Eccellente marzimino!
LEPORELLO (*a parte*): Questo pezzo di fagiano.
Piano piano vò inghiottir.
DON GIOVANNI (*a parte*): Sta mangiando quel marrano!
Fingerò di non capir.
(*Ora la musica è di* Le nozze di Figaro *di Mozart.*)
LEPORELLO: Questa poi la conosco pur troppo!
DON GIOVANNI: Leporello!
LEPORELLO: Padron mio!
DON GIOVANNI: Parla schietto, mascalzone!
LEPORELLO: Non mi lascia una flessione
Le parole proferir.
DON GIOVANNI: Mentre io mangio, fischia un poco.
LEPORELLO: Non sò far.
DON GIOVANNI: Cos'è?
LEPORELLO: Scusate!
Sì eccellente è il vostro cuoco,
Che lo volli anch'io provar!
(*Entra* DONNA ELVIRA.)
DONNA ELVIRA (*a* DON GIOVANNI): L'ultima prova
Dell'amor mio
Ancor vogl'io
Fare con te.
Più non rammento
Gl'inganni tuoi,
Pietate io sento.
DON GIOVANNI *e* LEPORELLO (*a parte*): Cos'è? cos'è?
DONNA ELVIRA: Da te non chiede
Quest'alma oppressa
Della sua fede
Qualche mercè.
(*S'inginocchia.*)

LEPORELLO: It conforms to your own merits.

DON GIOVANNI: Ah, what a delicious meat pie!

LEPORELLO: Ah, what a huge appetite! What gigantic mouthfuls! It takes my breath away!

DON GIOVANNI: More pie!

LEPORELLO: Here it is!

(*The music continues.*)

Long live *I Litiganti!*

DON GIOVANNI: Pour the wine! Excellent!

LEPORELLO (*aside*): While he isn't looking I'll swallow down this piece of pheasant!

DON GIOVANNI (*aside*): The rascal is eating! I'll pretend not to notice.

(*Now the music is from Mozart's* Marriage of Figaro.)

LEPORELLO: I've heard that tune once too often!

DON GIOVANNI: Leporello!

LEPORELLO: My Lord!

DON GIOVANNI: Speak clearly, you rascal!

LEPORELLO: I have a cold that won't let me speak clearly.

DON GIOVANNI: While I'm eating, whistle a little.

LEPORELLO: I can't!

DON GIOVANNI: Why not?

LEPORELLO: Excuse me! Your cook is so excellent that I wanted to sample his art!

(DONNA ELVIRA *enters.*)

DONNA ELVIRA (*to* DON GIOVANNI): I want to give you the ultimate proof of my love. I no longer resent your deceit; I only pity you!

DON GIOVANNI *and* LEPORELLO (*aside*): What is this?

DONNA ELVIRA: This unhappy soul expects no gratitude for her fidelity!

(*She kneels.*)

DON GIOVANNI: Mi maraviglio!
Cosa volete?
Se non sorgete
Non resto in piè.

DONNA ELVIRA: Ah, non deridere
Gli affanni miei!

LEPORELLO (*a parte*): Quasi da piangere
Mi fa costei!

DON GIOVANNI: Io ti derido!
Cielo! perchè?
Che vuoi, mio bene?

DONNA ELVIRA: Che vita cangi!

DON GIOVANNI: Brava!

DONNA ELVIRA: Cor perfido!

DON GIOVANNI: Lascia ch'io mangi;
E se ti piace,
Mangia con me.

DONNA ELVIRA: Restati barbaro,
Nel lezzo immondo,
Esempio orribile
D'iniquità!

DON GIOVANNI: Vivan le femmine!
Viva il buon vino!
Sostegno e gloria
D'umanità!

LEPORELLO (*a parte*): Se non si muove
Al suo dolore,
Di sasso ha il core,
O cor non hà!

DONNA ELVIRA (*esce precipitosamente*): Ah!

DON GIOVANNI: Che grido è questo mai?
Va a veder che cos'è stato!

LEPORELLO (*va alla porta*): Ah!

DON GIOVANNI: Che grido indiavolato!
Leporello, che cos'è?

LEPORELLO (*ritorna*): Ah, signor, per carità,
Non andate fuor di quà!
L'uom di sasso, l'uomo bianco—
Ah, padrone, io gelo, io manco!

DON GIOVANNI: I'm astounded! What do you want? If you won't get up, I'll have to kneel as well.

DONNA ELVIRA: Ah, don't ridicule my grief!

LEPORELLO (*aside*): She almost makes me cry!

DON GIOVANNI: I, ridicule you? Heavens, why? What do you ask of me, my dear?

DONNA ELVIRA: I want you to change your way of life!
DON GIOVANNI: Brava!
DONNA ELVIRA: Evil heart!
DON GIOVANNI: Let me continue with my supper, and if you like, you are welcome to join me.

DONNA ELVIRA: Stay there, you wretch; everyone will despise you as a horrible example of depravity!

DON GIOVANNI: Long live the women! Long live good wine! Forever may they sustain and exalt humanity!

LEPORELLO (*aside*): If he isn't moved by her grief, his heart is made of stone!

DONNA ELVIRA (*rushing out*): Ah!!!

DON GIOVANNI: Why is she screaming? Go out and see what has happened!

LEPORELLO (*going to the door*): Ah!!!

DON GIOVANNI: What an infernal cry! Leporello, what did she see?

LEPORELLO (*returning*): Ah, my Lord, for pity's sake, don't go out there! There's a man of stone, a white man—ah, my master, I'm freezing, I'm fainting! If you could see his size. If you could hear his footstep—ta, ta, ta, ta!

Se vedeste che figura.
Se sentiste come fa—
Ta, ta, ta, ta!
DON GIOVANNI: Non capisco niente affatto.
Tu sei matto in verità!
LEPORELLO: Ah sentite!
(*Si batte alla porta.*)
DON GIOVANNI: Qualcun batte.
Apri!
LEPORELLO: Io tremo!
DON GIOVANNI: Apri, dico!
LEPORELLO: Ah!
DON GIOVANNI: Matto!
Per togliermi d'intrico
Ad aprir io stesso andrò!
LEPORELLO: Non vò più veder l'amico,
Pian pianin si m'asconderò.
(*Si nasconde sotto la tavola. Entra la statua del* COMMENDA-
TORE.)
IL COMMENDATORE: Don Giovanni, a cenar teco
M'invitasti—e son venuto!
DON GIOVANNI: Non l'avrei giammai creduto,
Ma farò quel che potrò!
Leporello, un'altra cena
Fa che subito si porti!
LEPORELLO: Ah, padron, siam tutti morti!
DON GIOVANNI: Vanne dico!
IL COMMENDATORE: Ferma un pò!
Non si pasce di cibo mortale
Chi si pasce di cibo celeste;
Altre cure, più gravi di queste,
Altra brama quaggiù mi guidò!
DON GIOVANNI: Parla dunque—che chiedi? che vuoi?

LEPORELLO: La terzana d'avere mi sembra,
E le membra fermar più non so.
IL COMMENDATORE: Parlo, ascolta! più tempo non ho!

DON GIOVANNI: Parla, parla! ascoltando ti sto.

IL COMMENDATORE: Tu m'invitasti a cena,

DON GIOVANNI: I don't understand a word you're saying. Are you insane?

LEPORELLO: Ah, listen!

(*Somebody knocks at the door.*)

DON GIOVANNI: Someone's knocking! Open the door!

LEPORELLO: I'm frozen with terror.

DON GIOVANNI: Open, I say!

LEPORELLO: Ah!

DON GIOVANNI: Fool! To clarify this mystery I'll open the door myself.

LEPORELLO: I can't bear to look at him any more: I'll quietly hide!

(*He hides. The marble statue of the* COMMENDATORE *enters.*)

COMMENDATORE: Don Giovanni! You invited me to dinner—and here I am!

DON GIOVANNI: I would never have believed it, but I'll continue to act out the play! Leporello, another setting! Bring it immediately!

LEPORELLO: Ah, dear master, we're all dead!

DON GIOVANNI: Go, I command you!

COMMENDATORE: No, remain here! I have no need of earthly food, I who feast on heavenly substance; other concerns, more urgent, have brought me here!

DON GIOVANNI: Speak then— What do you ask? What do you demand?

LEPORELLO: I seem to have a fever, and I cannot move my limbs.

COMMENDATORE: I'll speak, and you must listen! I have very little time!

DON GIOVANNI: Speak then! I'm listening to you.

COMMENDATORE: You invited me to dinner. Now you, too,

Il tuo dover or sai;
Rispondimi: verrai
Tu a cenar meco?
LEPORELLO: Oibò! oibò! tempo non hà—scusate!
DON GIOVANNI: A torto di viltate
Tacciato mai sarò!
IL COMMENDATORE: Risolvi!
DON GIOVANNI: Ho già risolto.
IL COMMENDATORE: Verrai?
LEPORELLO: Dite di no!
DON GIOVANNI: Ho fermo il core in petto;
Non ho timor: verrò!
IL COMMENDATORE: Dammi la mano in pegno!
DON GIOVANNI: Eccola. Ohimè!
Che gelo è questo mai!
IL COMMENDATORE: Pentiti, cangia vita.
È l'ultimo momento!
DON GIOVANNI: No, no—ch'io non mi pento,
Vanne lontan da me!
IL COMMENDATORE: Pentiti, scelerato!
DON GIOVANNI: No, vecchio infatuato!
IL COMMENDATORE: Pentiti!
DON GIOVANNI: No!
IL COMMENDATORE: Sì!
DON GIOVANNI: No! No!
IL COMMENDATORE: Ah tempo più non v'è!
(IL COMMENDATORE *parte. Fiamme di sottera.*)
DON GIOVANNI: Da qual tremore insolito
Sento assalir gli spiriti!
Dond'escono quei vortici
Di foco pien d'orror?
CORO (*di sottera*): Tutto a tue colpe è poco,
Vieni c'è un mal peggior!
DON GIOVANNI: Chi l'anima mi lacera!
Chi m'agita le viscere!
Che strazio ohimè! che smania
Che inferno! che terror!
LEPORELLO: Che ceffo disperato!
Che gesti di dannato!

know your duty. Answer: Will you come to dine with me?

LEPORELLO: Oh, no, he hasn't time—please excuse him!
DON GIOVANNI: Nobody will ever accuse me of the crime of cowardice!
COMMENDATORE: Resolve, then!
DON GIOVANNI: I've already decided.
COMMENDATORE: Will you come, then?
LEPORELLO: Tell him no!
DON GIOVANNI: My heart is firm in my breast. I have no fear: I'll come!
COMMENDATORE: Give me your hand in pledge!
DON GIOVANNI: Take it! Oh, what a chill I feel!

COMMENDATORE: Repent! Change your way of life! It's your last chance!
DON GIOVANNI: No, no—I will never repent! Go—don't torment me!
COMMENDATORE: Repent, vile scoundrel!
DON GIOVANNI: No, you insane old man!
COMMENDATORE: Repent!
DON GIOVANNI: No!
COMMENDATORE: Yes!
DON GIOVANNI: No! no!
COMMENDATORE: Now there is no more time!
(*The* COMMENDATORE *exits. Flames appear from below.*)
DON GIOVANNI: This is a new terror. Spirits surround me! From where do those whirlwinds come? Those horrible flames?

CHORUS (*from below*): There is little enough punishment for your sins. There are worse pains yet to come!
DON GIOVANNI: What tears my soul? What rends my body? What pains, ah, God! Ah, what misery!

LEPORELLO: A desperate face! He is damned! What shouts! What lamentations!

Che gridi! che lamenti!
Come mi fa terror!
DON GIOVANNI: Ah!!!
(*È perso nelle fiamme. Entrano* DONNA ANNA, DONNA EL-
VIRA, ZERLINA, DON OTTAVIO *e* MASETTO.)
DONNA ANNA, DONNA ELVIRA, ZERLINA, DON OTTAVIO, MA-
SETTO: Ah dov'è il perfido,
Dov'è l'indegno!
Tutto il mio sdegno
Sfogar io vo'.
DONNA ANNA: Solo mirandolo
Stretto in catene
Alle mie pene
Calma darò!
LEPORELLO: Più non sperate
Di ritrovarlo!
Più non cercate!
Lontano andò.
DONNA ANNA, DONNA ELVIRA, ZERLINA, DON OTTAVIO, MA-
SETTO: Cos'è? favella!
Via, presto, sbrigati!
LEPORELLO: Venne un colosso—
Ma se non posso!
Trà fume e fuoco—
Badate un poco—
L'uomo di sasso—
Fermate il passo—
Giusto là sotto—
Diede il gran botto—
Giusto là il diavolo se'l trangugiò!
DONNA ANNA, DONNA ELVIRA, ZERLINA, DON OTTAVIO, MA-
SETTO: Stelle! che sento!
LEPORELLO: Vero è l'evento.
DONNA ANNA, DONNA ELVIRA, ZERLINA, DON OTTAVIO, MA-
SETTO: Ah, certo è l'ombra
Che l'(m')incontrò!
DON OTTAVIO (*a* DONNA ANNA): Or che tutti, o mio tesoro,
Vendicati siam del cielo,
Porgi, porgi a me un ristoro,
Non mi far languire ancor!
DONNA ANNA: Lascia, o caro, un anno ancora,

DON GIOVANNI: Ah!!!
(*The flames engulf him.* DONNA ANNA, DONNA ELVIRA, ZER-
LINA, DON OTTAVIO, *and* MASETTO *enter.*)
DONNA ANNA, DONNA ELVIRA, ZERLINA, DON OTTAVIO,
MASETTO: Ah, where is the criminal? We want to bend him
to our wrath!

DONNA ANNA: To see him bound in chains would comfort
my misery!

LEPORELLO: Don't expect to see him again; I don't know
where he is. He's gone far away.

DONNA ANNA, DONNA ELVIRA, ZERLINA, DON OTTAVIO,
MASETTO: Where is he? Tell us! Quickly, let us know!

LEPORELLO: A giant came here—but I can't describe him!
There were flames and smoke—the man was made of stone
—he walked into this room, and then—then the devil
dragged my master down below!

DONNA ANNA, DONNA ELVIRA, ZERLINA, DON OTTAVIO,
MASETTO: Heavens! What is he saying?
LEPORELLO: That's exactly how it happened.
DONNA ANNA, DONNA ELVIRA, ZERLINA, DON OTTAVIO,
MASETTO: Ah, that must have been the ghost that I saw.

DON OTTAVIO (*to* DONNA ANNA): Now that all are avenged
by heaven, my darling, give me some comfort—don't let
me languish forever!

DONNA ANNA: Let me wait another year, my darling, until

Allo sfogo del mio cor!
Al desio chi t'adora,
Ceder deve un fido amor.
DON OTTAVIO: Al desio di chi m'adora,
Ceder deve un fido amor.
DONNA ELVIRA: Io men vado in un ritiro a finir la vita mia.
ZERLINA e MASETTO: Noi, a casa andiamo, a cenar in compagnia!
LEPORELLO: Ed io vado all'osteria a trovar padron miglior.
ZERLINA, LEPORELLO, MASETTO: Resti dunque quel birbon con Proserpina e Pluton!
E noi tutti, o buona gente ripetiam allegramente l'antichissima canzon!
TUTTI: Questo è il fin di chi fa mal!
E de'perfidi la morte alla vita è sempre ugual!

my heart is ready. Your faithful love will yield to the desire of the woman who adores you.

DON OTTAVIO: My faithful love will yield to the desire of the woman I adore.

DONNA ELVIRA: I'll retire to a convent to end my life.

ZERLINA *and* MASETTO: We'll go home to have our dinner!

LEPORELLO: And I'll go to the inn to find a better master!

ZERLINA, LEPORELLO, MASETTO: Let that evil one remain in hell, with Proserpina and Pluto! And all of us meanwhile will repeat the oldest of songs!

ALL: This is the end of evildoers! The fate of sinners is always equal to their crimes!

COSÌ
FAN
TUTTE

An opera
in two acts

Music by
Wolfgang Amadeus Mozart
(K. 588)

Words by
Lorenzo da Ponte

INTRODUCTION

Così fan tutte was first produced in Vienna in January 1790, the third and final collaboration of Mozart and Da Ponte. Da Ponte's brilliant libretto is his only original work of the three; the wager that forms the basis of the plot was said to have been suggested by a contemporary incident. If *The Marriage of Figaro* marks the peak of Mozart's warmly realistic comedy, *Così fan tutte* is surely the ultimate comedy of artificiality. In its hard, glittering surface, it can be likened to the plays of Congreve. A work of wisdom and sophistication, and of impeccable stylistic grace, *Così fan tutte* portrays the coming-of-age of four utterly immature young people. The explicit theme is love and the fidelity of women, but actually, Don Alfonso's defense of reason and compromise might be applied in many other situations, and it provides a philosophical basis rare among operatic works.

The purpose of the opera may best be illustrated by examining its contrived, symmetrical structure. There are six characters: two pairs of young lovers, contrasted with Don Alfonso, the unembittered philosopher, and Despina, the worldly-wise maid. At the beginning, Don Alfonso may seem to be a disgruntled cynic when his sane admonitions are contrasted with the ravings of the wildly romantic younger men, but when we meet the ladies whom they characterize as paragons of virtue, we begin to see that Don Alfonso is simply being realistic. In *Così fan tutte,* the principal function of the characters is to fit into the general pattern, but it is also true that each possesses a definite individuality. Dorabella may be shallower than Fiordiligi, Ferrando more rhapsodical than Guglielmo, but all four young people share one common characteristic—they make no allowances for anything less than perfection in the ones they love. Don Alfonso deplores this attitude toward life; he knows that human beings cannot live up to such expectations, and he chooses to impart this knowledge by a joke that will give a maximum of instruction with a minimum of lasting pain.

Despina, utterly charming and utterly unscrupulous, is Don Alfonso's structural counterpart. She is a less elegant personification of his attitude toward life—make the best of every situation, and get what you can out of it! Newer to the art of deception, she does not recognize the officers in their Albanian disguises, but once she becomes part of the plot she makes it clear that Don Alfonso has found a worthy fellow conspirator.

Così fan tutte is one of those unusual works of art in which the original purpose of the creators is totally apparent in the final product. We feel no confusion or counter-pull; all is harmony and coherence. Unique for its music and libretto, the opera must also be regarded philosophically; it shows us a means of coming to terms with life, a philosophical approach that Mozart and Da Ponte, typical of the age of reason, found most effective. "Don't expect too much of people," they advise us, "and you'll never be disappointed." This is a philosophy that requires balance, self-confidence, and a sense of humor, and it is impossible for those incapable of severe self-examination. *Così fan tutte* does not attempt to present a flattering picture of humanity, nor one that is noble, but a true one.

For this reason, perhaps, *Così fan tutte*, in spite of its delightful music and engaging comedy, will never be quite as popular as the warmly human *Marriage of Figaro* or the challenging, enigmatic *Don Giovanni*. But a small group of its admirers will always regard it as the most perfect of Mozart's operas, ironically expressive of the quintessence of a philosophy and of an age.

SYNOPSIS

ACT ONE

In a tavern in Naples, two young officers, Ferrando and Guglielmo, sing the praises of their sweethearts, Fiordiligi and Dorabella. The officers' older friend, Don Alfonso, claims that a faithful woman has never existed, and never will, and he offers to prove his theory if the young men will follow his orders for the next twenty-four hours. The officers agree to a wager that they see no prospect of losing, and cheerfully propose a toast to the God of Love.

That morning, as Fiordiligi and Dorabella await their lovers, Don Alfonso arrives with bad news—the first link in his plot. The officers have been suddenly ordered off to war, he says, but they are permitted one last farewell before they go. To the young men's great delight, the ladies appear to be inconsolable.

Don Alfonso then enlists the aid of Despina, the sisters' maid, telling her that her mistresses need diversion in their loneliness. He presents the two officers, now fantastically disguised as noblemen from Albania. Despina pronounces them too grotesque to be taken seriously; the ladies are horrified at this invasion of their privacy, and Fiordiligi indignantly dismisses the "Albanians" from the house. When Ferrando and Guglielmo jubilantly demand their money from Don Alfonso, he recommends patience: the twenty-four hours have not yet run their course.

As the ladies bewail their solitude, the two "Albanians" rush in, proclaiming that they are dying of unrequited love, and have taken poison to hasten the process. Don Alfonso suggests a doctor, and returns with Despina, who is disguised as a worker of miracles, able to cure all ailments with a magnet. The men suddenly recover, and proclaim their love. From the very vehemence of the ladies' denials, it is evident that their resolve is beginning to weaken.

ACT TWO

After listening to Despina's worldly advice, the ladies conclude that they can amuse themselves with the newcomers without absolute infidelity to their lovers. In a joyous duet, each sister selects the other's former sweetheart to concentrate her attentions upon. First Dorabella succumbs to Guglielmo's ardent wooing; with somewhat more resistance, Fiordiligi yields to Ferrando's impassioned pleas.

Don Alfonso explains to the outraged young men that their sweethearts are no better or worse than all women: men must accept the instability of women, and love them anyway. As the ladies are about to marry their new suitors, Don Alfonso announces that the two officers have just returned from the battlefield. The "Albanians" hide, and a few minutes later, Ferrando and Guglielmo enter, clad in their officer's uniforms. Almost immediately they discover a false marriage contract, complete with signatures, as well as Despina, dressed, this time, as a notary. Explanations follow, and Dorabella and Fiordiligi, in spite of their resentment of the joke that has been played upon them, have no choice but to forgive and forget. All join in a chorus praising the man who is guided by reason; he will accept good and ill fortune alike, with philosophic calm.

CHARACTERS

FERRANDO, *an officer in love with* DORABELLA   *Tenor*
GUGLIELMO, *an officer in love with* FIORDILIGI   *Baritone*
DON ALFONSO, *the officers' older friend*   *Bass or Baritone*
FIORDILIGI ⎫ *two sisters of Ferrara,*   *Soprano*
DORABELLA ⎭ *living in Naples*   *Soprano or Mezzo-soprano*
DESPINA, *the sisters' maid*   *Soprano*
CHORUS *of soldiers, peasants, and servants*

The action takes place within the space of twenty-four hours, in and around FIORDILIGI *and* DORABELLA'S *house in Naples, during the mid-eighteenth century.*

ATTO PRIMO

Scena I

Una taverna a Napoli. DON ALFONSO, FERRANDO *e* GUGLIELMO *bevono.*

1. Terzetto

FERRANDO: La mia Dorabella
Capace non è,
Fedel quanto bella
Il cielo la fè!

GUGLIELMO: La mia Fiordiligi
Tradirmi non sa,
Uguale in lei credo
Costanza e beltà!

DON ALFONSO: Ho i crini già grigi,
Ex cathedra parlo
Ma tali litigi
Finiscano quà.

FERRANDO *e* GUGLIELMO: No, detto ci avete
Ch'infid'esser ponno
Provar cel'dovete,
Se avete onestà.

DON ALFONSO: Tai prove lasciamo—

FERRANDO *e* GUGLIELMO: No, no le vogliamo:
O fuori la spada,
Rompiam l'amistà!

DON ALFONSO: O pazzo desire!
Cercar di scoprire
Quel mal che trovato
Meschini ci fa.

FERRANDO *e* GUGLIELMO: Sul vivo mi tocca,
Chi lascia di bocca
Sortir un accento
Che torto le fa.

Recitativo

GUGLIELMO: Fuor la spada! sciegliete qual di noi più vi piace.

DON ALFONSO: Io son uomo di pace, e duelli non fo, se non a mensa.

Scene I

A tavern in Naples. DON ALFONSO, FERRANDO, *and* GU-
GLIELMO *are drinking.*

1. *Trio*

FERRANDO: My Dorabella is incapable of deceit. Heaven
made her as faithful as she is beautiful!

GUGLIELMO: My Fiordiligi could never betray me! I know
that her constancy equals her beauty!

DON ALFONSO: I'm older than you are; your experience
doesn't compare with mine. But we'll finish this argument
here and now.

FERRANDO *and* GUGLIELMO: No! Whoever has intimated
that our sweethearts might be unfaithful must prove it to
us if he has any honor.

DON ALFONSO: Let's forget about such proofs—
FERRANDO *and* GUGLIELMO: No, no, we demand them! Or
else draw your sword, for our friendship is at an end!

DON ALFONSO: I warn you, don't insist! It will only make
you miserable. He who looks for trouble is always bound
to find it.

FERRANDO *and* GUGLIELMO: When anyone utters a word
that might wrong my sweetheart it's a matter of life and
death to me!

Recitative

GUGLIELMO: Draw your sword! Choose whichever of us
you like!
DON ALFONSO: I'm a peaceful man, and I don't use steel
except at dinner.

FERRANDO: O battervi, o dir subito, perchè d'infedeltà la nostre amanti sospettate capaci.

DON ALFONSO: Cara semplicità, quanto mi piace!

FERRANDO: Cessate di scherzar, o giuro al cielo—

DON ALFONSO: Ed io, giuro alla terra, non scherzo, amici miei: solo saper vorrei che razza d'animali son queste vostre belle, se han come tutti noi carne, ossa, e pelle, se mangian come noi, se veston gonne, alfin, se dee, se donne son.

FERRANDO e GUGLIELMO: Son donne; ma son tali, son tali!

DON ALFONSO: E in donne pretendete di trovar fedeltà? Quanto mi piaci mai, semplicità!

2. Terzetto

È la fede delle femmine
Come l'araba fenice,
Che vi sia, ciascum lo dice,
Dove sia,
Nessun lo sa.

FERRANDO: La fenice è Dorabella.

GUGLIELMO: La fenice è Fiordiligi.

DON ALFONSO: Non è questa, non è quella,
Non fu mai, non vi sarà.

Recitativo

FERRANDO: Scioccherie di poeti!

GUGLIELMO: Scempiaggini di vecchi!

DON ALFONSO: Or bene, udite, ma senza andar in collera: qual prova avete voi, che ognor contanti vi sien le vostre amanti; chi vi fè sicurtà, che invariabili sono i lor cori?

FERRANDO: Lunga esperienza—

GUGLIELMO: Nobil educazion—

FERRANDO: Pensar sublime—

GUGLIELMO: Analogia d'umor—

FERRANDO: Disinteresse—

GUGLIELMO: Immutabil carattere—

FERRANDO: Promesse—

GUGLIELMO: Proteste—

FERRANDO: Giuramenti—

FERRANDO: Either accept our challenge or tell us at once why you believe that our sweethearts are capable of infidelity!

DON ALFONSO: What sweet simplicity! How very charming!

FERRANDO: Stop your joking, or I swear by heaven—

DON ALFONSO: And I swear by the earth. I'm not joking, my friends. I would only like to know what kind of creatures these ladies are; if they're made of bone, flesh, and skin; if they eat like us; if they wear skirts; in a word, if they're goddesses or women.

FERRANDO *and* GUGLIELMO: They're women, but such women, such women!

DON ALFONSO: And you expect to find fidelity in women? How delightfully naïve!

2. Trio

Women's faith is like the Phoenix of Arabia; everyone tells you that it exists, but nobody can tell you where to find it.

FERRANDO: Dorabella is a model of faith.

GUGLIELMO: So is Fiordiligi!

DON ALFONSO: You're both wrong; a faithful woman has never existed and never will!

Recitative

FERRANDO: Ridiculous poetic nonsense!

GUGLIELMO: You're becoming senile!

DON ALFONSO: Very well; now listen to me, but without losing your tempers. What proof have you that your sweethearts will always be faithful to you? How do you know that their hearts will never change?

FERRANDO: Long experience—

GUGLIELMO: Noble education—

FERRANDO: Sublime thoughts—

GUGLIELMO: Great respect for love—

FERRANDO: Careful observation—

GUGLIELMO: Unshakable principles—

FERRANDO: Promises—

GUGLIELMO: Protestations—

FERRANDO: Oaths—

DON ALFONSO: Piani, sospir, carezze, svenimenti. Lasciatemi un po' ridere!

FERRANDO: Cospetto! finite di deriderci?

DON ALFONSO: Pian piano; e se toccar con mano oggi vi fo che come l'altre sono?

GUGLIELMO: Non si può dar!

FERRANDO: Non è!

DON ALFONSO: Giochiam?

FERRANDO: Giochiamo.

DON ALFONSO: Cento zecchini.

GUGLIELMO: E mille, se volete.

DON ALFONSO: Parola.

FERRANDO: Parolissima.

DON ALFONSO: E un cenno, un motto, un gesto, giurate di non far di tutto questo alle vostre Penelopi?

FERRANDO: Giuriamo.

DON ALFONSO: Da soldati d'onore?

GUGLIELMO: Da soldati d'onore.

DON ALFONSO: E tutto quel farete ch'io vi dirò di far?

FERRANDO: Tutto!

GUGLIELMO: Tuttissimo!

DON ALFONSO: Bravissimi!

FERRANDO e GUGLIELMO: Bravissimo! Signor Don Alfonsetto! A spese vostre or ci divertiremo. E de' cento zecchini, che faremo?

3. *Terzetto*

FERRANDO: Una bella serenata
Far io voglio alla mia dea.

GUGLIELMO: In onor di Citerea
Un convito io voglio far.

DON ALFONSO: Sarò anch'io de' convitati?

FERRANDO e GUGLIELMO: Ci sarete, sì, Signor!

TUTTI: E che brindis replicati
Far vogliamo al Dio d'amor. (*Escono.*)

Scena II

La casa delle due sorelle. FIORDILIGI *e* DORABELLA *guardano i ritratti degli amanti.*

DON ALFONSO: Tears, sighs, caresses, swoonings! Let me laugh for just a moment!

FERRANDO: Good God! Will you ever stop laughing at us?

DON ALFONSO: Be calm. Suppose that today I could make you certain that they're just like all the others?

GUGLIELMO: You couldn't do it!

FERRANDO: It isn't true!

DON ALFONSO: Shall we bet?

FERRANDO: Certainly.

DON ALFONSO: A hundred gold pieces?

GUGLIELMO: Or a thousand if you like.

DON ALFONSO: On my word of honor.

FERRANDO: Absolutely!

DON ALFONSO: And you swear not to disclose our bet to the ladies by a nod, a motion, a gesture?

FERRANDO: We swear.

DON ALFONSO: On your honor as soldiers?

GUGLIELMO: On our honor as soldiers.

DON ALFONSO: And you'll do everything that I ask you to do?

FERRANDO: Everything!

GUGLIELMO: Absolutely everything!

DON ALFONSO: Bravissimi!

FERRANDO and GUGLIELMO: Bravissimo! Dear little Don Alfonso! We'll amuse ourselves at your expense! Now, how shall we spend those hundred gold pieces?

   3. *Trio*

FERRANDO: I will see that my goddess is beautifully serenaded!

GUGLIELMO: I'll hold a banquet in honor of Venus!

DON ALFONSO: Will I be among the guests?

FERRANDO and GUGLIELMO: You'll be there of course, my Lord!

ALL: We'll all drink endless toasts to the God of Love! (*Exit.*)

   Scene II

The sisters' house. FIORDILIGI *and* DORABELLA *are admiring their lovers' portraits.*

4. Duetto

FIORDILIGI: Ah guarda, sorella, se bocca più bella,
Se aspetto più nobile si può ritrovar.

DORABELLA: Osserva tu un poco
Osserva che foco ha ne' sguardi,
Se fiamme, se dardi non sembran scoccar.

FIORDILIGI: Si vede un sembiante
Guerriero ed amante.

DORABELLA: Si vede una faccia
Che alletta, che alletta,
E minaccia.

FIORDILIGI *e* DORABELLA: Io sono felice!
Se questo mio core
Mai cangia desio,
Amore, mi faccia vivendo penar.

Recitativo

FIORDILIGI: Mi par, che stamattina volontieri farei la pazzarella. Ho un certo foco, un certo pizzicor entro le vene
—quando Guglielmo viene—se sapessi, che burla gli vo far.

DORABELLA: Per dirti il vero, qualche cosa di nuovo anch'io nell'alma provo: io giurerei, che lontane non siam da gli imenei.

FIORDILIGI: Dammi la mano: io voglio astrologarti: uh, che bell'Emme! e questo un Pi: va bene: Matrimonio Presto.

DORABELLA: Affè, che ci avrei gusto.

FIORDILIGI: Ed io non ci avrei rabbia.

DORABELLA: Ma che diavol vuol dir che i nostri sposi ritardano a venir?
(*Entra* DON ALFONSO.)

FIORDILIGI: Eccoli!

DORABELLA: Non son essi; è Don Alfonso, l'amico lor.

FIORDILIGI: Ben venga il Signor Don Alfonso.

DON ALFONSO: Riverisco.

DORABELLA: Cos'è? Perche quì solo? Voi piangete? Parlate per pietà! Che cosa è nato? L'amante—

FIORDILIGI: L'idol mio—

DON ALFONSO: Barbaro fato!

4. Duet

FIORDILIGI: Look here, sister! Could one ever find a more sensitive mouth or a more noble expression?

DORABELLA: Just look at this picture! What fire glows in his eyes! How they flame and sparkle!

FIORDILIGI: Here you see the portrait of a lover and a warrior!

DORABELLA: Here is a face that at once attracts and threatens me!

FIORDILIGI *and* DORABELLA: I'm so very happy! If my heart ever changes, may the God of Love take revenge upon me!

Recitative

FIORDILIGI: Really, I feel a little giddy this morning. I have a certain restlessness, a rather ticklish feeling— When Guglielmo comes here—who knows what joke I'll play on him?

DORABELLA: To tell the truth, I also feel a little different this morning. I could swear that our wedding day will come very soon!

FIORDILIGI: Give me your hand; I'll tell your fortune! Oh, what a lovely *M*! And here's a *P*—that means you'll be married promptly!

DORABELLA: I wouldn't object to that.

FIORDILIGI: It wouldn't make me unhappy, either.

DORABELLA: But why on earth are our fiancés so late? (*Enter* DON ALFONSO.)

FIORDILIGI: Here they are!

DORABELLA: No, it's Don Alfonso, their friend.

FIORDILIGI: We're honored, dear Don Alfonso!

DON ALFONSO: The honor is mine.

DORABELLA: What is it? Why are you alone here? Why are you weeping? Tell us, for heaven's sake! What has happened? My beloved—

FIORDILIGI: My Guglielmo—

DON ALFONSO: Fate has been cruel!

5. *Aria*

Vorrei dir, e cor non ho,
Balbettando il labbro va—
Fuor la voce uscir non può—
Ma mi resta mezza quà.
Che farete?
Che farò?
Oh che gran fatalità!
Dar di peggio non si può, ah non si può
Ho di voi, di lor pietà.

Recitativo

FIORDILIGI: Stelle! per carità, Signor Alfonso, non ci fate morir.

DON ALFONSO: Convien armarvi, figlie mie, di costanza.

DORABELLA: Oh Dei! qual male è addivenuto mai, qual caso rio? Forse è morto il mio bene?

FIORDILIGI: È morte il mio?

DON ALFONSO: Morti non son, ma poco men che morti.

DORABELLA: Feriti?

DON ALFONSO: No.

FIORDILIGI: Ammalati?

DON ALFONSO: Neppur.

FIORDILIGI: Che cosa dunque?

DON ALFONSO: Al marzial campo ordin regio li chiama.

FIORDILIGI *e* DORABELLA: Ohimè! Che sento!

FIORDILIGI: E partiran?

DON ALFONSO: Sul fatto!

DORABELLA: E non v'è modo d'impedirlo?

DON ALFONSO: Non v'è.

FIORDILIGI: Ne un solo addio?

DON ALFONSO: Gli infelici non hanno coraggio di vedervi; ma se voi lo bramate, son pronti.

DORABELLA: Dove son?

DON ALFONSO: Amici, entrate!
(*Entrano* GUGLIELMO *e* FERRANDO.)

5. *Aria*

I really ought to tell you, but I don't have the heart—my lips tremble; my voice is not at my command—I have a lump in my throat. What will happen? What will you do? Oh, what a great disaster! Nothing worse could have occurred—I pity them, and I pity you!

Recitative

FIORDILIGI: Heavens! For pity's sake, Don Alfonso, don't frighten us to death!

DON ALFONSO: You must arm yourselves with courage, my dear girls.

DORABELLA: O God, what evil fate! What a dreadful catastrophe! Is my darling dead?

FIORDILIGI: And mine?

DON ALFONSO: Dead? No, not yet. But they're little better than dead.

DORABELLA: Wounded?

DON ALFONSO: No.

FIORDILIGI: Ill?

DON ALFONSO: Not really.

FIORDILIGI: Then what has happened?

DON ALFONSO: The King's orders have called them to the battlefield.

FIORDILIGI *and* DORABELLA: O heavens, how horrible!

FIORDILIGI: And when do they leave?

DON ALFONSO: This moment!

DORABELLA: Isn't there any way to save them?

DON ALFONSO: I'm afraid not.

FIORDILIGI: Can't we say good-by?

DON ALFONSO: The poor things haven't the courage to face you. But if you insist, they're ready.

DORABELLA: Where are they?

DON ALFONSO: My friends, you may come in now.
(*Enter* GUGLIELMO *and* FERRANDO.)

6. Quintetto

GUGLIELMO: Sento, o Dio!
Che questo piede
È restio nel girle avante.

FERRANDO: Il mio labbro palpitante
Non più detto pronunziar.

DON ALFONSO: Nei momenti i più terribili
Sua virtù l'eroe palesa.

FIORDILIGI e DORABELLA: Or ch'abbiam la nuova intesa,
A voi resta a fare il meno;
Fate core,
A entrambe in seno,
Immergeteci l'acciar.

FERRANDO e GUGLIELMO: Idol mio! la sorte incolpa se ti
deggio abbandonar!

DORABELLA: Ah no no, non partirai!

FIORDILIGI: No crudel, non te ne andrai!

DORABELLA: Voglio pria cavarmi il core.

FIORDILIGI: Pria ti vo morire ai piedi.

FERRANDO (*a parte a* DON ALFONSO): Cosa dici?

GUGLIELMO (*a parte a* DON ALFONSO): Te n'avveddi?

DON ALFONSO (*a parte a* FERRANDO *e* GUGLIELMO): Saldo
amico, finem lauda!

TUTTI: Il destin così defrauda,
Le speranze de' mortali,
Ah, chi mai fra tanti mali,
Chi mai puo la vita amar?

Recitativo

FERRANDO: O cielo! questo è il tamburo funesto, che a
divider mi vien dal mio tesoro.

DON ALFONSO: Ecco amici, la barca.

FIORDILIGI: Io manco.

DORABELLA: Io moro.
(*Entrano i soldati e contadini.*)

8. Coro

Bella vita militar!
Ogni dì si cangia loco,
Oggi molto, doman poco,
Ora in terra ed or sul mar.

6. Quintet

GUGLIELMO: My feet are powerless to move!

FERRANDO: My lips cannot speak!

DON ALFONSO: A hero's courage shines forth even in life's blackest moments!

FIORDILIGI *and* DORABELLA: Now that we have heard the sad news, you must end our misery. Take courage, and plunge your swords into our breasts!

FERRANDO *and* GUGLIELMO: My darling! Only cruel fate could make me leave you!

DORABELLA: Ah, no, no, you mustn't leave me!

FIORDILIGI: No, cruel one, I won't let you go!

DORABELLA: I'll tear my own heart first!

FIORDILIGI: I'll die right here at your feet!

FERRANDO (*aside to* DON ALFONSO): What do you say now?

GUGLIELMO (*aside to* DON ALFONSO): Are you listening?

DON ALFONSO (*aside to* FERRANDO *and* GUGLIELMO): Softly, my friends; he who laughs last always laughs best!

ALL: So destiny betrays the hopes of mortals. In the midst of such tragedy, how is it possible to regard life with any kindness?

Recitative

FERRANDO: Heavens, there is the funeral drum that divides me from my beloved!

DON ALFONSO: There is the boat, my friends.

FIORDILIGI: I'm fainting!

DORABELLA: I'm dying!

(*A group of soldiers and peasants enter.*)

8. CHORUS

A soldier's life is joyous! What pleasure to be able to travel from place to place—today everything—tomorrow nothing. Sometimes we go by land and sometimes by sea. The music of horns and trumpets, the bursting of bombs and cannon

Il fragor di trombe e pifferi,
Lo sparar di schioppi, e bombe,
Forza accresce al braccio, e all' anima
Vaga sol di trionfar.
Bella vita militar!

Recitativo

DON ALFONSO: Non v'è più tempo, amici, andar conviene,
ove il destino, anzi il dover v'invita.

FIORDILIGI: Mio cor—

DORABELLA: Idolo mio—

FERRANDO: Mio ben—

GUGLIELMO: Mia vita—

FIORDILIGI: Ah per un sol momento—

DON ALFONSO: Del vostro reggimento già è partita la barca,
raggiungerla convien coi pochi amici che su legno più lieve
attendendo vi stanno.

FERRANDO *e* GUGLIELMO: Abbracciami, idol mio!

FIORDILIGI *e* DORABELLA: Muojo d'affano.

9. Quintetto

FIORDILIGI: Di scrivermi ogni giorno!
Giurami, vita mia!

DORABELLA: Due volte ancora tu
Scrivimi, se puoi.

FERRANDO: Sii certa, sii certa,
O cara!

GUGLIELMO: Non dubitar,
Non dubitar, mio bene!

DON ALFONSO (*a parte*): Io crepo se non rido.

FIORDILIGI: Sii costante a me sol!

DORABELLA: Serbati fido!

FERRANDO: Addio!

GUGLIELMO: Addio!

FIORDILIGI *e* DORABELLA: Addio!

FIORDILIGI, DORABELLA, FERRANDO, GUGLIELMO: Mi si divide il cor,
Bell' idol mio!
Addio!
(*Escono* FERRANDO *e* GUGLIELMO.)

balls, gives strength to our arms and to our spirits! A soldier's life is joyous!

Recitative

DON ALFONSO: There's no more time, my friends, you must go where destiny and duty call you!

FIORDILIGI: My darling!

DORABELLA: My dearest!

FERRANDO: My sweetest!

GUGLIELMO: My life!

FIORDILIGI: Ah, only for a moment!

DON ALFONSO: Your regiment's ship is already gone; you must go with some people who are waiting for you with a smaller boat.

FERRANDO *and* GUGLIELMO: Kiss me, my darling!

FIORDILIGI *and* DORABELLA: I'm dying of grief!

9. *Quintet*

FIORDILIGI: Swear to write to me every day!

DORABELLA: Or twice a day if you can!

FERRANDO: I'll certainly do it, my darling!

GUGLIELMO: Don't doubt me, my dearest!

DON ALFONSO (*aside*): If I don't laugh at them, I shall burst!

FIORDILIGI: Be true to me only!

DORABELLA: Keep your faith!

FERRANDO: Good-by!

GUGLIELMO: Good-by!

FIORDILIGI *and* DORABELLA: Good-by!

FIORDILIGI, DORABELLA, FERRANDO, GUGLIELMO: O my love, my heart is torn with grief!

(FERRANDO *and* GUGLIELMO *exit.*)

Recitativo

DORABELLA: Dove son?

DON ALFONSO: Son partiti.

FIORDILIGI: Oh dipartenza crudelissima amara!

DON ALFONSO: Fate core, carissime figliuole; guardate, da lontano vi fan cenno con mano i cari sposi.

FIORDILIGI: Buon viaggio, mia vita!

DORABELLA: Buon viaggio!

FIORDILIGI: Oh Dei! come veloce se ne va quella barca! già sparisce! già non si vede più. Deh faccia il cielo ch'abbia prospero corso.

DORABELLA: Faccia che al campo giunga con fortunati auspici.

DON ALFONSO: E a voi salvi gli amanti, e a me gli amici.

10. Terzettino

FIORDILIGI, DORABELLA, DON ALFONSO: Soave sia il vento,
Tranquilla sia l'onda,
Ed ogni elemento
Benigno risponda
Ai nostri desir!
(FIORDILIGI *e* DORABELLA *partono.*)

Recitativo

DON ALFONSO: Non son cattivo comico! va bene; al concertato loco i due campioni di Ciprigna, e di Marte mi staranno attendendo; or senza indugio, raggiungerli conviene. Quante smorfie, quante buffonerie! Tanto meglio per me, cadran più facilmente: questa razza di gente è la più presta a cangiarsi d'umore. Oh poverini! per femmina giocar cento zecchini?

10A. Aria

Nel mare solca,
E nell' arena semina,
E il vago vento
Spera in rete accogliere
Chi fonda sue speranze
In cor di femmina.
(*Esce* DON ALFONSO. *Entra* DESPINA, *chi porta di cioccolatte.*)

Recitative

DORABELLA: Where are they?

DON ALFONSO: They've gone.

FIORDILIGI: Oh, most cruel, most bitter departure!

DON ALFONSO: Take heart, my dearest daughters! Look, they're waving to you from far away.

FIORDILIGI: Good fortune to my darling!

DORABELLA: Good fortune!

FIORDILIGI: O God! How quickly they're disappearing in that boat! It has already vanished. May heaven protect them on their journey!

DORABELLA: I pray that they will arrive at the battlefield refreshed and courageous!

DON ALFONSO: May heaven protect your lovers, and my friends!

10. Trio

FIORDILIGI, DORABELLA, DON ALFONSO: May the winds blow gently and the waves be calm—may every element look benignly on our desires!

(FIORDILIGI *and* DORABELLA *exit.*)

Recitative

DON ALFONSO: I'm not a bad actor; it's going very well. These two disciples of Venus and of Mars will be awaiting me at the appointed place. Now I must go to meet them, without delaying. What sighs—what languishings! What ridiculous nonsense! So much the better for me—they'll be tempted that much more easily. The more sighs and tears, the more vulnerable women become to a change of lovers. Those poor boys—to bet a hundred gold pieces on woman's fidelity!

10A. Aria

One might as well try to plow the sea or cultivate the desert, or to catch the wild wind in a net, as to trust the heart of a woman!

(DON ALFONSO *exits. Enter* DESPINA, *with a tray of hot chocolate.*)

Recitativo

DESPINA: Che vita maledetta è il far la cameriera! Dal mattino alla sera si fa, si suda, si lavora, e poi di tanto, che si fa, nulla è per noi. È mezza ora, che sbatto, il cioccolatte è fatto, ed a me tocca restar ad odorarlo a secca bocca? Non è forse la mia come la vostra? o garbate Signore, che a voi dessi l'essenza e a me l'odore? per Bacco, vo assagiarlo: com' è buono! Vien gente! oh ciel! son le padrone. (FIORDILIGI e DORABELLA *entrano*.) Madame, ecco la vostra collazione. Diamine! cosa fate?

FIORDILIGI e DORABELLA: Ah!

DESPINA: Che cosa è nato?

FIORDILIGI: Ov' è un acciaro!

DORABELLA: Un veleno, dov è!

DESPINA: Padrone, dico!

DORABELLA: Ah scostati! paventa il tristo affetto d'un disperato affetto. Chiudi quelle fenestre—odio la luce—odio l'aria che spiro—odio me stessa! Chi schernisce il mio duol? chi mi consola? Deh fuggi, per pietà! fuggi, lasciami sola.

11. Aria

Smanie implacabili,
Che m'agitate,
Entro quest' anima
Più non cessate,
Finchè l'angoscia
Mi fa morir.
Esempio misero
D'amor funesto,
Darò all' Eumenidi,
Se viva resto
Col suono orribile
De' miei sospir.

Recitativo

DESPINA: Signora Dorabella, Signora Fiordiligi, ditemi, che cosa è stato?

DORABELLA: Oh terribil disgrazia!

DESPINA: Sbrigatevi in buon' ora.

Recitative

DESPINA: A chambermaid has a thankless life! From morning until evening, I work, I slave, I labor, and I get nothing out of it for myself! The chocolate has been ready for half an hour, and I have to stand here and smell it while my mouth is watering! Why aren't I as good as they are? O my dear Ladies, who apportioned you the substance and me the aroma? By heaven, I'm going to taste it! Oh, how lovely! I hear someone coming—O Lord, here are my ladies!

(FIORDILIGO *and* DORABELLA *enter.*)

My Ladies, here's your breakfast. What on earth has happened?

FIORDILIGI *and* DORABELLA: Ah!

DESPINA: What can it be?

FIORDILIGI: Give me a dagger!

DORABELLA: I'm going to take poison!

DESPINA: What is it, my Ladies?

DORABELLA: Out of my sight! Respect the madness of a desperate love! Close all the windows—I hate the light—I hate the air I breathe—I hate myself! Who will comfort my grieving? Who will console me? Then leave me, I beg you—leave me to my sorrow!

11. Aria

Horrible agony that tortures me—consume my soul until I expire! I'm the miserable victim of a tragic love. While I still am living I'll frighten the Furies themselves with the horrible sound of my groans and sighs!

Recitative

DESPINA: My lady Dorabella, my lady Fiordiligi, tell me what has happened!

DORABELLA: Oh, horrible misfortune!

DESPINA: Tell me at once!

FIORDILIGI: Da Napoli partiti sono gli amanti nostri.

DESPINA: Non c'è altro? Ritorneran.

DORABELLA: Chi sa!

DESPINA: Come, chi sa? Dove son iti?

DORABELLA: Al campo di battaglia.

DESPINA: Tanto meglio per loro: li vedrete tornar carchi d'alloro. Ma non parliam di ciò, sono ancor vivi, e vivi torneran; ma son lontani, e più tosto che invani pianti perdere tempo, pensate a divertirvi.

FIORDILIGI: Divertirci?

DESPINA: Sicuro e quel ch'è meglio far all' amor come assassine, e come faranno al campo i vostri cari amanti.

DORABELLA: Non offender così quelle alme belle, di fedeltà, d'intatto amore esempi.

DESPINA: Via, via, passaro i tempi da spacciar queste favole ai bambini.

12. Aria

In uomini, in soldati,
Sperare fedeltà?
In uomini sperare fedeltà?
In soldati sperare fedeltà,
Non vi fate sentir per carità!
Di pasta simile son tutti quanti:
Le fronde mobili, l'aure incostanti
Han più degli uomini stabilità.
Mentite lagrime,
Fallaci sguardi,
Voci ingannevoli,
Vezzi bugiardi,
Son le primarie
Lor qualità.
In noi non amano che il cor diletto,
Poi ci dispregiano, neganci affetto,
Nè val da' barbari chieder pietà.
Paghiam, o femmine, d'ugual moneta
Questa malefica razza indiscreta;
Amiam per comodo, per vanità.

(FIORDILIGI e DORABELLA *escono e* DESPINA *ritorna alla sua stanza. Entra* DON ALFONSO.)

FIORDILIGI: Our lovers have left Naples.

DESPINA: That's all? They'll come back.

DORABELLA: Who knows?

DESPINA: What do you mean? Where have they gone?

DORABELLA: To the battlefield.

DESPINA: So much the better for them; you'll see them next covered with laurels! But let's not speak of that; they're still alive, and they'll be alive when they come back; and rather than wasting your time in idle tears, you must think of amusing yourselves.

FIORDILIGI: Amusing ourselves?

DESPINA: Certainly! And, more than that, you must make love to others, just as your dear lovers are doing at the front!

DORABELLA: Don't cast aspersions on those beautiful, faithful souls; they are veritable models of fidelity.

DESPINA: Come, now—let's not tell each other fairy tales!

12. Aria

You expect fidelity in men? In soldiers? Don't let anyone hear you, for heaven's sake! Men are all alike: fluttering leaves and inconstant winds have much more stability! Lying tears, false glances, deceiving promises, charming lies—those are their most usual tricks! They only use us for their pleasure, then they despise us, denying us any affection. It does no good to expect pity from these monsters! My Ladies, men are evil and indiscreet; let's pay them in their own coin—let's make love for convenience and vanity, just as they do!

(FIORDILIGI *and* DORABELLA *exit, as* DESPINA *returns to her own room.* DON ALFONSO *enters.*)

Recitativo

DON ALFONSO (*lo stesso*): Che silenzio! che aspetto di tristezza spirano queste stanze! Poverette! non han già tutto il torto: bisogna consolarle; infin che vanno i due creduli sposi, com' io loro commisi, a mascherarsi, pensiam cosa può farsi—temo un po' per Despina—quella furba potrebbe riconoscerli; potrebbe rovesciarmi le macchine, vedremo— se mai farà bisogno un regaletto a tempo, un zechinetto per una cameriere è un gran scongiuro—(*forte*) Despinetta!

DESPINA (*dalla sua stanza*): Chi batte?

DON ALFONSO: Oh!

(*Entra* DESPINA.)

DESPINA: Ih!

DON ALFONSO: Despina mia, di te bisogno avrei.

DESPINA: Ed io niente di voi.

DON ALFONSO: Ti vo fare del ben.

DESPINA: A una fanciulla un vecchio come lei non può far nulla.

DON ALFONSO: Parla piano ed osserva.

(*Le mostra un pezzo d'oro.*)

DESPINA: Me lo dona?

DON ALFONSO: Sì, se meco sei buona.

DESPINA: E che vorebbe? È l'oro il mio giulebbe.

DON ALFONSO: Ed oro avrai; ma ci vuol fedeltà.

DESPINA: Non c'è altro? Son quà.

DON ALFONSO: Prendi ed ascolta. Sai, che le tue padrone han perduti gli amanti.

DESPINA: Lo so.

DON ALFONSO: Tutti i lor pianti, tutti deliri loro ancor tu sai.

DESPINA: So tutto.

DON ALFONSO: Or ben; se mai per consolarle un poco, e trar, come diciam, chiodo per chiodo, tu ritrovassi il modo, da metter in lor grazia due soggetti di garbo che vorrieno provar, già mi capisci. C'è una mancia per te di venti scudi, se li fai riuscir.

Recitative

DON ALFONSO (*to himself*): What silence! What a tragic atmosphere permeates these rooms! Poor girls! The joke is only beginning; now we must try to console them. Meanwhile, I'll bring in their lovers, disguised as I directed them. But I'm a bit apprehensive about Despina— that vixen might recognize them and upset all my plans. Let's see. If I ever need to bribe her, a little money is always persuasive to a chambermaid. (*aloud*) Despinetta!

DESPINA (*from her room*): Who's knocking?

DON ALFONSO: I!

(DESPINA *enters.*)

DESPINA: You?

DON ALFONSO: My dear Despina, I have great need of your assistance.

DESPINA: And I have no need of yours.

DON ALFONSO: I only want to do you a favor.

DESPINA: At your age you can do no favors for young girls like me!

DON ALFONSO: Be quiet, and look at this.

(*He shows her a gold piece.*)

DESPINA: Is that for me?

DON ALFONSO: Yes, if you'll be kind to me.

DESPINA: Well, what would you like? Perhaps I can help you.

DON ALFONSO: You may keep the money; all I ask is your co-operation.

DESPINA: Nothing else? I'm ready!

DON ALFONSO: Take it then, and listen. You know that your mistresses have temporarily lost their lovers.

DESPINA: I know it.

DON ALFONSO: You've seen their tears and their extravagant grief?

DESPINA: I certainly have!

DON ALFONSO: Well then, if you had a chance to console them a little, and to replace one nail with another, as the saying goes, I'm sure that you'd be glad to do it. I know two charming young men who would like to try their luck. You understand me? If you'll help them, I'll give you twenty gold pieces.

DESPINA: Non mi dispiace questa proposizione. Ma con quelle buffone basta, udite: son giovani? son belli? e sopra tutto hanno una buona borsa i vostri concorrenti?

DON ALFONSO: Han tutto quello che piacer può alle donne di giudizio. Li vuoi veder?

DESPINA: E dove son?

DON ALFONSO: Son lì: li posso far entrar?

DESPINA: Direi di si.

(*Entrano* FERRANDO *e* GUGLIELMO *travestati da albinasi.*)

13. Sestetto

DON ALFONSO: Alla bella Despinetta
Vi presento, amici miei;
Non dipende che da lei,
Consolar il vostro cor.

FERRANDO *e* GUGLIELMO: Per la man,
Che lieto io bacio,
Per quei rai di grazia pieni,
Fa che volga a me sereni
I begli occhi il mio tesor.

DESPINA (*fra se, ridendo*): Che sembianze!
Che vestiti!
Che figure!
Che mustacchi!
Io non so, se son Vallacchi?
O se Turchi son costor?
Vallacchi, Turchi,
Turchi, Vallacchi?

FERRANDO *e* GUGLIELMO: Or la cosa è appien decisa,
Se costei non ci ravisa
Non c'è più nesun timor.

DON ALFONSO (*a* DESPINA): Che ti par di quell' aspetto?

DESPINA: Per parlarvi schietto, schietto,
Hanno un muso fuor dell' uso,
Vera antidoto d'amor!
Che figure, che mustacchi!

FIORDILIGI *e* DORABELLA (*da lontano*): Ehi, Despina! olà Despina!

DESPINA: Le padrone.

DON ALFONSO (*a* DESPINA): Ecco l'istante!
Fa con arte:

DESPINA: I don't dislike your proposition. But those stupid women! Only tell me—are your friends young, handsome, and above all, rich?

DON ALFONSO: They are all that could please a woman of discrimination. Would you like to see them?

DESPINA: But where are they?

DON ALFONSO: They're waiting outside. May they come in?

DESPINA: I don't see why not.

(FERRANDO *and* GUGLIELMO *enter, disguised as Albanians.*)

13. Sextet

DON ALFONSO: I present you, my friends, to the lovely Despinetta. She certainly can help you to console the pangs of your love.

FERRANDO *and* GUGLIELMO: I kiss your hands, and I hope that I can induce your mistresses' beautiful eyes to look kindly upon us!

DESPINA (*to herself, laughing*): What appearances! What costumes! What figures! What mustaches! I don't know if these creatures came from Rumania or from Turkey!

FERRANDO *and* GUGLIELMO: Now the matter is decided; if Despina can't recognize us, there's no longer any reason for fear!

DON ALFONSO (*to* DESPINA): Well, what do you think of them?

DESPINA: To speak frankly, the strangeness of their appearance would be an antidote to love!

FIORDILIGI *and* DORABELLA (*off-stage*): Eh, Despina, where are you, Despina?

DESPINA: My Ladies!

DON ALFONSO (*to* DESPINA): This is the crucial moment! Manage it craftily; I'll leave you alone.

Io quì m'ascondo.
(DON ALFONSO *parte*. *Entrano* FIORDILIGI *e* DORABELLA.)
FIORDILIGI *e* DORABELLA: Ragazzaccia tracotante!
Che fai lì con simil gente?
Falli uscire immantinente,
O ti so pentir con lor.
DESPINA, FERRANDO, GUGLIELMO: Ah, madame! perdonate!
Al bel piè languir mirate
Due meschin, di vostro merto,
Spasimanti adorator.
FIORDILIGI *e* DORABELLA: Giusti numi! cosa sento?
Dell' enorme tradimento,
Chi fu mai l'indegno autor?
DESPINA, FERRANDO, GUGLIELMO: Deh calmate, quello sdegno.
FIORDILIGI *e* DORABELLA: Ah, che più non ho ritegno!
Tutta piena ho l'alma in petto
Di dispetto e di terror!
DESPINA, FERRANDO, GUGLIELMO: Mi da un poco di sospetto,
Quella rabbia e quel furor!
Qual diletto è a questo petto,
Quella rabbia e quel furor!
(DON ALFONSO *entra*.)

Recitativo

DON ALFONSO: Che susurro! che strepito, che scompiglio è mai questo! siete pazze, care le mie ragazze? volette sollevar il vicinato? cosa avete? ch' è nato?

DORABELLA: Oh ciel! mirate uomini in casa nostra?

DON ALFONSO: Che male c'è?

FIORDILIGI: Che male? in questo giorno? dopo il caso funesto?

DON ALFONSO: Stelle! sogno, o son desto? amici miei, miei dolcissimi amici! Voi quì? come? perchè? quando! in qual modo? Numi! quanto ne godo! (*a parte a* FERRANDO *e* GUGLIELMO) Secondatemi.

FERRANDO: Amico Don Alfonso!

GUGLIELMO: Amico caro!

DON ALFONSO: Oh, bella improvisata!

(DON ALFONSO *exits.* FIORDILIGI *and* DORABELLA *enter.*)

FIORDILIGI *and* DORABELLA: Presumptuous girl! What are you doing here with people of that sort? Make them leave this instant, or you'll be sorry and so will they!

DESPINA, FERRANDO, GUGLIELMO: Ah, my ladies, pardon us! You see two unhappy men, passionate adorers of your virtues, languishing at your beautiful feet!

FIORDILIGI *and* DORABELLA: Heavens! What is this? Who is responsible for this horrible outrage?

DESPINA, FERRANDO, GUGLIELMO: Please calm your anger!

FIORDILIGI *and* DORABELLA: Now I can't control myself any longer! My whole soul is filled with horror and disdain!

DESPINA, FERRANDO, GUGLIELMO: I suspect this rage and fury; it doesn't quite ring true!
(DON ALFONSO *enters.*)

Recitative

DON ALFONSO: What noise! What a racket! What confusion! Have you gone insane, my dear girls? Do you want to call in all the neighborhood? What has happened? Tell me!

DORABELLA: O God! Look for yourself! Strange men in our house of sorrow!

DON ALFONSO: What harm is there in that?

FIORDILIGI: What harm? Today! After our tragic parting!

DON ALFONSO: Good heavens! Am I awake or dreaming? My friends, my dearest friends! Are you really here? How? Why? By land or sea? Good Lord, this is wonderful. (*aside to* FERRANDO *and* GUGLIELMO) Bear me out.

FERRANDO: My friend Don Alfonso!

GUGLIELMO: My dearest friend!

DON ALFONSO: Oh, happy surprise!

DESPINA: Li conoscete voi?

DON ALFONSO: Se li conosco! questi sono i più dolci amici ch'io m'abbia in questo mondo, e vostri ancor saranno.

FIORDILIGI: E in casa mia che fanno?

GUGLIELMO: Ai vostri piedi due rei, due delinquenti, ecco madame! Amor—

FIORDILIGI: Numi! che sento?

FERRANDO: Amor, il nume, si possente per voi, qui ci conduce.

GUGLIELMO: Vista appena la luce di vostre fulgidissime pupille—

FERRANDO: Che alle vive faville—

GUGLIELMO: Farfallette amorose e agonizzanti—

FERRANDO: Vi voliamo davanti—

GUGLIELMO: Ed ai lati ed a retro!

FERRANDO e GUGLIELMO: Per implorar pietade in flebil metro!

FIORDILIGI: Stelle! che ardir!

DORABELLA: Sorella! che facciamo?

14. Recitativo ed Aria

FIORDILIGI: Temerari, sortite fuori di questo loco! e non profani l'alito infausto degli infami detti nostro cor, orecchio, e nostri affetti! Invan per voi, per gli altri invan si cerca le nostre alme sedur: l'intatta fede che per noi già si diede ai cari amanti saprem loro serbar infino a morte, a dispetto del mondo e della sorte.
Come scoglio immoto resta
Contra i venti e la tempesta,
Così ognor quest' alma è forte
Nella fede e nell' amor.
Con noi nacque quello face,
Che ci piace, e ci consola;
E potrà la morte sola,
Far che cangi affetto il cor.
Rispettate, anime ingrate,
Questo esempio di costanza,
E una barbara speranza
Non vi renda audaci ancor.

Recitativo

FERRANDO: Ah, non partite!

DESPINA: Do you know these people?

DON ALFONSO: Do I know them? They are the dearest friends that I have in this world, and they will be your friends as well.

FIORDILIGI: But what are they doing in our house?

GUGLIELMO: Two rude and unworthy men kneel at your feet! Love—

FIORDILIGI: Heavens! What are you saying?

FERRANDO: Love, that overwhelming force, drove us here.

GUGLIELMO: As soon as we beheld the eloquence of your radiant eyes—

FERRANDO: They flashed flames—

GUGLIELMO: We were transformed into amorous, agonized butterflies—

FERRANDO: We flew before you—

GUGLIELMO: And fluttered back and forth!

FERRANDO *and* GUGLIELMO: We implore your pity in sweet, poetic measures!

FIORDILIGI: Heavens! What boldness!

DORABELLA: Sister, what shall we do?

14. Recitative and Aria

FIORDILIGI: Audacious intruders, leave this house immediately! Don't profane this unfortunate hearth with your infamous words! Spare our hearts, our ears, and our affections! It is vain for you or anyone else to attempt to seduce our souls! We shall keep the faith that we have pledged to our dear lovers until the hour of our death, in spite of all the world, and fate's adversity!

I stand firm as a rock against all winds and tempests! My soul will always be strong in faith and in love. My constancy consoles my grief, and only death can change my heart's affection. You, ungrateful creatures, must respect my example of fidelity—let it extinguish your false audacious hopes!

Recitative

FERRANDO: You must not leave us!

GUGLIELMO: Ah, barbara restate! (*a parte a* DON ALFONSO)
Che vi pare?

DON ALFONSO (*a parte*): Aspettate! (*forte*) Per carità ragazze, non mi fate più far trista figura.

DORABELLA: E che pretendereste?

DON ALFONSO: Eh nulla; ma mi pare che un pocchin di dolcezza—alfin son galant uomini e sono amici miei.

FIORDILIGI: Come! e udire dovrei?

GUGLIELMO: Le nostre pene e sentirne pietà! A voi davanti spirar vedrete i più fedeli amanti.

15. Aria
Non siate ritrosi
Occhietti vezzosi,
Due lampe amorosi
Vibrate un po' quà.
Felici rendeteci
Amate con noi,
E noi felicissimi
Faremo anche voi.
Guardate, toccate,
Il tutto osservate:
Siam due cari matti,
Siam forti e ben fatti,
E come ognun vede,
Sia merto, sia caso,
Abbiamo bel piede,
Bell' occhio, bel naso,
Guardate bel piede,
Osservate bell'occhio,
Toccate bel naso,
Il tutto osservate:
E questi mustacchi
Chiamare si possono
Trionfi degli uomini,
Penacchi d'amor,
(*Escono* FIORDILIGI, DORABELLA *e* DESPINA; GUGLIELMO *continua, ridendo.*)
Trionfi,
Penacchi, mustacchi!
16. Terzetto
DON ALFONSO: E voi ridete?

GUGLIELMO: Ah, cruel ones, do not go! (*aside to* DON ALFONSO) What do you say now?

DON ALFONSO (*aside*): Wait a little longer! (*aloud*) For pity's sake, my dear girls, don't behave like the tragic Muses!

DORABELLA: And what would you like us to do?

DON ALFONSO: Oh, nothing in particular; only I thought that you might be polite—after all, these two gentlemen are my friends.

FIORDILIGI: What! And must we listen to their proposals?

GUGLIELMO: If you knew how we are suffering, you would pity us. You'll see us die here before you, we who love you so faithfully!

15. Aria

Don't be so prudish; return our loving glances with your beautiful eyes! We'll all be so happy! Love us, and we'll all be ecstatic with joy! Look at us, touch us, observe us carefully. We're strong and virile. Anyone can see that we possess every merit—beautiful feet, lovely eyes, charming noses! And one might call these mustaches the triumph of masculinity, a symbol of love!

(FIORDILIGI, DORABELLA, *and* DESPINA *exit.* GUGLIELMO *goes on, laughing.*)

A triumph! A symbol! Mustaches!

16. Trio

DON ALFONSO: And you can laugh at this?

FERRANDO *e* GUGLIELMO: Certo, ridiamo.

DON ALFONSO: Ma cosa avete?

FERRANDO *e* GUGLIELMO: Già lo sappiamo—

DON ALFONSO: Ridete piano.

FERRANDO *e* GUGLIELMO: Parlate invano.

DON ALFONSO: Se vi sentissero,
Se vi scoprissero,
Si guasterebbe tutto l'affar,
Si guasterebbe
Tutto l'affar.

FERRANDO *e* GUGLIELMO: Ah che dal ridere,
L'alma dividere,
Ah, ah, ah, ah, ah, ah, ah, ah,
Ah, che le viscere
Sento scoppiar.

DON ALFONSO: Mi fa da ridere
Questo lor ridere,
Ma so che in piangere
Dee terminar.

Recitativo

Si può sapere un poco la cagion di quel riso?

GUGLIELMO: Oh cospettaccio, non vi pare che abbiam giusta ragione, il mio caro padrone?

FERRANDO: Quanto pagar volete, e a monte è la scommessa?

DON ALFONSO: Intanto silenzio e ubbidienza fino a doman mattina.

GUGLIELMO: Siamo soldati, e amiam la disciplina.

DON ALFONSO: Or bene: andate un poco ad attendermi entrambi in giardinetto, colà vi manderò gli ordini miei.

GUGLIELMO: Ed oggi non si mangia?

FERRANDO: Cosa serve: a battaglia finita fia la cena per noi più saporita.

(*Escono* DON ALFONSO *e* GUGLIELMO.)

17. Aria

Un' aura amorosa
Del nostra tesoro
Un dolce ristoro

FERRANDO *and* GUGLIELMO: Of course we're laughing!

DON ALFONSO: But what's so amusing?

FERRANDO *and* GUGLIELMO: Already we know—

DON ALFONSO: Don't laugh so loudly!

FERRANDO *and* GUGLIELMO: That your sarcasm was misguided.

DON ALFONSO: Be quiet! If they overhear you, the whole affair will be spoiled!

FERRANDO *and* GUGLIELMO: My heart will burst from laughing! Ha, ha! My sides are splitting!

DON ALFONSO: Their laughter makes me laugh in turn, for it must end in tears!

Recitative

Won't you tell me the reason for this laughter?

GUGLIELMO: Oh, good Lord, doesn't it seem to you that we have good reason, my dear fellow conspirator?

FERRANDO: When will you pay us and call off the bet?

DON ALFONSO: You promised silence and obedience until tomorrow morning.

GUGLIELMO: We're soldiers, and we're used to discipline.

DON ALFONSO: Very well; go for a walk now, and wait for me together in that little garden. There I'll give you my further instructions.

GUGLIELMO: Then we'll have no dinner?

FERRANDO: Not today. Tomorrow, when the bet is won, we'll relish the banquet even more fully!

(DON ALFONSO *and* GUGLIELMO *exit.*)

17. Aria

The sweet ambiance of love will bring delightful consolation to my soul! When the heart is nourished with fond dreams of love, no other joy is needed.

Al cor porgerà.
Al cor che nudrito
Da speme, d'amore,
D'un esca migliore
Bisogna non ha.
(*Esce* FERRANDO. *Entrano* FIORDILIGI *e* DORABELLA.)

18. Finale

FIORDILIGI *e* DORABELLA: Ah! che tutta in un momento
Si cangiò la sorte mia,
Ah, che un mar pien di tormento,
È la vita omai per me.
Finchè meco il caro bene
Mi lasciar le ingrate stelle,
Non sapea cos' eran pene,
Non sapea languir cos' è—no!

FERRANDO *e* GUGLIELMO (*dall interno*): Si mora, sì, si mora,
Onde appagar le ingrate.

DON ALFONSO (*dall interno*): C'è una speranza ancora,
Non fate, oh dei, non fate!

FIORDILIGI *e* DORABELLA: Stelle, che grida orribili!

FERRANDO *e* GUGLIELMO: Lasciatemi!

DON ALFONSO: Aspettate!
(*Entrano i tre uomini.*)

FERRANDO *e* GUGLIELMO: L'arsenico mi liberi
Di tanta crudeltà.

FIORDILIGI *e* DORABELLA: Stelle, un velen fu quello?

DON ALFONSO: Veleno buono e bello,
Che ad essi in pochi istanti
La vita toglierà.

FIORDILIGI *e* DORABELLA: Il tragico spettacolo
Gelare il cor mi fa!

FERRANDO *e* GUGLIELMO: Barbare, avvicinatevi:
D'un disperato affetto
Mirate il tristo effetto
E abbiate almen pietà.

FIORDILIGI, DORABELLA, FERRANDO, DON ALFONSO, GUGLI-
ELMO: Ah! che del sole il raggio
Fosco per me diventa.
Tremo, le fibre e l'anima

(FERRANDO *exits*. FIORDILIGI *and* DORABELLA *enter*.)

18. *Finale*

FIORDILIGI *and* DORABELLA: Ah! How everything has changed in the space of an hour! Life is now like a stormy ocean for me! While my dear lover was near me, I never knew the meaning of suffering or pain!

FERRANDO *and* GUGLIELMO (*off-stage*): Only our death can appease these ungrateful women!

DON ALFONSO (*off-stage*): There's still a ray of hope. O God—don't do it!

FIORDILIGI *and* DORABELLA: Heavens, what horrible cries!

FERRANDO *and* GUGLIELMO: Leave us to our tragic destinies!

DON ALFONSO: Wait a moment!

(*The three men enter.*)

FERRANDO *and* GUGLIELMO: Arsenic will liberate us from their cruelty!

FIORDILIGI *and* DORABELLA: Heavens! Have they really taken poison?

DON ALFONSO: A most effective poison, one that will take their lives in a matter of minutes!

FIORDILIGI *and* DORABELLA: This tragic sight freezes my heart!

FERRANDO *and* GUGLIELMO: Cruel women, look at us! You'll see the effect of a desperate passion, and perhaps at last you'll be moved by pity!

FIORDILIGI, DORABELLA, FERRANDO, DON ALFONSO, GUGLIELMO: The sun's light is darkening! I'm trembling—my nerves and spirit are faltering—my tongue and lips cannot form a word!

Par che mancar si senta,
Nè può la lingua o il labbro
Accenti articolar.
DON ALFONSO: Giacchè a morir vicini
Sono quei meschinelli
Pietade almeno a quelli
Cercate di mostrar.
FIORDILIGI *e* DORABELLA: Gente, accorrete, gente!
Nessuno, o dio, ci sente!
Despina! Despina!
DESPINA (*dall interno*): Chi mi chiama?
FIORDILIGI *e* DORABELLA: Despina! Despina!
(*Entra* DESPINA.)
DESPINA: Cosa vedo!
Morti i meschini io credo,
O prossimi a spirar.
DON ALFONSO: Ah che pur troppo è vero:
Furenti, disperati
Si sono avvelenati,
Oh amore singolar!
DESPINA: Abbandonar i miseri
Saria per voi vergogna,
Soccorrerli bisogna.
FIORDILIGI *e* DORABELLA: Cosa possiam mai far?
DESPINA: Soccorrerli bisogna.
Di vita ancor dan segno,
Colle pietose mani
Fate un po lor sostegno. (*a* DON ALFONSO)
E voi con me correte:
Un medico un antidoto
Voliamo a ricercar.
(DESPINA *e* DON ALFONSO *partono.*)
FIORDILIGI *e* DORABELLA: Dei! che cimento è questo!
Evento più funesto
Non si potea trovar!
FERRANDO *e* GUGLIELMO (*a parte*): Più bella comediola
Non si potea trovar!
FIORDILIGI *e* DORABELLA: Sospiran gl'infelici!
FIORDILIGI: Che facciamo?
DORABELLA: Tu che dici?

DON ALFONSO: Poor boys, now that they're so near to death, you might at least show them some pity!

FIORDILIGI *and* DORABELLA: Help! Somebody, help us! O God, nobody hears us! Despina! Despina!

DESPINA (*off-stage*): Who's calling me?
FIORDILIGI *and* DORABELLA: Despina! Despina!
(DESPINA *enters.*)
DESPINA: What on earth! The poor things seem to be dead, or very near it!

DON ALFONSO: Ah, that's only too true; they were in a fury of despair; they poisoned themselves! Oh, what a strange, desperate love!

DESPINA: It would be shameful to abandon these poor wretches; we must help them!

FIORDILIGI *and* DORABELLA: Whatever can we do?
DESPINA: They still seem to be breathing. We must support them gently. (*to* DON ALFONSO) And you must come with me to find a doctor or an antidote!
(DESPINA *and* DON ALFONSO *exit.*)

FIORDILIGI *and* DORABELLA: God! What a dreadful situation! One couldn't imagine a more tragic sight!

FERRANDO *and* GUGLIELMO (*aside*): One couldn't find a funnier comedy anywhere!
FIORDILIGI *and* DORABELLA: The poor things are sighing!
FIORDILIGI: What shall we do?
DORABELLA: What do you say?

FIORDILIGI: In momenti si dolenti
Chi potria li abbandonar?
DORABELLA: Che figure interessanti!
FIORDILIGI: Possiam farci un poco avanti.
DORABELLA: Ha fredissima la testa.
FIORDILIGI: Fredda, fredda è ancora questa.
DORABELLA: Ed il polso?
FIORDILIGI: Io non gliel' sento.
DORABELLA: Questo batte lento, lento.
FIORDILIGI e DORABELLA: Ah se tarda ancor l'aita,
Speme più non v'è di vita.
FERRANDO e GUGLIELMO (*a parte*): Più domestiche e trattabili
Sono entrambe diventate,
Sta a veder
Che lor pietade
Va in amore a terminar.
FIORDILIGI e DORABELLA: Poverini, poverini!
La lor morte
Mi farebbe lagrimar.
(*Entra* DON ALFONSO, *con* DESPINA, *travestita da medico.*)
DON ALFONSO: Eccovi il medico,
Signore belle.
FERRANDO e GUGLIELMO (*a parte*): Despina in maschera,
Che trista pelle!
DESPINA: Salvete amabiles
Bones puelles.
FIORDILIGI e DORABELLA: Parla un linguaggio
Che non sappiamo.
DESPINA: Come comandano dunque parliamo,
So il greco e l'arabo,
So il turco e il vandalo,
Lo sveco e il tartaro
So ancor parlar.
DON ALFONSO: Tanti linguaggi per se conservi, per se conservi.
Quei miserabili per ora osservi,
Preso hanno il tossico, che si può far?
FIORDILIGI e DORABELLA: Signor Dottore, che si può far?

FIORDILIGI: We can't leave them alone at such a critical moment!

DORABELLA: They have very interesting faces!

FIORDILIGI: We can go a little nearer.

DORABELLA: This one's head is cold as ice.

FIORDILIGI: So is this one's.

DORABELLA: And the pulses?

FIORDILIGI: I don't feel it.

DORABELLA: His is beating very slowly.

FIORDILIGI *and* DORABELLA: Ah, if only help would come! There will soon be no hope!

FERRANDO *and* GUGLIELMO (*aside*): They have become so intimate and maternal. Now let's see if their pity will turn into love!

FIORDILIGI *and* DORABELLA: Poor things! If they should die, I would feel dreadful!

(*Enter* DON ALFONSO, *with* DESPINA, *who is disguised as a doctor.*)

DON ALFONSO: Here's the doctor, noble ladies!

FERRANDO *and* GUGLIELMO (*aside*): Despina disguised; what a joke!

DESPINA: Salvete amabiles bones puelles.

FIORDILIGI *and* DORABELLA: He speaks a strange language that we don't understand.

DESPINA: I'll speak whatever language you command me to. I know Greek and Arabic, Turkish and Vandal, Swedish and Tartaric; I can speak them all.

DON ALFONSO: Keep your languages to yourself for the present. Please examine these miserable young men. They've taken poison; what can you do for them?

FIORDILIGI *and* DORABELLA: Most honored Doctor, what can be done?

DESPINA: Saper bisognami
Pria la cagione
E quindi l'indole
Della pozione;
Se calda
O frigida,
Se poca
O molta
Se in una volta,
Ovvere in più.

FIORDILIGI, DORABELLA, DON ALFONSO: Preso han l'arsenico,
signor Dottore,
Quì dentro il bebbero.
La causa è amore
Ed in un sorso sel mandar giù.

DESPINA: Non vi affannate,
Non vi turbate,
Ecco una prova di mia virtù.
(*Prenda un magnete dalla sua manica, e l'agita sopra i due
uomini.*)

FIORDILIGI, DORABELLA, DON ALFONSO: Egli ha di un ferro
La man fornita.

DESPINA: Questo è quel pezzo
Di calamita
Pietra Mesmerica,
Ch' ebbe l'origine
Nell' Alemagna,
Che poi sì celebre
Là in Francia fù.
(GUGLIELMO *e* FERRANDO *si muovono le braccia.*)

FIORDILIGI, DORABELLA, DON ALFONSO: Come si muovono,
Torcono, scuotono,
In terra il cranio
Presto percuotono.

DESPINA (*gesticola col magnete*): A lor la fronte
Tenete sù.

FIORDILIGI *e* DORABELLA: Eccoci pronte.

DESPINA: Tenete forte,
Coraggio!
Or liberi
Siete da morte.

DESPINA: First I must know the cause, and then the nature of the poisoning. Was it warm or cold? A little or much? Was it one dose or several?

FIORDILIGI, DORABELLA, DON ALFONSO: They've taken arsenic, Doctor; they drank it right here, driven by disappointed love; they swallowed it down in one gulp!

DESPINA: Don't disturb yourselves— Now I will reveal my scientific skill!
(*She takes a magnet from her sleeve, and waves it over the two young men.*)

FIORDILIGI, DORABELLA, DON ALFONSO: He has a huge piece of iron in his hand!
DESPINA: This is a piece of Doctor Mesmer's magnetic stone. It was first discovered in Germany, and then became celebrated in France as well.
(GUGLIELMO *and* FERRANDO *move their arms.*)

FIORDILIGI, DORABELLA, DON ALFONSO: How they're moving, turning and twisting! Their heads are inclining toward the ground!

DESPINA (*gesturing with the magnet*): Now hold their heads up!
FIORDILIGI *and* DORABELLA: Here, they're ready!
DESPINA: Hold them tightly, tightly, tightly; have courage! Now they will both be saved from death!

FIORDILIGI, DORABELLA, DON ALFONSO: Attorno guardano:
Forze riprendono:
Ah questo medico vale un Perù.

FERRANDO e GUGLIELMO (*fingono di ravvivare*): Dove son!
Che loco è questo?
Chi è colui? color chi sono?
Son di Giove innanzi al trono?
Sei tu Palla, o Citerea?
No tu sei l'alma mia dea;
Ti ravviso al dolce viso:
E alla man ch'or ben conosco
E che sola è il mio tesor.

DESPINA e DON ALFONSO: Son effetti ancor del tosco,
Non abbiate alcun timor.

FIORDILIGI e DORABELLA: Sàra ver, ma tante smorfie
Fanno torto al nostro onor.

FERRANDO e GUGLIELMO (*a parte*): Dalla voglia che ho di
ridere,
Il polmon mi scoppia ognor. (*forte*)
Per pietà, bell' idol mio!
Volgi a me le luci liete!

FIORDILIGI e DORABELLA: Più resister non poss' io!

FERRANDO e GUGLIELMO (*si saltano subito*): Dammi un bacio, o mio tesoro,
Un sol bacio, o qui mi moro!

FIORDILIGI e DORABELLA: Stelle, un bacio?

DESPINA e DON ALFONSO: Secondate
Per effetto di bontate.

FIORDILIGI e DORABELLA: Ah, che troppo si richiede
Da una fida onesta amante
Oltraggiata è la mia fede,
Oltraggiato è questo cor.

DESPINA e DON ALFONSO (*a parte*): Un quadretto più gio-
condo
Non si vide in tutti il mondo,
Quel che più mi fa da ridere
È quell' ira e quel furor.

FIORDILIGI e DORABELLA: Disperati, attossicati,
Ite al diavol quanti siete;
Tardi in ver vi pentirete
Se più cresce il mio furor.

FIORDILIGI, DORABELLA, DON ALFONSO: See them stirring;
they're regaining their strength! Ah, this doctor is worth
his weight in gold!

FERRANDO and GUGLIELMO (*pretending to revive*): Where
am I? What place is this? Who is he? And who are you?
Am I before the throne of Jupiter? Are you Athena or
Venus? No, you are the goddess of my soul! Once again
I see your lovely face, and by your beloved touch I recog-
nize my love!

DESPINA and DON ALFONSO: It's the influence of poison;
don't listen to what they say.

FIORDILIGI and DORABELLA: That may be true, but such
passion wrongs our honor!

FERRANDO and GUGLIELMO (*aside*): My chest is going to
burst from holding back my laughter! (*aloud*) Have pity!
Let your beautiful eyes shine upon us!

FIORDILIGI and DORABELLA: I can't bear it any longer!

FERRANDO and GUGLIELMO (*suddenly leaping up*): Give
me a kiss! O my darling! Only one kiss, and then I can die!

FIORDILIGI and DORABELLA: Heavens, a kiss?

DESPINA and DON ALFONSO: Go ahead; it's only kindness!

FIORDILIGI and DORABELLA: Ah, that's too much to ask of
an honest woman! My heart and my soul are outraged
by your request!

DESPINA and DON ALFONSO (*aside*): One couldn't find a
more amusing scene in all this world! How their raging
makes me laugh!

FIORDILIGI and DORABELLA: Take your poison to the devil.
You'll repent it if you try my patience any longer!

DESPINA *e* DON ALFONSO: In poch' ore lo vedrete
Per virtù del magnetismo
Finire quel parossismo,
Torneranno al primo umor.

FERRANDO *e* GUGLIELMO (*a parte*): Un quadretto più giocondo
Non s'è visto in questo mondo,
Ma non so se finta o vera
Sia quell' ira
E quel furor.

DESPINA *and* DON ALFONSO: You'll see that in no time the magnet will end their spasms. They'll be just as good as new.

FERRANDO *and* GUGLIELMO (*aside*): One couldn't find a more amusing scene in all this world! But I'm beginning to doubt whether their rage is real or feigned!

ATTO SECONDO

Una stanza nella casa delle due sorelle. DESPINA *aiuta* FIORDILIGI *e* DORABELLA *a vestirsi.*

Recitativo

DESPINA: Andate là, che siete due bizzarre ragazze!

FIORDILIGI: Oh cospettaccio! cosa pretenderesti?

DESPINA: Per me nulla.

FIORDILIGI: Per chi dunque?

DESPINA: Per voi.

DORABELLA: Per noi?

DESPINA: Per voi. Siete voi donne, o no?

FIORDILIGI: E per questo?

DESPINA: E per questo dovete far da donne.

DORABELLA: Ciò è?

DESPINA: Tratter l'amore en bagatelle. Le occasioni belle non negliger giammai! cangiar a tempo, a tempo esser costanti, coquettizar con grazia, prevenir la disgrazia sì comune a chi si fida in uomo, mangiar il fico, e non gittare il pomo.

FIORDILIGI (*a parte*): Che diavolo! (*forte*) Tai cose falle tu, se n'hai voglia.

DESPINA: Io già le faccio. Ma vorrei che anche voi per gloria del bel sesso faceste un po' lo stesso!

19. Aria

Una donna a quindici anni
Dee saper ogni gran moda,
Dove il diavolo ha la coda,
Cosa è bene, e mal cos' è,
Dee saper le maliziette,
Che innamorano gli amanti,
Finger riso, finger pianti,

A room in the sisters' house. DESPINA *is helping* FIORDILIGI *and* DORABELLA *to dress.*

Recitative

DESPINA: Well, you are certainly two very strange girls!

FIORDILIGI: For goodness' sake, what do you expect of us?

DESPINA: For myself—nothing.

FIORDILIGI: For whom, then?

DESPINA: For you!

DORABELLA: For us?

DESPINA: Yes, for you. Are you women or not?

FIORDILIGI: Isn't that quite evident?

DESPINA: Well, if you are women, you must behave like women!

DORABELLA: Which means?

DESPINA: You must realize that love should not be serious. Never reject a chance to have some fun! There are times when you must be changeable and times when you must be constant. You must know how to flirt gracefully, always avoiding the common disgrace of those who trust in men. In short, you must know how to have your cake and eat it at the same time!

FIORDILIGI (*aside*): How outrageous! (*aloud*) You may do those things if you want to.

DESPINA: That's how I always do them. But for the honor and glory of our sex, I would like you both to follow my example!

19. Aria

By the time a girl is fifteen she must know the ways of the world! She must know where the devil's tail is, what is good and what is bad! She must learn the little lies that fascinate a lover, how to feign laughter or tears, and how to invent plausible excuses! She must be able to deal with a hundred suitors at the same time; she must speak to a thousand with her eyes; she must give hope to all men

Inventar i bei perchè.
Dee in un momento
Dar retta a cento,
Colle pupille
Parlar con mille,
Dar speme a tutti,
Sien belli o brutti,
Saper nascondersi,
Senza confondersi,
Senza arrossire,
Saper mentire,
E qual regina
Dall' alto soglio
Col posso e voglio farsi ubbidir. (*a parte*)
Par ch'abbian gusto
Di tal dottrina, (*forte*)
Viva Despina
Che sa servir! (*Parte.*)

Recitativo

FIORDILIGI: Sorella, cosa dici?

DORABELLA: Io son stordita dallo spirto infernal di tal ragazza.

FIORDILIGI: Ma credimi è una pazza. Ti par che siamo in caso di seguir suoi consigli?

DORABELLA: Oh certo se tu pigli pel rovescio il negozio.

FIORDILIGI: Anzi io lo piglio per il suo vero dritto: Ma i nostri cori?

DORABELLA: Restano quel che sono; per divertirsi un poco, e non morire della malinconia non si manca di fè, sorella mia.

FIORDILIGI: Questo è ver.

DORABELLA: Dunque, per intenderci bene, qual vuoi scieglier per te de' due Narcisi?

FIORDILIGI: Decidi tu, sorella.

DORABELLA: Io già decisi.

20. Duetto

Prenderò quel brunettino,
Che più lepido mi par.

FIORDILIGI: Ed intanto io col biondino
Vo un po ridere e burlar.

whether they're handsome or ugly, and know how to hide
her plans without confusion, and to lie without blushing!
With these talents she'll be obeyed like a queen on the
highest throne. (*aside*) It seems that my advice appeals to
them! (*aloud*) Trust in Despina—I'll be your guide!
(*Exits.*)

Recitative

FIORDILIGI: Sister, what do you say?

DORABELLA: I'm amazed at that girl's diabolical cynicism!

FIORDILIGI: I think she's crazy. Does she believe that we'll
follow her advice?

DORABELLA: Certainly not—if you undertake to stop the
whole business.

FIORDILIGI: I estimate it at its true value. And our devotion?

DORABELLA: We're still devoted. To amuse oneself a little
and not to die of melancholy is not the same as breaking
one's faith, my dear sister.

FIORDILIGI: There is some truth in that.

DORABELLA: Well, then? Let's understand each other—
which gentleman is your choice?

FIORDILIGI: You decide it, sister.

DORABELLA: I have decided!

20. Duet

I'll take that sweet little dark one; he seems more vivacious
to me.

FIORDILIGI: And I will laugh and joke with the nice little
blond one.

DORABELLA: Scherzosetta ai dolci detti
Io di quel risponderò.

FIORDILIGI: Sospirando i sospiretti
Io dell' altro imiterò.

DORABELLA: Mi dirà, "ben mio, mi moro."

FIORDILIGI: Mi dirà, "mio bel tesoro!"

FIORDILIGI e DORABELLA: Ed intanto che diletto,
Che spassetto io proverò!

(*Entrano* FERRANDO e GUGLIELMO *con* DON ALFONSO e DES ·
PINA.)

21. Duetto

FERRANDO e GUGLIELMO: Secondate, aurette amiche,
Secondate i miei desiri,
E portate i miei sospiri
Alla dea di questo cor.
Voi, che udiste mille volte
Il tenor delle mie pene;
Ripetete al caro bene,
Tutto quel che udiste allor.

Recitativo

FIORDILIGI e DORABELLA: Cos' è tal mascherata?

DESPINA (*a* FERRANDO e GUGLIELMO): Animo, via, coraggio: avete perso l'uso della favella?

FERRANDO: Io tremo, e palpito dalla testa alle piante.

GUGLIELMO: Amor lega la membra a vero amante.

DON ALFONSO: Da brave incorraggiteli.

FIORDILIGI: Parlate!

DORABELLA: Liberi dite pur quel che bramate!

FERRANDO: Madama—

GUGLIELMO: Anzi madame—

FERRANDO: Parla pur tu.

GUGLIELMO: No, no, parla pur tu.

DON ALFONSO: Oh! cospetto del diavolo! lasciate tali smorfie del secolo passato: Despinetta, terminiam questa festa, fa tu con lei, quel ch'io farò con questa.

(*Prende la mano di* DORABELLA; DESPINA *prende la mano di* FIORDILIGI.)

DORABELLA: I'll parody his sweet speeches.

FIORDILIGI: I'll mock his sighs.

DORABELLA: Mine will say: "My dearest, I'm dying!"

FIORDILIGI: Mine will say: "My darling, you're so beautiful!"

FIORDILIGI *and* DORABELLA: And, in any case, how amusing it will be!

(FERRANDO *and* GUGLIELMO *enter with* DON ALFONSO *and* DESPINA.)

21. Duet

FERRANDO *and* GUGLIELMO: Echo my desires, friendly breezes, and carry my sighs to the goddess of my heart! You who have heard the story of my suffering a thousand times, repeat it once again to my dear love!

Recitative

FIORDILIGI *and* DORABELLA: What is the meaning of this performance?

DESPINA (*to* FERRANDO *and* GUGLIELMO): Hurry, speak up now! Have you lost the use of your tongues?

FERRANDO: I'm trembling from head to foot.

GUGLIELMO: Emotion paralyzes the limbs of a true lover.

DON ALFONSO: Dear ladies, please encourage them.

FIORDILIGI: Speak!

DORABELLA: You may tell us whatever you like!

FERRANDO: Dear lady!

GUGLIELMO: Or rather, both dear ladies!

FERRANDO: You tell them.

GUGLIELMO: No, you.

DON ALFONSO: Oh, the devil! Leave such bashfulness to our grandparents. Despinetta, let's end this farce; you speak for the ladies; I'll speak for my friends.

(*He takes* DORABELLA'S *hand;* DESPINA *takes* FIORDILIGI'S *hand.*)

22. *Quartetto*

La mano a me date,
Movetevi un pò! (*ai due giovani uomini*)
Se voi non parlate,
Per voi parlerò. (*a* FIORDILIGI *e* DORABELLA)
Perdono vi chiede
Un schiavo tremante,
V'offese, lo vede,
Ma solo un istante;
Or pena, ma tace!

FERRANDO *e* GUGLIELMO: Tace!

DON ALFONSO: Or lasciavi in pace!

FERRANDO *e* GUGLIELMO: In pace!

DON ALFONSO: Non può quel che vuole,
Vorrà, quel che può.

FERRANDO *e* GUGLIELMO: Non può quel che vuole,
Vorrà quel che può.

DON ALFONSO: Su! via! rispondete!
Guardate, e ridete?

DESPINA: Per voi la risposta (*risponde per le donne*)
A loro darò.
Quello ch'è stato, è stato,
Scordiamci del passato.
Rompasi omai quel laccio,
Segno di servitù;
A me porgete il bracio:
Nè sospirate più.

DESPINA *e* DON ALFONSO (*a parte*): Per carità partiamo,
Quel che san far veggiamo,
Le stimo più
Del diavolo,
S'ora non cascan giù. (*Partono.*)

Recitativo

FIORDILIGI: Oh che bella giornata!

FERRANDO: Caldetta anzi che no.

DORABELLA: Che vezzosi arboscelli!

GUGLIELMO: Certo, certo: son belli: han più foglie che frutti.

FIORDILIGI: Quei viali come sono leggiadri; volete passeggiar?

22. Quartet

Give me your hand; now, try to respond gracefully. (*to the two young men*) If you won't speak to these ladies, I'll find the words for you. (*to* FIORDILIGI *and* DORABELLA) A trembling slave begs for your pardon. It is true that I offended you, but only for a moment. Now I will gladly suffer in silence!

FERRANDO *and* GUGLIELMO: In silence!

DON ALFONSO: I'll leave you in peace!

FERRANDO *and* GUGLIELMO: In peace!

DON ALFONSO: If you desire it, I'll disappear from your sight.

FERRANDO *and* GUGLIELMO: If you desire it, I'll disappear from your sight.

DON ALFONSO: Come on, then! Answer me! You're watching? And smiling?

DESPINA: I'll supply their answer. (*replying for the ladies*) What is past is finished; let's forget all about it. Now we must sever the bonds of a former love which has become only slavery. Give me your hands and don't grieve any longer!

DESPINA *and* DON ALFONSO (*aside*): Let's leave them all together; we'll see what will happen. I'll respect them more than the devil himself if they can resist temptation now! (*Exit.*)

Recitative

FIORDILIGI: Oh, what a beautiful day!

FERRANDO: It's a little warm.

DORABELLA: What charming arbors!

GUGLIELMO: Yes, yes, the trees are pretty, but they have more leaves than fruit.

FIORDILIGI: What interesting pathways; would you like to walk?

FERRANDO: Son pronto, o cara, ad ogni vostro cenno.

FIORDILIGI: Troppa grazia!

FERRANDO (*a parte a* GUGLIELMO): Eccoci alla gran crisi.

FIORDILIGI: Cosa gli avete detto?

FERRANDO: Eh gli raccomandai di divertirla bene.

(FIORDILIGI *e* FERRANDO *partono*.)

DORABELLA: Passeggiamo anche noi?

GUGLIELMO: Come vi piace. Ahimè!

DORABELLA: Che cosa avete?

GUGLIELMO: Io mi sento si male, si male, anima mia, che mi par di morire.

DORABELLA (*a parte*): Non otterà nientissimo. (*forte*) Saranno rimasugli del velen che beveste.

GUGLIELMO: Ah che un veleno assai più forte io bevo in questi crudi e focosi mongibelli amorosi!

DORABELLA: Sarà veleno calido; fatevi un poco fregeo.

GUGLIELMO (*le offre una fermaglia col suo quadro*): Questa picciola offerta d'accettare degnatevi.

DORABELLA: Un core?

GUGLIELMO: Un core; è simbolo di quello ch'arde, languisce e spasima per voi.

DORABELLA: L'accetto.

GUGLIELMO (*a parte*): Infelice Ferrando! (*forte*) Oh che diletto!

23. *Duetto*

Il core vi dono,
Bell'idolo mio;
Ma il vostro vo'anch'io,
Via datelo a me.

DORABELLA: Mel date, lo prendo,
Ma il mia non vi rendo,
Invan me'l chiedete,
Più meco non è.

GUGLIELMO: Se teco non l'hai,
Perchè batte quì?

DORABELLA: Se a me tu lo dai,
Che mai balza lì?

FERRANDO: I'm ready to do your slightest bidding, dear.

FIORDILIGI: You're very kind.

FERRANDO (*aside to* GUGLIELMO): This is the critical moment.

FIORDILIGI: What did you say to him?

FERRANDO: I was only wishing him a pleasant walk. (FIORDILIGI *and* FERRANDO *exit.*)

DORABELLA: Shall we walk, too?

GUGLIELMO: As you wish—O God!

DORABELLA: What is the matter?

GUGLIELMO: I feel so ill—so ill, my darling, that I think I'm going to die!

DORABELLA (*aside*): That won't get him anywhere! (*aloud*) It must be the after effects of the poison.

GUGLIELMO: Ah, but I drank a stronger poison from your beautiful eyes!

DORABELLA: Oh, what intoxicating poison! You should walk in the fresh air!

GUGLIELMO (*offering her a locket with his picture*): Will you deign to accept this small present?

DORABELLA: A heart?

GUGLIELMO: A heart, symbolic of this one that languishes and beats for you!

DORABELLA: I'll accept it.

GUGLIELMO (*aside*): Poor Ferrando! (*aloud*) Oh, I'm delighted!

   23. Duet

I give you my heart, my beautiful goddess, but I desire yours in return. Come, give it to me.

DORABELLA: I'll accept the gift of your heart, but I can't return my own. You ask me for it in vain; it's no longer in my possession.

GUGLIELMO: If your heart is gone, why does it beat here?

DORABELLA: If your heart is mine, what do I feel beating here?

DORABELLA *e* GUGLIELMO: E il mio coricino,
Che più non è meco,
Ei venne a star teco,
Ei batte così.

GUGLIELMO: Qui lascia che metta.

DORABELLA: Ei qui non può star.

GUGLIELMO: T'intendo, furbetta.

DORABELLA: Che fai?

GUGLIELMO: Non guardar.

DORABELLA: Nel petto un Vesuvio d'avere mi par!

GUGLIELMO (*a parte*): Ferrando meschino! possibil non par. (*forte*)
L'occhietta a me gira.

DORABELLA: Che brami?

GUGLIELMO: Rimira, rimira,
Se meglio può andar.

DORABELLA *e* GUGLIELMO: Oh cambio felice,
Di cori e d'affetti!
Che nuovi diletti,
Che dolce penar!

(*Partono* DORABELLA *e* GUGLIELMO. *Entrano* FIORDILIGI *e* FERRANDO.)

Recitativo

FERRANDO: Barbara! perchè fuggi?

FIORDILIGI: Ho visto un aspide, un' idra, un basilisco!

FERRANDO: Ah! crudel, ti capisco! L'aspide, l'idra, il basilisco, e quanto i libici deserti han di più fiero, in me solo tu vedi.

FIORDILIGI: È vero, è vero. Tu vuoi tormi la pace.

FERRANDO: Ma per farti felice.

FIORDILIGI: Cessa di molestarmi!

FERRANDO: No ti chiedo ch'un guardo!

FIORDILIGI: Partiti!

FERRANDO: Non sperarlo, se pria gli occhi men fieri a me non giri. O ciel! ma tu mi guardi e poi sospiri? (*Parte.*)

FIORDILIGI: Ei parte—senti—ah no—partir si lasci, so tolga ai sguardi miei l'infausto oggetto della mia debolezza. A qual cimento il barbaro mi pose! Un premio è questo ben

DORABELLA *and* GUGLIELMO: It must be my own heart which is now beating in your breast.

GUGLIELMO: Now let me put this locket on you.
DORABELLA: You mustn't put it there.
GUGLIELMO: I understand you, you vixen.
DORABELLA: What are you doing?
GUGLIELMO: Don't look!
DORABELLA: Vesuvius seems to be erupting in my breast!
GUGLIELMO (*aside*): Poor Ferrando; I wouldn't have believed it! (*aloud*) Now, open your eyes.

DORABELLA: Where shall I look?
GUGLIELMO: Look down there. Isn't it better that way?

DORABELLA *and* GUGLIELMO: Oh, happy change of heart! What new delight I feel, what sweet pain!
(DORABELLA *and* GUGLIELMO *exit.* FERRANDO *and* FIORDILIGI *enter.*)

Recitative
FERRANDO: Cruel one! Why do you shun me?
FIORDILIGI: I've seen an asp, a hydra, a basilisk!
FERRANDO: Ah, now I understand you! You see in me all the fiercest animals of the jungle!
FIORDILIGI: It's true, I confess it. You're trying to destroy my peace.
FERRANDO: But only to make you happy.
FIORDILIGI: Stop pursuing me!
FERRANDO: I ask only a kind glance!
FIORDILIGI: Leave me!
FERRANDO: No, never! First you must turn your beautiful eyes to mine. O God! You look at me and then you sigh? (*Exits.*)
FIORDILIGI: He's gone! Come back! No—let him go—let the unhappy object of my weakness be concealed from my sight. He has plunged me into a horrible dilemma!

dovuto a mie colpe; In tale istante dovea di nuovo amante,
i sospiri ascoltar? l'altrui querele dovea volger in gioco?
Ah, questo core a ragione condanni, o giusto amore! Io
ardo e l'ardor mio non è più effetto d'un amor virtuoso: è
smania, affanno, rimorso, pentimento, leggerezza, perfidia,
e tradimento!

25. *Rondo*

Per pietà, ben mio, perdona,
All'error d'un alma amante
Fra quest' ombre, e queste piante
Sempre ascoso, oh Dio, sarà.
Svenerà quest'empia voglia
L'ardir mio, la mia costanza,
Perderà la rimembranza,
Che vergogna e orror mi fa.
A chi mai mancò di fede
Questo vano ingrato cor?
Si dove a miglior mercede,
Caro bene, al tuo candor!
(FIORDILIGI *parte. Entrano* GUGLIELMO *e* FERRANDO.)

Recitativo

FERRANDO: Amico, abbiamo vinto!

GUGLIELMO: Un ambo, o un terno?

FERRANDO: Una cinquina, amico; Fiordiligi è la modestia
in carne.

GUGLIELMO: Niente meno?

FERRANDO: Nientissimo; sta attento e ascolta come fù. Mi
discaccia superba, mi maltratta, mi fugge, testimonio ren-
dendomi e messaggio, che una femmina ell'è senza pa-
raggio.

GUGLIELMO: Bravo tu, bravo io, brava la mia Penelope!
Lascia un po ch'io ti abbracci per si felice augurio, o mio
fido Mercurio.

FERRANDO: E la mia Dorabella? Come s'è diportata? Oh non
ho neppur dubbio assai conosco quella sensibil alma.

GUGLIELMO: Eppur un dubbio parlando ti a quattr'occhi,
non saria mal, se tu l'avessi!

FERRANDO: Come?

GUGLIELMO: Dico così per dir. (*a parte*) Avrei piacere d'in-
dorargli la pillola.

But I surely deserved as much for my foolishness! At such a sad time I should never have listened to the pleas of a new lover! Should I have treated it all as a joke? No—truly my heart is guilty. Gods of Love! I am aflame, and my love is not virtuous! It is madness, suffering, remorse, repentance, perfidy, and finally—betrayal!

25. *Rondo*

For pity's sake, my Guglielmo, grant me pardon for the errors of a loving soul. O God, they will be hidden forever among my tears and sorrows. Let my future constancy obscure the memory of this evil desire that has caused me such horror and shame. How could this vain, ungrateful heart have broken its promises? My darling, you deserved better recompense for your fidelity!

(FIORDILIGI *exits.* GUGLIELMO *and* FERRANDO *enter.*)

Recitative

FERRANDO: My friend, we've won the bet!

GUGLIELMO: Doubly or triply?

FERRANDO: Five times over, my friend; Fiordiligi is modesty personified.

GUGLIELMO: Nothing less?

FERRANDO: Exactly; listen and you'll hear what happened. She dismissed me proudly; she rebuffed me, fled from me, giving me proof that she's a woman beyond emulation.

GUGLIELMO: Good for you, good for me, good for Fiordiligi. Let me embrace you for your good fortune.

FERRANDO: And my Dorabella? How did she behave? But I have no doubt— I know that faithful soul too well.

GUGLIELMO: And yet a doubt might enter your mind, if I may speak to you frankly.

FERRANDO: What?

GUGLIELMO: Oh, I was only joking. (*aside*) I wish there were some way to make it easier for him!

FERRANDO: Stelle, cesse ella forse alle lusinghe tue?

GUGLIELMO: Certo! anzi in prova di suo amor, di sua fede questo bel ritrattino ella mi diede.

FERRANDO: Il mio ritratto! Ah perfida!

GUGLIELMO: Ove vai?

FERRANDO: A trarle il cor dal scellerato petto, e a vendicar, il mio tradito affetto.

GUGLIELMO: Fermati!

FERRANDO: No, mi lascia!

GUGLIELMO: Sei tu pazzo? vuoi tu precipitarti per una donna, che non val due soldi? (*a parte*) Non vorrei, che facesse qualche corbelleria!

FERRANDO: Numi! tante promesse e lagrime, e sospiri, e giuramenti in sì pocchi momenti come l'empia obliò!

GUGLIELMO: Per Bacco io non lo so!

FERRANDO: Che fare or deggio! a qual partito, A qual idea mi appiglio? Abbi di me pietà, dammi consiglio!

GUGLIELMO: Amico, non saprei qual consiglia a te dar!

FERRANDO: Barbara! ingrata! in un giorno! in poch'ore!

GUGLIELMO: Certo un caso quest'è da far stupore.

26. *Aria*

Donne mie, la fate a tanti!
A tanti, a tanti, a tanti, a tanti!
Che se il ver vi deggio dir,
Se si lagnano gli amanti,
Li commincio a compatir.
Io vo bene al sesso vostro,
Lo sapete, ognun lo sà,
Ogni giorno ve lo mostro,
Vi do segno d'amistà.
Ma quel farla a tanti e tanti,
A tanti e tanti,
M'avvilisce in verità.
Mille volte il brando presi,
Per salvar il vostro onor,
Mille volte vi difesi
Colla bocca, e più col cor.

FERRANDO: Heavens! Did she yield to your advances? But now—you are joking—she loves only me.

GUGLIELMO: Certainly. And in proof of her love and her faith she gave me this charming little portrait of you.

FERRANDO: My portrait! Ah, the traitress!

GUGLIELMO: Where are you going?

FERRANDO: To tear her heart from her breast, and to avenge my betrayed affection!

GUGLIELMO: Stop!

FERRANDO: No, let me go!

GUGLIELMO: Are you insane? You're going to such trouble for a woman who isn't worth two pennies? (*aside*) I wouldn't want him to do anything rash!

FERRANDO: Heavens, so many promises, tears, sighs, oaths —how could she have forgotten them in so short a time?

GUGLIELMO: Don't ask me!

FERRANDO: Where shall I go now? What shall I do? What comfort can I find? Have pity on me! Give me some advice.

GUGLIELMO: My friend, I don't know what advice to give you.

FERRANDO: She's cruel, ungrateful! Forgotten in a day— in an hour!

GUGLIELMO: It's certainly most amazing!

26. Aria

My dear ladies, must you eternally behave this way? Really, I begin to understand why your lovers complain about you. I adore your sex: you know it; everyone knows it. I show it every day. I constantly give you pledges of my devotion. But now this eternal behavior of yours is beginning to disgust me. I've drawn my sword a thousand times to avenge your honor. A thousand times I've defended you, believing my own words. But really, again and again, your behavior is most offensive! You're charming; you're lovable. Heaven gave you your beauty, and graces encircle you from head to foot. But, over and over, the way that you treat men

Ma quel farla a tanti e tanti,
A tanti e tanti,
E un vizietto seccator.
Siete vaghe, siete amabili,
Più tesori il ciel vi diè;
E le grazie vi circondano,
Dalla testa sino ai piè.
Ma, ma, ma la fate a tanti e tanti,
A tanti e tanti,
Che credibile non è.
Ma la fate a tanti a tanti,
A tanti a tanti, a tanti,
Che se gridano gli amanti,
Hanno certo un gran perchè.
(*Entra* DON ALFONSO.)

Recitativo

DON ALFONSO: Bravo! questa è costanza.

FERRANDO: Andate, o barbaro, per voi misero sono.

DON ALFONSO: Via se sarete buono vi tornerò l'antica calma. Udite: Fiordiligi a Guglielmo si conserva fedel, e Dorabella infedel a voi fù.

FERRANDO: Per mia vergogna.

GUGLIELMO: Caro amico, bisogna far delle differenze in ogni cosa, ti pare che una sposa mancar possa a un Guglielmo? Intanto mi darete cinquanta zecchinetti.

DON ALFONSO: Volontieri: pria però di pagar vo che facciamo qualche altra esperienza. Venite; io spero mostrarvi ben che folle è quel cervello, che sulla frasca ancor vende l'uccello.

(DON ALFONSO, FERRANDO *e* GUGLIELMO *escono. Entrano* DESPINA *e* DORABELLA.)

DESPINA: Ora vedo che siete una donna di garbo.

DORABELLA: Invan, Despina, di resister tentai.

DESPINA: Corpo di satanasso, questo vuol dir saper! tanto di raro noi povere ragazze abbiamo un po di bene, che bisogna pigliarlo allor ch'ei viene. Ma ecco la sorella, che ceffo!

(*Entra* FIORDILIGI.)

FIORDILIGI: Sciagurate! ecco per colpa vostra in che stato

is unbelievable! If your lovers find cause for complaint they most certainly have their reasons!
(DON ALFONSO *enters.*)

Recitative

DON ALFONSO: Well! That's fidelity for you!

FERRANDO: Leave me alone; you're the cause of all my misery!

DON ALFONSO: If you'll be calm, your peace will be restored. Listen; Fiordiligi has proved herself true to Guglielmo, while Dorabella was unfaithful to you.

FERRANDO: To my shame.

GUGLIELMO: Dear friend, we must always make allowances in everything. Do you think a woman could ever fail a Guglielmo? Meanwhile, I'd like my fifty gold pieces.

DON ALFONSO: Gladly. But before paying, I want to make one more test. Come along; I hope to show you how unwise it is to count your chickens before they're hatched!
(DON ALFONSO, FERRANDO, *and* GUGLIELMO *exit.* DESPINA *and* DORABELLA *enter.*)

DESPINA: Now I see that you're really behaving as a woman should!

DORABELLA: I couldn't resist him, Despina.

DESPINA: Good heavens, we women have so little chance to amuse ourselves that we must take it as it comes. But here's your sister. What a frown!
(FIORDILIGI *enters.*)

FIORDILIGI: Little wretch, it's your fault that I find myself

mi trovo! Ma non so, come mai si può cangiar in un sol giorno un core.

DORABELLA: Che domanda ridicola! siam donne! e poi tu com' hai fatto!

FIORDILIGI: Io saprò vincermi.

DESPINA: Voi non saprete nulla.

FIORDILIGI: Farò, che tu lo veda.

DORABELLA: Credi sorella, è meglio che tu ceda! (*Parte.*)

FIORDILIGI: Despina! Despina!

DESPINA: Cosa c'è!

FIORDILIGI: Tieni un po questa chiave e senza replica, senza replica alcuna, prendi nel guardaroba, e quì mi porta due spade, due cappelli, e due vestiti de nostri sposi.

DESPINA: E che volete fare?

FIORDILIGI: Vanne, non replicare.

DESPINA (*a parte*): Comanda in abregè donna Arroganza.

FIORDILIGI: Vanne, sei cavalli di posta voli un servo ordinar, di a Dorabella che parlar le vorrei.

DESPINA: Sarà servita. (*a parte*) Questa donna mi par di senno uscita. (*Parte.*)

FIORDILIGI: L'abito di Ferrando sarà buono per me.

29. Duetto

Fra gli amplessi, in pochi istanti,
Giungerò del fido sposo,
Sconosciuta a lui davanti
In quest' abito verrò.
Oh che gioja il suo bel core
Proverà nel ravvisarmi!
(FERRANDO *entra inapproviso;* GUGLIELMO *e* DON ALFONSO *si nascondono in dietro.*)
FERRANDO: Ed intanto di dolore
Meschinello, io mi morrò!
FIORDILIGI: Cosa veggio!
Son tradita!
Deh, partite!
FERRANDO: Ah no, mia vita:

in this situation. I don't understand how a heart can change in a single day!

DORABELLA: What a silly question; we're women! How was your stroll?

FIORDILIGI: I know how to resist temptation!

DESPINA: Don't be too sure of that!

FIORDILIGI: You'll see that I'm in earnest.

DORABELLA: Believe me, sister, you'd do better to yield! (*Exits.*)

FIORDILIGI: Despina! Despina!

DESPINA: What's the matter?

FIORDILIGI: Take this key, and without questions, without telling anyone, go to the wardrobe trunk and find two swords, two hats, and two uniforms that belong to our fiancés.

DESPINA: What will you do with them?

FIORDILIGI: Go; don't argue with me!

DESPINA (*aside*): My Lady Arrogance is on her high horse!

FIORDILIGI: Get me a horse, and a servant to ride with me. And tell Dorabella that I would like to speak to her.

DESPINA: My lady shall be served. (*aside*) I think she's gone insane! (*Exits.*)

FIORDILIGI: The hat and uniform will disguise me beyond recognition.

29. Duet

Soon I shall be with my faithful lover again. At first he won't know me in that uniform, but then how happy he will be to see me again!

(FERRANDO *enters suddenly, as* GUGLIELMO *and* DON ALFONSO *hide upstage.*)

FERRANDO: And meanwhile I'll die of grief!

FIORDILIGI: Who is this? I'm betrayed! Please leave me!

FERRANDO: Ah no, my darling! Kill me, instead, with this

Con quel ferro di tua mano
Questo cor tu ferirai,
E se forza oh Dio non hai,
Io la man ti reggerò.

FIORDILIGI: Taci, ahimè! son abbastanza
Tormentata ed infelice!

FERRANDO: Ah che omai la sua costanza—

FIORDILIGI: Ah, che omai la mia costanza—

FIORDILIGI e FERRANDO: A quei sguardi, a quel che dice,
Incomincia a vacillar.

FIORDILIGI: Sorgi, sorgi!

FERRANDO: Invan lo credi.

FIORDILIGI: Per pietà, da me che chiedi?

FERRANDO: Il tuo cor, o la mia morte.
Cedi cara!

FIORDILIGI: Ah non son, non son più forte!
Dei, consiglio!

FERRANDO: Volgi a me pietoso il ciglio,
In me sol trovar tu puoi
Sposo, amante, e più, se vuoi,
Idol mio, più non tardar.

FIORDILIGI: Giusto ciel!
Crudel! hai vinto.
Fa di me quel che ti par!

FIORDILIGI e FERRANDO: Abbracciamci, o caro bene,
E un conforto a tante pene
Sia languir di dolce affetto,
Di diletto sospirar.
(*Partono* FIORDILIGI *e* FERRANDO. GUGLIELMO *emerge dal
suo nascondiglio.*)

Recitativo

GUGLIELMO: Oh poveretto me! cosa ho veduto! cosa ho
sentito mai!
(DON ALFONSO *emerge dal suo nascondiglio.*)

DON ALFONSO: Per carità! silenzio!

GUGLIELMO: Mi pelerei la barba! mi graffierei la pelle! e
darei colle corna entro le stelle, fu quella Fiordiligi? la
Penelope, l'Artemisia del secolo! briccona, assassina fur-
fante, ladra, cagna!

sword. If you haven't the courage, I myself will guide your hand!

FIORDILIGI: O God! Don't talk like that— I've suffered enough unhappiness already!
FERRANDO: Ah, her constancy is beginning to fail—
FIORDILIGI: Ah, my constancy is beginning to fail—
FIORDILIGI *and* FERRANDO: Judging from glances and sighs.

FIORDILIGI: Go away!
FERRANDO: I won't leave you!
FIORDILIGI: For pity's sake, what do you want of me?
FERRANDO: Either your heart, or my own death. Yield, my darling!
FIORDILIGI: Ah, I'm not strong enough! God, assist me!

FERRANDO: Turn your eyes upon me, out of pity; only in me will you find the husband of your fondest dreams. My dearest, don't hesitate!

FIORDILIGI: O God! Cruel one, you have conquered! I will do whatever you desire.

FIORDILIGI *and* FERRANDO: Kiss me, O my darling, and let sweet affection and sighs of pleasure comfort us for so much suffering and pain!
(FIORDILIGI *and* FERRANDO *exit.* GUGLIELMO *comes out of his hiding place.*)

Recitative
GUGLIELMO: Oh, what shame! What have I seen? What have I heard!
(DON ALFONSO *comes out of his hiding place.*)
DON ALFONSO: Be quiet, for heaven's sake!
GUGLIELMO: I'll tear my hair out! I'll pull my skin off! I'm forever branded with the cuckold's horns! Was that Fiordiligi, the chaste, virtuous Penelope? Wretch! Vixen! Liar! Slut!

DON ALFONSO: Lasciamolo sfogar.
(*Entra* FERRANDO.)
FERRANDO: Ebben!
GUGLIELMO: Dov'è!
FERRANDO: Chi? la tua Fiordiligi?
GUGLIELMO: La mia Fior, Fior di diavolo, che strozzi lei prima e dopo me!
FERRANDO: Tu vedi bene, v'han delle differenze in ogni cosa, un poco di più merto—
DON ALFONSO: Dunque restate celibi in eterno.
FERRANDO *e* GUGLIELMO: Mancheran forse donne ad uomin come noi?
DON ALFONSO: Non c'è abbondanza d'altro. Ma l'altre, che faran, se ciò fer queste? in fondo voi le amate queste vostre cornacchie spennacchiate.
FERRANDO *e* GUGLIELMO: Ah pur troppo! Pur troppo!

DON ALFONSO: Ebben pigliatele com' elle son. Frattanto un' ottava ascoltatte:felicissimi voi, se la imparete.

30. *Aria*
Tutti accusan le donne,
Ed io le scuso,
Se mille volte al dì cangiano amore,
Altri un vizio lo chiama,
Ed altri un uso, ed a me par
Neccesità del core.
L'amante che si trova al fin deluso
Non condanni l'altrui, ma il proprio errore:
Giàcche giovani, vecchie, e belle e brutte,
Ripetete con me: Così fan tutte!
FERRANDO, GUGLIELMO, DON ALFONSO: Così fan tutte!
(*Partono* DON ALFONSO, FERRANDO *e* GUGLIELMO. *Entra* DESPINA, *con* CORO *dei servi.*)

31. *Finale*
DESPINA: Fate presto, o cari amici,
Alle faci il foco date,
E la mensa preparate
Con ricchezza e nobiltà!
Delle nostre padroncine
Gl'imenei son già disposti:

DON ALFONSO: Let him rave.

(FERRANDO *enters.*)

FERRANDO: Well, now?

GUGLIELMO: Where is she?

FERRANDO: Who? Your Fiordiligi?

GUGLIELMO: My Fiordiligi can go to the devil! Let him take her, and then me!

FERRANDO: You must understand that we must always make allowances in everything. All women are the same.

DON ALFONSO: Then both of you intend to remain celibate?

FERRANDO *and* GUGLIELMO: Men like us are irresistible to women.

DON ALFONSO: I don't doubt it. But what makes you think you will suffer less at the hands of others? At the bottom of your hearts you still love your unfaithful sweethearts.

FERRANDO *and* GUGLIELMO: Ah, yes, beyond reason! Beyond reason!

DON ALFONSO: Well then, accept them as they are. And now listen to a sermon. Perhaps you can learn something from it!

30. Aria

Everyone condemns women for being so changeable, but I excuse them for it. Others call it a custom or a vice, but to me it seems a necessity of the heart. The lover who at the end finds himself deceived should blame only his own folly; for the young, the old, the beautiful, even the ugly—repeat this now with me: They all do it!

FERRANDO, GUGLIELMO, DON ALFONSO: They all do it!

(DON ALFONSO, FERRANDO, *and* GUGLIELMO *exit.* DESPINA *enters with a* CHORUS *of servants.*)

31. Finale

DESPINA: Hurry up, my dear friends; light all the candles, and see that the supper is ready; prepare it all with richness and grace! We must await the celebration, and the music must begin as soon as our dear mistresses appear!

E voi gite ai vostri posti
Finchè i sposi vengon quà.

CORO: Facciam presto, o cari amici,
Alle faci il foco diamo,
E la mensa preparate
Con ricchezza e nobiltà.

(*Entra* DON ALFONSO.)

DON ALFONSO: Bravi, bravi!
Ottimamente!
Che abbondanza, che eleganza!
Una mancia conveniente
L'un e l'altro a voi darà.
Le due coppie omai si avvanzano,
Fate plauso al loro arrivo,
Lieto canto e suon giulivo
Empia il ciel d'ilarità.

DESPINA *e* DON ALFONSO: La più bella comediola
Non s'è vista, o si vedrà. (*Partono.*)

CORO: Benedetti i doppi conjugi,
E le amabili sposine:
Splenda lor il ciel benefico,
Ed a guisa di galline
Sien di figli ognor prolifiche
Che le agguaglino in beltà.

(*Entrano* FIORDILIGI, DORABELLA, FERRANDO *e* GUGLIELMO.)

FIORDILIGI, DORABELLA, FERRANDO, GUGLIELMO: Come par
che qui prometta
Tutto gioja e tutto amore!
Della cara Despinetta
Certo il merito sarà.
Radoppiate il lieto suono,
Replicate il dolce canto,
E noi qui seggiamo intanto
In maggior giovialità.

CORO: Beneditti i doppi conjugi— (*Esce.*)

FERRANDO *e* GUGLIELMO: Tutto, tutto, o vita mia,
Al mio foco, or ben risponde!

FIORDILIGI *e* DORABELLA: Pel mio sangue l'allegria
Cresce, cresce e si diffonde!

FERRANDO *e* GUGLIELMO: Sei pur bella!

FIORDILIGI *e* DORABELLA: Sei pur vago!

FERRANDO *e* GUGLIELMO: Che bei rai!

CHORUS: Yes, we'll hurry to light the candles, and prepare a rich and noble supper.
(DON ALFONSO *enters*.)

DON ALFONSO: Bravo! You've done well! What abundance! What elegance! I shall see that you're suitably rewarded. Now the two couples will enter; cheer them as they come in. Let the sound of rejoicing fill the air with happiness.

DESPINA *and* DON ALFONSO: The best part of the comedy will now be seen. (*Exit*.)
CHORUS: God bless the brides and bridegrooms, may heaven rain its joys upon them, and may they have many children just as handsome as they are!
(FIORDILIGI, DORABELLA, FERRANDO, *and* GUGLIELMO *enter*.)

FIORDILIGI, DORABELLA, FERRANDO, GUGLIELMO: Now it seems that everything promises us joy and love! Certainly we must thank Despina, who has made all this possible. Let the happy chorus continue, and we will sit here and listen, in the greatest happiness!

CHORUS: God bless the brides and bridegrooms— (*Exits*.)
FERRANDO *and* GUGLIELMO: Now everything responds to my love!
FIORDILIGI *and* DORABELLA: My happiness is infinite!

FERRANDO *and* GUGLIELMO: You're so beautiful!
FIORDILIGI *and* DORABELLA: You're so charming!
FERRANDO *and* GUGLIELMO: What beautiful eyes!

FIORDILIGI *e* DORABELLA: Che bella bocca!

TUTTI: Tocca e bevi,
Bevi e tocca,
Tocca, bevi,
Tocca, tocca, bevi, bevi, tocca!

FIORDILIGI, DORABELLA, FERRANDO: E nel tuo, nel mio bicchiero
Si sommerga ogni pensiero,
E non resti più memoria
Del passatto ai nostri cor.

GUGLIELMO (*a parte*): Ah, bevessero del tossico
Queste volpi senza onor!
(*Entra* DON ALFONSO, *con* DESPINA *travestita da notajo.*)

DON ALFONSO: Miei Signori, tutto è fatto;
Col contratto nuziale
Il notajo è sulle scale
E ipso facto qui verrà.

FIORDILIGI, DORABELLA, FERRANDO, GUGLIELMO: Bravo,
bravo! passi subito.

DON ALFONSO: Vò a chiamarlo:
Eccolo quà.

DESPINA: Augurandovi ogni bene,
Il notajo Beccavivi
Coll' usata a voi sen viene
Notariale dignità!
E il contratto stipulato
Colle regole ordinarie,
Nelle forme giudiziarie,
Pria tossendo, poi sedendo
Clara voce leggerà.

FIORDILIGI, DORABELLA, FERRANDO, GUGLIELMO: Bravo,
bravo, in verità!

DESPINA: Per contratto da me fatto
Si congiunge in matrimonio
Fiordiligi con Sempronio,
E con Tizio Dorabella,
Sua legitima sorella,
Quelle Dame ferraresi,
Questi nobili albinesi,
E per dote e contradote—

FIORDILIGI *and* DORABELLA: What beautiful mouths!

ALL: Let's drink and toast one another!

FIORDILIGI, DORABELLA, FERRANDO: And let all thought be submerged in our glasses, and never again shall we recall the past.

GUGLIELMO (*aside*): Ah, I wish we could all drink poison! Those unfaithful sluts!

(DON ALFONSO *enters, with* DESPINA *disguised as a notary.*)

DON ALFONSO: My Lords, everything is done; the lawyer has arrived with the marriage contract, and he'll be here at once.

FIORDILIGI, DORABELLA, FERRANDO, GUGLIELMO: Let him come in!

DON ALFONSO: I'll call him. Here he is.

DESPINA: Wishing you every joy, the lawyer Beccavivi has come to lead you into the dignity of the married state. Here's the contract, stipulated according to the ordinary forms and the judicial rules. First I'll cough, then I'll sit down and read it aloud to you.

FIORDILIGI, DORABELLA, FERRANDO, GUGLIELMO: Very well, go on, quickly!

DESPINA: By this contract that I've drawn up, I hereby join you in matrimony! Fiordiligi with Sempronio, Tizio with Dorabella, the former's legitimate sister. These are ladies of Ferrara, those are nobles from Albania, and as for the dowries and the gifts—

FIORDILIGI, DORABELLA, FERRANDO, GUGLIELMO: Cose note,
cose note!
Vi crediamo,
Ci fidiamo, soscriviam,
Date pur quà!
DESPINA *e* DON ALFONSO: Bravi, bravi, in verità!
CORO (*da lontano*): Bella vita militar!
Ogni dì si cangia loco,
Oggi molto, e doman poco,
Ora in terra ed or sul mar.
FIORDILIGI, DORABELLA, DESPINA, FERRANDO, GUGLIELMO:
Che rumor! che canto è questo!
DON ALFONSO: State cheti; io vò a guardar. (*va alla fines-
tra*)
Misericordia!
Numi del cielo!
Che caso orribile!
Io tremo! io gelo!
Gli sposi vostri—
FIORDILIGI *e* DORABELLA: Lo sposo mio!
DON ALFONSO: In questo istante
Tornano, o Dio, ed alla riva
Sbarcano già!
FIORDILIGI, DORABELLA, FERRANDO, GUGLIELMO: Cosa mai
sento!
Barbara stelle! in tal momento,
Che si farà?
FIORDILIGI *e* DORABELLA: Presto partite!
Presto fuggite!
DESPINA, FERRANDO, GUGLIELMO, DON ALFONSO: Ma se li
veggono?
Ma se li incontrano?
FIORDILIGI *e* DORABELLA: Là, là celatevi, per carità!
(*Escono* FERRANDO *e* GUGLIELMO.)
Numi! soccorso!
Numi consiglio!
Chi dal periglio ci salverà?
Chi?
DON ALFONSO: Rasserenatevi,
Ritranquillatevi!
In me fidatevi,
Ben tutto andrà.
FIORDILIGI *e* DORABELLA: Mille barbari pensieri

FIORDILIGI, DORABELLA, FERRANDO, GUGLIELMO: It's all noted! We believe you, and we'll all sign it now; give it to us!

DESPINA *and* DON ALFONSO: Everything is going well!
CHORUS (*off-stage*): A soldier's life is joyous! What pleasure to be able to travel from place to place—today everything—tomorrow nothing. Sometimes we go by land and sometimes by sea!
FIORDILIGI, DORABELLA, DESPINA, FERRANDO, GUGLIELMO: What's that song? I've heard it before!
DON ALFONSO: Be quiet; I'll go and see. (*going to window*) Good Lord, this is horrible! I'm trembling! I'm dizzy! Your former fiancés—

FIORDILIGI *and* DORABELLA: Our former fiancés?
DON ALFONSO: They've come home again, and they're disembarking at this moment!

FIORDILIGI, DORABELLA, FERRANDO, GUGLIELMO: What are you saying? How horrible! Now what can we do?

FIORDILIGI *and* DORABELLA: Leave us at once! You must escape!
DESPINA, FERRANDO, GUGLIELMO, DON ALFONSO: But if they come here? If we meet them?

FIORDILIGI *and* DORABELLA: You must hide yourselves somewhere.
(FERRANDO *and* GUGLIELMO *exit.*)
Heaven help us! Fate, assist us! Who will save us from this peril?

DON ALFONSO: Reassure yourselves! Be calm! Trust in me, and all will go well.

FIORDILIGI *and* DORABELLA: A thousand horrible thoughts

Tormentando il cor mi vanno,
Se discoprono l'inganno,
Ah, di noi che mai sarà!
(DESPINA *si nasconde sotto una tavola. Entrano* FERRANDO
e GUGLIELMO, *vestiti da soldati, come prima.*)
FERRANDO e GUGLIELMO: Sani e salvi agli amplessi amorosi,
Delle nostre fidissime amanti,
Ritorniamo di gioja esultanti,
Per dar premio alla lor fedeltà.
DON ALFONSO: Giusti Numi! Guglielmo! Ferrando!
O che giubilo! qui,
Come,
E quando?
FERRANDO e GUGLIELMO: Richiamati da regio contrordine,
Pieni il cor di contento e di gaudio,
Ritorniamo alle spose adorabili,
Ritorniamo alla vostro amistà.
GUGLIELMO (*a* FIORDILIGI): Ma cos'è quel pallor, quel silenzio?
FERRANDO (*a* DORABELLA): L'idol mio, perchè mesto si stà?

DON ALFONSO: Dal diletto confuse ed attonite,
Mute, mute si restano là.
FIORDILIGI e DORABELLA (*a parte*): Ah, che al labbro le
voci mi mancano,
Se non moro, un prodigio sarà.
GUGLIELMO: Permettete che sia posto
Quel baul in quella stanza.
(GUGLIELMO *guarda sotto la tavola.*)
Dei! che veggio! un uom nascosto?
Un notajo? qui che fa?
(DESPINA *emerge, vestita come prima.*)
DESPINA: Non Signor non è un notajo,
È Despina mascherata,
Che dal ballo or è tornata,
E a spogliarsi, venne quà.
FIORDILIGI e DORABELLA: La Despina, la Despina!
Non capisco come và.
DESPINA: Una furba che m'agguagli
Dove mai si troverà!
FERRANDO e GUGLIELMO: Una furba uguale a questa,
Dove mai si troverà?

are whirling in my head. If they discover our deceit, whatever will become of us?

(DESPINA *hides under a table,* FERRANDO *and* GUGLIELMO *enter, dressed in their officer's uniforms.*)

FERRANDO *and* GUGLIELMO: Safe and sound, we joyously return to the embraces of our most faithful sweethearts, whose fidelity deserves this reward.

DON ALFONSO: Good heavens! Guglielmo! Ferrando! What joy! You've returned! Tell us how and when!

FERRANDO *and* GUGLIELMO: We were called back to Naples by the King's orders. Our hearts are full of joy and love, as we return to our adorable sweethearts and to you, our most beloved friend!

GUGLIELMO (*to* FIORDILIGI): But why are you so pale and so silent?

FERRANDO (*to* DORABELLA): My darling, why are you so sad?

DON ALFONSO: They're confused and bewildered by happiness.

FIORDILIGI *and* DORABELLA (*aside*): I simply can't speak. If I don't die here and now, it will be miraculous!

GUGLIELMO: Will you permit us to leave our baggage here?
(GUGLIELMO *looks under the table.*)
Heavens, what's down there? A man in hiding! A lawyer! What is going on?
(DESPINA *comes out, dressed as before.*)

DESPINA: No, my Lord; I'm not a lawyer, but Despina, in disguise. I've just come home from a masked ball, and I was taking off my costume when you arrived.

FIORDILIGI *and* DORABELLA: The lawyer is Despina! I don't understand this at all!

DESPINA: Where on earth will you find anybody as clever as I am?

FERRANDO *and* GUGLIELMO: Where on earth will you find anybody as clever as Despina?

DON ALFONSO (*a parte a* FERRANDO *e* GUGLIELMO): Già
cadar lasciai le carte,
Raccoglietele con arte.

FERRANDO: Ma che carte sono queste?

GUGLIELMO: Un contratto nuziale?

FERRANDO *e* GUGLIELMO: Giusto ciel! voi qui scriveste,
Contradirci omai non vale,
Tradimento, tradimento,
Ah si faccia il scoprimento;
E a torrenti, a fiumi, a mari
Indi il sangue scorrerà!

FIORDILIGI *e* DORABELLA: Ah! Signor son rea di morte
E la morte io sol vi chiedo,
Il mio fallo tardi vedo,
Con quel ferro un sen ferite
Che non merita pietà!

FERRANDO *e* GUGLIELMO: Cosa fù?

FIORDILIGI *e* DORABELLA (*indicando* DON ALFONSO *e* DES-
PINA): Per noi favelli
Il crudel, la seduttrice.

DON ALFONSO: Troppo vero è quel che dice,
E la prova è chiusa lì!

(FERRANDO *e* GUGLIELMO *escono precipitosomente*.)

FIORDILIGI *e* DORABELLA: Dal timor io gelo, io palpito:
Perchè mai li discoprì!

(FERRANDO *entrando, senza la barba, ma coi vestiti del
suo travestito albanese*.)

FERRANDO (*a* FIORDILIGI): A voi s'inchina
Bella damina!
Il Cavaliere dell' Albania.

(GUGLIELMO, *entrando, col ritratto di* DORABELLA.)

GUGLIELMO (*a* DORABELLA): Il ritrattino
Pel coricino,
Ecco io le rendo
Signora mia.

FERRANDO *e* GUGLIELMO (*a* DESPINA): Ed al magnetico
Signor Dottore
Rendo l'onore
Che meritò.

FIORDILIGI, DORABELLA, DESPINA: Stelle! che veggo!
Al duol non reggo!

DON ALFONSO (*aside to* FERRANDO *and* GUGLIELMO): The contract is on the floor; pick it up, and read it aloud!

FERRANDO: What's this paper?

GUGLIELMO: A marriage contract?

FERRANDO *and* GUGLIELMO: Good Lord, you have both signed it! Your guilt is obvious!

FIORDILIGI *and* DORABELLA: Ah, I'm truly guilty, and I want you to kill me! I see my crime too late; kill me with your sword; I don't deserve your mercy!

FERRANDO *and* GUGLIELMO: Explain your betrayal!

FIORDILIGI *and* DORABELLA (*pointing to* DON ALFONSO *and* DESPINA): They beguiled us, that cruel man and that unprincipled girl!

DON ALFONSO: That's perfectly true, and you will find the proof hidden in the next room.

(FERRANDO *and* GUGLIELMO *rush out.*)

FIORDILIGI *and* DORABELLA: I'm shivering and shaking with terror— Why did he show them their hiding place?

(FERRANDO *enters, without his false beard, but with the clothing of his Albanian disguise.*)

FERRANDO (*to* FIORDILIGI): I bow to you, my sweet lady! I'm the noble Albanian lord!

(GUGLIELMO *enters with the portrait that he took from* DORABELLA.)

GUGLIELMO (*to* DORABELLA): I'll give you back my portrait in exchange for that little heart, my dear lady!

FERRANDO *and* GUGLIELMO (*to* DESPINA): And to the wonderful magnetic doctor let all honor be shown!

FIORDILIGI, DORABELLA, DESPINA: Heavens! This is dreadful! I cannot endure it!

FERRANDO, GUGLIELMO, DON ALFONSO (*a parte*): Son stupefatte!
Son mezze matte!

FIORDILIGI *e* DORABELLA (*indicando* DON ALFONSO): Ecco
là il barbaro che c'ingannò.

DON ALFONSO: V'ingannai, ma fu l'inganno
Disinganno ai vostri amanti,
Che più saggi omai saranno
Che faran quel ch'io vorrò.
Quà le destre, siete sposi,
Abbracciatevi e tacete.
Tutti quattro ora ridete,
Chi'io già risi e riderò.

FIORDILIGI *e* DORABELLA: Idol mio, se questo è vero,
Colla fede e coll' amore
Compensar saprò il tuo core,
Adorarti ognor saprò!

FERRANDO *e* GUGLIELMO: Te lo credo, gioja bella,
Ma la prova io far non vò.

DESPINA: Io non so se questo è sogno,
Mi confondo, mi vergogno:
Manco mal se a me l'han fatta,
Che a molt' altri
Anch'io la fò.

TUTTI: Fortunato l'uom', che prende
Ogni cosa pel buon verso,
E tra i casi, e le vicende
Da ragion guidar si fà.
Quel che suole altrui far piangere
Fia per lui cagion di riso,
E del mondo in mezzo i turbini,
Bella calma troverà.

FERRANDO, GUGLIELMO, DON ALFONSO (*aside*): They're amazed and stupefied! They're overwhelmed!

FIORDILIGI *and* DORABELLA (*pointing to* DON ALFONSO): You are the monster who deceived us!

DON ALFONSO: I only deceived you in order to free your lovers from their illusions. They will be wiser now, and I hope they'll follow my advice. Be reconciled: get married! Kiss each other and make it up! See the humor here; laugh, as I have laughed and will laugh again!

FIORDILIGI *and* DORABELLA: My darling, if this is true, I'll console your heart with faith and love; I will love you forever!

FERRANDO *and* GUGLIELMO: I believe you, my dearest—but this time I ask for no proof!

DESPINA: I don't know whether I'm awake or dreaming; I'm so confused and embarrassed. It seems that Don Alfonso has deceived me, when I thought that I was deceiving all the others!

ALL: Fortunate is the man who is able to make the best of all adversity! Through all vicissitudes he can let Reason be his guide. That which makes others weep will be a cause of laughter for him. And, even in the midst of a whirlwind, he will find a center of tranquillity!

A CATALOG OF SELECTED

DOVER BOOKS

IN ALL FIELDS OF INTEREST

A CATALOG OF SELECTED DOVER
BOOKS IN ALL FIELDS OF INTEREST

CONCERNING THE SPIRITUAL IN ART, Wassily Kandinsky. Pioneering work by father of abstract art. Thoughts on color theory, nature of art. Analysis of earlier masters. 12 illustrations. 80pp. of text. 5⅜ x 8½.　　　　　0-486-23411-8

CELTIC ART: The Methods of Construction, George Bain. Simple geometric techniques for making Celtic interlacements, spirals, Kells-type initials, animals, humans, etc. Over 500 illustrations. 160pp. 9 x 12. (Available in U.S. only.)　　　0-486-22923-8

AN ATLAS OF ANATOMY FOR ARTISTS, Fritz Schider. Most thorough reference work on art anatomy in the world. Hundreds of illustrations, including selections from works by Vesalius, Leonardo, Goya, Ingres, Michelangelo, others. 593 illustrations. 192pp. 7⅛ x 10¼.　　　　　　　　　　0-486-20241-0

CELTIC HAND STROKE-BY-STROKE (Irish Half-Uncial from "The Book of Kells"): An Arthur Baker Calligraphy Manual, Arthur Baker. Complete guide to creating each letter of the alphabet in distinctive Celtic manner. Covers hand position, strokes, pens, inks, paper, more. Illustrated. 48pp. 8¼ x 11.　　0-486-24336-2

EASY ORIGAMI, John Montroll. Charming collection of 32 projects (hat, cup, pelican, piano, swan, many more) specially designed for the novice origami hobbyist. Clearly illustrated easy-to-follow instructions insure that even beginning papercrafters will achieve successful results. 48pp. 8¼ x 11.　　　0-486-27298-2

BLOOMINGDALE'S ILLUSTRATED 1886 CATALOG: Fashions, Dry Goods and Housewares, Bloomingdale Brothers. Famed merchants' extremely rare catalog depicting about 1,700 products: clothing, housewares, firearms, dry goods, jewelry, more. Invaluable for dating, identifying vintage items. Also, copyright-free graphics for artists, designers. Co-published with Henry Ford Museum & Greenfield Village. 160pp. 8¼ x 11.　　　　　　　　　　　　　　0-486-25780-0

THE ART OF WORLDLY WISDOM, Baltasar Gracian. "Think with the few and speak with the many," "Friends are a second existence," and "Be able to forget" are among this 1637 volume's 300 pithy maxims. A perfect source of mental and spiritual refreshment, it can be opened at random and appreciated either in brief or at length. 128pp. 5⅜ x 8½.　　　　　　　　　　　　0-486-44034-6

JOHNSON'S DICTIONARY: A Modern Selection, Samuel Johnson (E. L. McAdam and George Milne, eds.). This modern version reduces the original 1755 edition's 2,300 pages of definitions and literary examples to a more manageable length, retaining the verbal pleasure and historical curiosity of the original. 480pp. 5³⁄₁₆ x 8¼.　　　　　　　　　　　　　　0-486-44089-3

ADVENTURES OF HUCKLEBERRY FINN, Mark Twain, Illustrated by E. W. Kemble. A work of eternal richness and complexity, a source of ongoing critical debate, and a literary landmark, Twain's 1885 masterpiece about a barefoot boy's journey of self-discovery has enthralled readers around the world. This handsome clothbound reproduction of the first edition features all 174 of the original black-and-white illustrations. 368pp. 5⅜ x 8½.　　　　　　　　0-486-44322-1